Also by Joel Engel

ROD SERLING: THE DREAMS AND NIGHTMARES
OF LIFE IN THE TWILIGHT ZONE

ADDICTED

GENE RODDENBERRY

THE MYTH AND THE MAN
BEHIND STAR TREK

JOEL ENGEL

NEW YORK

Library of Congress Cataloging-in-Publication Data

Engel, Joel

      Gene Roddenberry : the myth and the man behind Star Trek / Joel Engel — 1st ed.

        p.   cm.

    Includes bibliographical references and index.

    ISBN 0–7868–6004–9

    1. Roddenberry, Gene. 2. Television producers and directors—United States—Biography. 3. Star Trek (Television program) I. Title.

PN1992.4.R55E54   1994

791.45'023'092—dc20

[B]   93–23723
                                           CIP

Designed by Robert Bull Design

10 9 8 7 6 5 4 3 2

To my wife, who gets up early every morning and lights the way.

And to my mother, who taught me when I was seven years old that the worst thing about lying was not that no one can trust you, but that you can trust no one.

ACKNOWLEDGMENTS

Literally hundreds of people and institutions provided generous assistance in the researching of this book; to thank them all properly is not possible. Some of them, however, must be singled out.

To Christopher Knopf and E. Jack Neuman: Thank you for sharing reminiscences of your friend. I owe the same thanks to Sam Rolfe, a wonderful and talented man who passed away in July 1993.

To Bob Justman: Thank you for the clarity and compassion of your memories.

To Harve Bennett: Thank you for sharing ten years' worth of wonderful and not so wonderful memories, and for your great kindnesses.

To Jon Povill: Thank you for your willingness to recall the big picture and the small detail.

To Brigitte Kueppers and Paul Camp at UCLA's theatre arts special collections department: Thank you for granting me access to the *Star Trek* collection, and for providing such a pleasant place to work.

To Ron Simon and Alden Gewirtz at the Museum of Television and Radio: Thank you for opening the museum to me, and for your time.

To Sam Peeples: Thank you for showing me the same kind of generosity that you showed Gene Roddenberry almost thirty years ago.

To Joe Bonino, head of records and identification for the Los

Angeles Police Department: Thank you for your courtesies, care, and concern.

To Leonard Nimoy, Dorothy Fontana, and David Gerrold: Thank you for your trust and your continued willingness to help me get the facts right.

To John D. F. Black and Mary Stilwell Black: Thank you for rolling out the memories in my company and for the best hamburgers of the year.

To Lauren Weinstein: Thank you for your expertise.

To Oscar Rothenberg: Thank you for donning a deerstalker hat and showing up Sherlock Holmes.

To Mary Ellen Strote: Thank you for your good taste, your talent, your judgment, your skill, your intelligence, your patience, and your friendship.

And to Christine Archibald: Thank you for asking me to the party, and then showing me around.

CONTENTS

FOREWORD

first met Gene Roddenberry in 1963 when I came to work as a secretary for his associate producer on *The Lieutenant*, a Marine Corps series at MGM. Except for the long, dark weekend of John Kennedy's assassination and funeral, working for Gene was fun. His writing was crisp; he was clear about what he wanted from his staff; he has a sense of humor. He listened when I told him I had six TV sales and aspired to be a full-time writer. When *The Lieutenant* was wrapping, Gene called ne into his office and asked me to read a ten- or eleven-page document and tell him what I thought of it. It was a basic format for a science fiction adventure series titled *Star Trek*. I loved it.

Gene and his agent went around town trying to find a studio that would take a chance on *Star Trek*. It landed at Desilu in Hollywood. NBC agreed to make a pilot in association with Desilu, and *Star Trek* began its long road toward series-hood. Writing "The Cage" required long hours, with me sitting behind my typewriter transcribing Gene's words from Dictaphone to script pages while he sat behind his desk dictating the next section. We were the "producer's office," and we became friends as well as colleagues.

Star Trek was a show that had a high cast, crew, and staff morale. People enjoyed working on the show because Gene went out of his way to make it a partnership. Birthdays were remembered; impromptu parties were arranged for the cast and crew after long weeks of shooting. Everyone cared about making *Star Trek* a good show, and everyone pitched in with enthusiasm.

Gene offered me a script assignment in the first thirteen episodes and followed it up with a second assignment immediately after the first. Having been with him through the two years of pilot creation, he said I knew the show as well as he did. He didn't seem to begrudge the fact that giving me the second assignment solidified my decision to leave his employ as a secretary to become a full-time writer. Instead, he told me he would appoint me as his story editor if I could rewrite an unworkable script quickly and to the satisfaction of the studio and the network. I did—and he did. Which began a year and a half of the happiest work and writing I did on staff for a long time.

Though we both left *Star Trek* as its third season began, Gene and I remained friends over the years. I became close to Majel Barrett and sometimes offered a shoulder to cry on while Gene went through his divorce. I applauded their wedding in Japan. I happily attended the "welcoming" party Gene and Majel gave for the birth of their son, Rod. I served as associate producer on the *Star Trek Animated* series. Even though we sometimes didn't see each other for long stretches of time because of the different demands in our lives, I always felt we were friends and that *Star Trek* was a special "home."

In late 1986, Gene called me and told me there was going to be a new *Star Trek* series. He wanted to include me in on it. I was sent a copy of the show bible in progress; and a stream of memos began to arrive at my home from David Gerrold and Bob Justman, who were already on staff. Gene surprised me by saying he'd decided I should write the series premiere episode. So the deal was set, and I once again signed on the Starship *Enterprise*.

At first, things seemed fine; but as 1987 progressed, I discovered there was something new on board—something new and unpleasant. Maybe it was too many years of Gene being hailed as the "Great Bird of the Galaxy," and being known only as the creator of *Star Trek*. Maybe it was too many years of watching other people write and produce *Star Trek* movies. Maybe it was noticing that other people (myself included) had been given credit for creating some of the popular aspects of the show—justly so, but it collided with the legend of Roddenberry the Creator.

While I didn't know the precise source of the problem, I did know I was included as one of the targets. No one but Gene could be recognized as a contributor to ideas for the show. No one else could write a final draft. Writer-producers on the series felt the same anger and outrage I did at being excluded from the production process—at being told not to visit the sets or speak to the actors—at watching perfectly good scripts being rewritten by Gene into something far less—at having their files prowled through and sometimes removed. Definitely gone were the days when a staff birthday was an occasion and the crew was rewarded with a party for hard work. In the space of nine months, no fewer than eight writing-staff members left the series. There was no high sense of morale and community; rather, the production offices were like an armed camp. Armed against Gene Roddenberry because of his alienating actions.

A twenty-four-year friendship and a lot of respect died during that long summer. I turned my back on Gene Roddenberry and *Star Trek* and walked away. I didn't know why Gene had chosen to behave as he did, but I didn't look back until this book was written. I found a lot of answers in it—some I never suspected.

Gene Roddenberry had a lot of fine qualities. He could charm the angels down from the sky with a line of blarney the Irish could admire. He often made great intuitive leaps of inventiveness to solve story problems. On his best days, his writing was clean and intelligent. He frequently was generous, sometimes overly so. But—like the little girl with the curl—when he was good, he was very, very good; and when he was bad, he was horrid. This book explains some of the reasons for both the good and the bad.

D. C. Fontana
November 1993

AUTHOR'S PREFACE

irst, a confession. *Star Trek* debuted the fall I entered high school, and ended its original run two weeks before I graduated. But despite the hallway buzz and the gasps of acclaim from several friends who were (and remain) passionate fans, I never watched a single episode. I had, as they say, other interests at the time. It wasn't until 1976 that I first became devoted to *Star Trek*. One summer evening I came home from work and switched on my old black and white Sony monitor, which was coincidentally set to the independent station that rented Paramount's syndication package. Before I could turn the dial (there was no remote), I became entranced, and I stayed that way throughout the hour. Only later did I learn that "Spock's Brain" is generally considered one of *Star Trek*'s poorest episodes. (I related to Bones McCoy's thinking that the rewiring of Spock's brain was as easy as child's play, and then his becoming discombobulated when he comprehended the job's infinite difficulty. The story, I was certain, had been written by someone who, like me, had been awakened by the brilliance of a dream that recedes before it can be remembered.) And indeed, each of the next seventy-eight weeknights that I made certain to be home at six o'clock, before the opening teaser, seemed to offer better and better viewing. One sensation that I recall with particular intensity was excitement inspired by the sudden belief that the future would be a wonderful place. Some of the episodes, I felt, were breathtaking, and I lamented having missed the excitement of watching them first run. Nothing—not time, nor repetition—has dulled their luster.

On December 7, 1979, I brought a stack of magazines and newspapers to keep me occupied while I stood on line for *Star Trek: The Motion Picture,* and was able to finish reading them in the four hours before I gained admission. My disappointment, which I heard reflected by virtually everyone else leaving the theater, was tempered by knowing that if the film could manage to earn enough money, there would be a *Star Trek II*—without the same mistakes. After *The Wrath of Khan,* I thought that *Star Trek* might continue forever, even if there weren't new episodes every week. And then in 1987, it became clear that *Star Trek* really would run forever, and there *were* new episodes every week.

When Gene Roddenberry died in October 1991, I realized that I knew little about him, apart from his *Star Trek* persona; I was aware of the myth but wasn't certain that it fit the mortal man. Some days later, I received an offer to find out: Hyperion asked if I'd be interested in writing his biography. Not wanting to rush in blindly, I called several acquaintances who had known and worked with Roddenberry. They assured me, without showing their cards, that there was a good story to tell. Still not satisfied, I spent several days in the reading room of UCLA's theater arts special collections department, where a treasure trove of *Star Trek* correspondence, scripts, memoranda, letters, and related documents are held. What I found there surprised me, and piqued my interest and enthusiasm for the project at hand.

Gene Roddenberry: The Myth and the Man Behind Star Trek is not, per se, a comprehensive biography of Gene Roddenberry's every waking moment, from birth to death. It is a study in character that relies on events and incidents to illuminate its subject. Soon after beginning my research I began to see an almost novelistic plot line. Roddenberry's predilections informed virtually every area of his life, which was reordered by his personality into a sort of traditional dramatic narrative, the events and details— plot—created by his character. The story has a beginning, a middle, and an end. Like the best stories, Roddenberry's continued to

surprise; each layer of onion, peeled away by word an
revealed another layer that eventually was peeled away
that remained was the core. If, in financial scandals, a re
told to "follow the money," with Roddenberry one fol
ambition.

As a storyteller, Roddenberry became his own grea
ation. While it's true that Gene Roddenberry made *Star*
even more true that *Star Trek* made Gene Roddenberry.

n September 24, 1992, eleven months to the day after Gene Roddenberry died, the Sci-Fi Channel began operations. For the previous month or so, the cable channel's satellite feed had been a continous loop of special effects on which a character generator counted back the seconds until zero—precisely 8:00 P.M. EDT on the day noted. At that moment, before *Star Wars* came on, a printed message appeared on screen: "The Sci-Fi Channel is dedicated to the memory of two science fiction pioneers."

The first name was that of Isaac Asimov, the "human writing machine" who authored about three hundred nonfiction science books and science fiction novels, as well as nearly a thousand magazine articles on a broad range of subjects; the man who devised the "Three Laws of Robotics" that even now continue to influence engineers in that field; a full professor of biochemistry, and a renowned researcher in the fields of kinetics, photochemistry, enzymology, and irradiation.

The second name was Gene Roddenberry's. Through *Star Trek*, his indirect impact on aspects of popular culture these last three decades has been eclipsed, arguably, only by Elvis Presley.

GENE
RODDENBERRY

CHAPTER ONE

Ad

Hominem

Memoriam

THE MORNING of November 1, 1991, broke clear and pleasantly cool over Los Angeles. Liz Wahlstedt rose early in the guest bedroom of her friend's suburban home, still tired after a night of jet-lagged sleep. She was in a hurry to get to the cemetery, though the service wouldn't begin for another six hours.

Liz hadn't known the deceased, nor was she a friend or relative of the family. She'd flown from Minneapolis not out of obligation but out of reverence. Gene Roddenberry's death, one week before, had devastated her. Having grown up during the cold war, with the relentless dread of nuclear holocaust, she believed that *Star Trek*'s vision of the future—at the time virtually unique in its optimism—had contributed to the world's survival. In homage to Chekov, the Russian ensign aboard Roddenberry's starship *Enterprise*, she'd chosen Russian for her language instruction during her hitch with the air force.

With Roddenberry now gone, Liz wondered what would become of *Star Trek: The Next Generation,* the phenomenally successful sequel to the original series, airing in first-run syndication. "The future of *Star Trek* reflects what might be for the future of humanity," she says. "*Star Trek* can affect how we see our own future. It's not that I think we're going to be beamed up tomorrow; it's just a TV show. But at the same time, it still has social importance."

The day after Roddenberry's death, Liz had read his obituary in the *Star Tribune*, noting that the memorial would be held the following Friday, one of her two days off. His widow, actress Majel Barrett, had invited the public.

By ten o'clock, four hours before the scheduled service, Liz had negotiated the Los Angeles freeways in her rented Ford Escort and found her way to Forest Lawn in the Hollywood Hills. Once inside the gate, she began looking for other fans. She wended slowly from the entrance, passing lush green lawns that were shaded by tall pines and decorated with statuary. She bore right at the "Old North Church" and kept going. Almost a mile from the entrance stood a huge rectangular building, one side covered completely by a mural depicting scenes from the American Revolution. "God gave us liberty. People who forsake God lose their liberty," read the inscription above the mural.

Taking in the cemetery's Hollywood-style opulence, Liz looked around for other fans; seeing no one, she wondered whether she'd come to the wrong place. Finally she spotted a well-dressed young man walking out of the building. She stopped him and asked if he knew where the Gene Roddenberry memorial service was to be. Right here, he said, in the Hall of Liberty.

At about the same time, forty miles to the southwest, a Toyota pickup pulled away from Don Maglio's Long Beach home. Its four passengers had rendezvoused sometime earlier that morning from points all over southern California. Don, who'd taken the day off from work, wore an original Captain Kirk uniform, as did Jill Bryant, a college student. Lorri Goldman, another student, wore an original *Star Trek* science officer's uniform. Nita Myer, Don's girlfriend, had donned her ordinary civilian clothes. Their driver was Don's mother, whose interest in the matter was to provide safe transportation for the four mourners, who'd all met at *Star Trek* conventions.

By the time they arrived at Forest Lawn, the first of what would be three hundred or so fans had already gathered around the area beside the Hall of Liberty to talk about the man and the shows—both "classic *Trek*," as they called it, and *The Next Gener-*

ation. That Don, Jill, and Lorri had dressed in their uniforms—they would be the only mourners so attired, except for one young woman who later showed up wearing Spock ears—sent twitters through the growing crowd. Most, like Liz Wahlstedt, believed that this was not the kind of event to which one wore a costume.

"I thought that wearing my uniform was a way of showing that the dream lives on, despite the death of the man who created it—that there's still hope for an optimistic future," says Don.

The fans watched as the limos bearing celebrities began pulling up. The atmosphere seemed more festive than solemn. It was a bright autumn day of almost religious beauty, if you were inclined to see God's handiwork in the clarity of such blue skies and brisk air.

Roddenberry, for one, had not been so inclined. A devotee of humanistic philosophy, he had disdained organized religion, having long before slammed the door on the Baptist teachings of his early childhood in the belief that religious faith was a vestige of a prerational age. In Roddenberry's universe, Man made the rules and Man could break the rules. And so the actors, writers, fans, family, and friends of Gene Roddenberry would soon witness a secular ceremony, not one presided over by clergy. Since the deceased had been cremated days before, there would be no graveside ceremony.

The invited guests were seated on the floor level of the Hall of Liberty. Fans filled the balcony. A photograph of a smiling Roddenberry adorned an easel at stage right. The familiar themes to the two *Star Treks* played over the loudspeakers. When the lights dimmed, the curtains opened on the stage, revealing a large screen on which was projected a montage of this-is-your-life photographs.

Nichelle Nichols, who portrayed communications officer Uhura during the first three seasons of *Star Trek* on television and in six feature films, sang two songs to a pianist's accompaniment: Paul McCartney's "Yesterday," followed by one she'd written herself, "Gene." She dedicated it to the "Great Bird of the Galaxy," the epithethical nickname conferred upon Roddenberry by producer and longtime friend Robert Justman.

Ray Bradbury spoke first, reminiscing about the friend whom, he said, he missed already:

> …I was over in Scottsdale last year, and three young men ran up, in their early thirties, and they said, "Oh, Mr. Roddenberry, you are so wonderful. We love you and we love your show and we hope it goes on forever." And I said, "Thank you, I'm glad you like my work." I learned to not disappoint these fans. To tell them the truth would be so terrible that their faiths would be destroyed. So I let them go away happy and it made me happy, too. You know, when I told some of my friends this, that I was going to be here today, two of them said, "What an honor, what an honor." And I hadn't thought of it until that moment. I was sad, first of all. It was going to be a burden. A sweet burden, but a burden. And when they said that twice, I said, "Yes, it is an honor. A great honor to be here to speak of an honorable man."

Oscar-winning actress Whoopi Goldberg spoke next. Five years before, she had asked Roddenberry whether she might have an irregularly recurring role on *The Next Generation*. "I amused him," she said, "and he asked, 'Why?' And when I explained to him that his was the only vision that had black people in the future [Nichelle Nichols as Lieutenant Uhura], he thought that was very bizarre. I guess he didn't realize how many of us saw us there." Roddenberry, she said,

> in fact changed the entire face of the world. Everywhere you go, no matter what country, they all love *Star Trek*. They all know that, somehow, the world can actually be better because of this one man's vision.
> What an honor to have been able to meet someone who changed the world without screaming and yelling and cursing out crazies, like some of us do. He just said, "No. This is my vision." And for once, people in charge listened. And twenty-five years later, a kid from the projects, and kids from all over the world and all over the country are standing here to celebrate Gene Roddenberry.

The accomplished screen and television writer Christopher Knopf, one of Roddenberry's closest friends, recalled a long ago afternoon at Dodger Stadium, when Roddenberry had told him the premise of a new television series idea he had, about a dirigible that takes to the air in the late nineteenth century with a crew of men and women who intend to explore the earth's unexplored regions.

Knopf then related an anecdote that seemed quintessentially Roddenberry: The two friends and their wives had just returned to the Roddenberry home after dining out. When the women disappeared into the house, Roddenberry dragged Knopf up the driveway to show off his recent acquisition, a motorcycle that was soaking wet from the rain. "Ever been on one?" Roddenberry asked.

"No," Knopf replied, "and it doesn't start now."

> In our blue suits, shirts, and ties, rain beating us to death, down the driveway we went on the Harley, onto Beverly Glen, leaning into a turn up Lindbrook; lots of leaning; traction suddenly history; the bike on its side, spinning about the asphalt.
> When we picked ourselves off the pavement, our suits torn to shreds, blood pouring out of our knees, the bike, what was left of it, plowed through a hedge, and we sat on the curb, trying to decide whether the wiser course was emergency hospital or a hot shower, Gene turned to me, with that sudden marvelous laugh of his.
> "Do you realize," he said, "you'll probably never do anything like this again. You've got to love it."

Near the end of his eulogy, when talking about *Star Trek,* Knopf injected a wistful note:

> Most of us would have made a mess of the eternal debate between good and evil, standing for justice and equality. Except that his choices, his words, the poetry and rhythm with which he used them, his philosophy and ideas were so many levels above what most of us as writers knew how to achieve. Never mesmerized by the sound of his own voice, he was a spectacular learner, providing insight, charm, compassion, humor, infusing his work with qualities of self-searching, putting us on paper, himself on paper, and the result you know: a seemingly ordinary man with extraordinary vision.

Another close friend, the writer-producer E. Jack Neuman, stepped to the podium. After noting that Roddenberry was the first writer to receive a star on the Hollywood Walk of Fame, Neuman recounted the time in 1956 when he met Roddenberry, who was then a few months removed from the Los Angeles Police Department. An aspiring television writer, Roddenberry had covertly arranged to sit next to the established professional, Neuman, on a flight from New York to Los Angeles. They talked for a long time, and had five rounds of drinks. Adequately fortified, Roddenberry admitted that he was scared. "What's to be scared about?" Neuman asked.

"I used to fly one of these things," Roddenberry replied.

Roddenberry was a golfer, Neuman said, by way of a metaphorical segue into a personal assessment of the man: "Aside from the fairways, Gene's expertise was in a little-known, very obscure, track-and-field event called self-effacement. In Hollywood it's practically extinct. Gene was the hands-down champion of self-effacement—unequaled, unrivaled, unchallenged; Gene owned the gold, the silver, and the bronze without even competing. He invented the event."

The final eulogist was Patrick Stewart, the actor who portrays Capt. Jean-Luc Picard on *The Next Generation*. Commanding the stage as only a trained Shakespearean can, he alluded to the deceased's cosmology by reciting dialogue Roddenberry had composed for an episode in the show's second season. Roddenberry had Picard answer the question of what happens to a body after death. Did the captain believe in the traditional concept of an afterlife, or in black nothingness? "Considering the marvelous complexity of our universe, its clockwork perfection balancing this against that, matter, energy, gravitation, time, dimension, happening, I believe that our existence must mean more than either of those choices. I prefer to believe that what we are goes beyond Euclidian and other practical measuring systems in ways we cannot yet fathom. Our existence is part of a reality beyond what we understand now as reality."

Stewart later recounted an incident that had occurred the previous spring. Former president Ronald Reagan had stopped by the set briefly to watch the filming. At the time, Roddenberry's deteriorating health had required that he use a wheelchair, but for standing and minor locomotion he used a cane. "[Reagan] and Gene stood side by side," Stewart said, "and somehow Gene's stick fell to the ground and at once the president bent on one knee to pick it up. And when this was referred to later, Mr. Reagan said, 'You know, in that moment, I felt I was being knighted.'

"Well, in one way or another, Gene graced all of us while he was alive, and he will go on doing so."

At the conclusion of Stewart's remarks, two men dressed in kilts played a particularly mournful version of "Amazing Grace" on bagpipes. Roddenberry's prerecorded voice could then be heard, reiterating his well-known sanguine forecast that reason and logic will, by the twenty-fourth century, lead that wondrous creature, the human being, into virtual utopia.

The mourners were directed outside. Fans and celebrities mingled together, waiting for the announced overhead fly-by—the so-called missing man formation. After thirty minutes, under a sky that had grown intensely blue in the late afternoon, four planes approached in a modified wedge formation. The lead plane broke formation while the other three flew on.

"I thought I would cry, but I didn't," Lorri Goldman says. "Even though it was sad, it was inspiring, too. It was a celebration, not like, 'Oh, gee, we lost him.' Well, it was that, too, but his life was so wonderful.

"And yet, I don't lionize the man. I've talked with some other people since and found out that, indeed, he wasn't Saint Gene."

Roddenberry had died, eight days before, of a heart attack in his doctor's Santa Monica office, his heart failure attributable to diabetes, hydrocephalus, alcoholism, and a series of strokes. The man extolled by five eulogizers and honored by several hundred guests had been a World War II bomber pilot, a commercial airline pilot for Pan American Airways, a police officer, and an episodic television writer of relatively minor distinction—until *Star Trek*.

In the last twenty-two years of his life, he never escaped the gravitational pull of that future universe. Nor had he wanted to. It was the wellspring from which sprang his pleasures and successes. Gene Roddenberry became a willing one-trick pony. But when it came time, in 1986, to re-create that universe anew for *The Next Generation,* he found that his pony had gone lame. He had to rely on others to get there—and felt entitled to the free ride. In his mind, he was the creator emeritus who'd made their work possible.

But *Star Trek* had never existed as Gene Roddenberry's proprietary domain—not in the twenty-third century, nor in the twenty-fourth. And despite his insistence, he had not entrusted it begrudgingly, because of lack of time, to other writers. No matter how persuasively he had convinced himself otherwise, the *Star Trek* realm had been, almost from the beginning, a dynamic cosmos with many gods, some less equal than others, but all of them contributors to the vision.

When the applause began, Roddenberry had walked out alone onto center stage, where he maintained that humans just three hundred years into the future—barely one tick of the evolutionary clock—will have overcome their frailties and foibles, and particularly their vanities. Irony explains why so few of those former fellow gods joined those who, on November 1, 1991, had come to pay their final respects: They had no respect left to pay.

CHAPTER TWO

The

Lieutenant

L ATE IN THE FALL of 1962, Gene Roddenberry stood outside the offices of producer Norman Felton's Arena Productions on the Metro-Goldwyn-Mayer lot. He straightened to his full six-foot-three-inch height and smoothed the rumpled corduroy pants and ill-fitting shirt that had become his trademark to people who knew him well. He checked his hair in a window's reflection and took a deep breath.

Roddenberry had come a long way in the seven years since leaving the Los Angeles Police Department to be a full-time television writer—but not far enough to satisfy himself. In the beginning, he'd done anything he could to meet producers who might buy stories, or to make the acquaintance of established writers who'd volunteer a quick tip. "He had these ears that stuck out, and he had a haircut that was going to last a long time," E. Jack Neuman recalls of the time Roddenberry maneuvered a seat next to him on a Los Angeles–bound flight. Neuman had been the writer-producer of a show called *West Point,* about army cadets in training, and Roddenberry wanted to write for it. His zeal impressed Neuman. It was determination that had driven him when he was a cop, daydreaming about someday being a professional writer. He'd looked up to working writers, guys who spent their days turning ideas into words and pages into dollars. At the time, he'd been a moonlighter, selling stories to cop shows like *Dragnet*—stories he'd either lived, heard about, or bought from other cops. Above all things, he'd wanted to support his family as a full-timer. That was one reason why, after getting off duty, he had hung out at the old Cock 'n Bull restaurant on Sunset Boulevard. Writers gathered there to pass happy hour and tell each other tales, which is probably how the place got its name. His other reason he shared with the pros: Cock 'n Bull bartenders poured with cast-iron hands.

"I was always interested in anybody who tried that hard," Neuman says.

In April 1956, Roddenberry sold his first *West Point* script, and over the next year wrote ten more, including a collaboration with Neuman. One of them had been a rewrite of a script by Sam Rolfe, who was then in the process of creating *Have Gun, Will Travel,* the witty thirty-minute series starring Richard Boone as the literate and moral gunfighter Paladin. Roddenberry eventually wrote twenty-seven *HGWT*s, the last just before meeting Felton.

Roddenberry didn't know Felton, but he'd written a script for one of Felton's shows, *Dr. Kildare.* As executive producer, Felton usually left the task of meeting with writers to his co-executive producer, Herbert Hirschmann, or to the two other producers, David Victor and Calvin Clements. After watching "A Distant Thunder," the episode based on Roddenberry's script about an aging, embittered army general who checks into Blair General Hospital, Felton took the unusual step of sending Roddenberry a note of appreciation. "Writers write scripts for episodic television, then the show is made, and nobody tells them that the script was any good," Felton says. "They just tell them what was wrong with it or that they should make it better. I wanted to tell him that I liked it, that I thought it was good." Felton was impressed by the sense of character he saw in the script, the pathos and insight.

Roddenberry's General Sparrow suffered physically from psychosomatic illnesses rooted in despair over having fought in three wars, none of them the war to end all wars. "Save more, save [patients] from this and that and they'll overpopulate the globe and die from swollen-belly hunger," he told Kildare after questioning the righteousness and necessity of waging both World Wars. "Or save them all, let them breed so they can be roasted to death by some new weapon from some new enemy."

Roddenberry was pleased by the compliments from one of television's top producers, a man supplying the NBC television network with two popular and high-quality shows (the other was *Eleventh Hour,* a sort of *Kildare* about psychiatrists). He had become a steady television writer with dozens of credits, although until *Have Gun, Will Travel* most were for undistinguished episodic series. In 1957, he'd even won a Writers Guild Award, in the best Western category, for a *Have Gun, Will Travel* script. He was making a satisfactory living, but he'd never get rich as just another episodic hack, and from the career plateau on which he found himself perched, he could see that he was probably closer to the bottom of the mountain than to the top.

"I'd like to write a pilot for you," Roddenberry told Felton when they met.

"Why not?" Felton declared. "What'd you have in mind?"

Roddenberry had previously written four pilots, all of them for Screen Gems and all of them failures. The first, in 1959, was called "Night Stick," about a cop whose beat is Greenwich Village. It never aired. The second, "333 Montgomery Street," about a criminal defense attorney, had been broadcast in June 1960 as a thirty-minute episode of *Alcoa Goodyear Theatre.* The third, "APO 923," about three servicemen stationed on an unnamed Polynesian island in 1943, also went unseen—except by network executives and ad agencies. The fourth, "Defiance County," was never filmed.

Now, pushing forty-two, he felt desperate to write a pilot that would make a network's fall schedule. As the show's creator, he would receive a fee every time an episode ran, whether he had written that episode's script or played golf. That's where Felton came in. Any pilot to come out of his Arena Productions stood a better than even chance of actually getting on the air. Better still, Felton might give him a chance to produce. The way Roddenberry had it figured, playwrights controlled the theater, directors the movies. In television, producers held the power. They hired other writers to formalize their ideas into scripts, and they made the real money.

Unfortunately, Roddenberry had brought nothing specific to the table. So the two men agreed to meet again. And then again.

Felton had a hunch about Roddenberry and was willing to gamble.

By the third meeting Felton had fashioned an amorphous treatment, inspired by Roddenberry's *Dr. Kildare* script, its theme being the humanity behind the military uniform. Their proposed show, he said, ought to focus on the life and times of a professional soldier, a young lieutenant, in the peacetime Marine Corps. Felton hadn't served, but he knew that Roddenberry had—as a B-17 pilot in the Army Air Corps during World War II, with eighty-nine South Pacific combat missions locked into memory.

Thanks to the Ashley-Famous talent agency, which happened to handle both Roddenberry and Felton—and excelled at packaging television series—a deal was struck. Using MGM's money, Arena Productions would fund the script, and if the pilot went to series, Roddenberry would be given a shot at producing, under executive producer Felton.

Ordinarily, Felton would have pitched the proposed show directly to NBC, the network that had bought his two current prime-time hits. But when he told the idea to MGM head Robert Weitman, Weitman enthusiastically suggested that the studio make the pilot as a "free-ball." Instead of gauging network interest first and receiving network money to finance the pilot's production, the studio would bear the considerable production costs. This would entitle them to pitch the finished product to all three networks and, Weitman hoped, cut a better deal. If a network said no to a pilot after financing it, the deal was dead, because its financing conferred exclusive broadcast rights.

Weitman saw in this deal a way to assuage MGM's board of directors, who had been infuriated by his having given away distribution rights and profit participation to NBC on *Dr. Kildare.* A savvy deal made on behalf of *The Lieutenant* might recoup some of his prestige and confidence. He believed that all three networks, not just NBC alone, would jump through hoops for the next series from Norman Felton—and would be willing to pay more for it. Usually, the license fee networks paid to broadcast each episode of most shows left the studio that owned and financed the show in the red, hoping to transform the deficit into profits through future syndication (they'd then hide the profits through questionable accounting procedures). But given the possibility of a bidding war, a higher fee might leave MGM with a cash surplus during production.

Roddenberry balked, reasoning that a network which hadn't committed itself through pilot money could more easily say no. But at the time he had zero leverage and two choices: acquiescing or walking away. This pilot script was to be his one-way ticket out of Palookaville. The studio, obligated contractually to Arena's pilot needs, insisted on a free-ball arrangement. As Felton explained it, MGM's board of directors, led by Random House publisher Bennett Cerf, had been wanting to bow out of the unprofitable television production business for several seasons in order to concentrate on feature films. Its only two successes in the home medium were Felton's, and it rankled the directors that the producer owned a larger stake in the shows' profits than they did.

On January 10, 1963, Roddenberry's script of "A Very Private Affair" made the rounds at Arena Productions. It introduced the lead character of William T. (Tiberius) Rice, second lieutenant, U.S. Marine Corps. Rice, somewhere in his early twenties and a recent graduate of the Naval Academy in Annapolis, Maryland, reports to his new assignment at Camp Pendleton, California. His superior, Captain Rambridge, sends Rice to investigate assault charges against a Private Eckles in third platoon, who has whacked a corporal on the head. Rice resists, believing that all the plum assignments for recently arrived second looies will have been taken by the time he completes the investigation, which on the surface appears to be routine and therefore undeserving of his presumably considerable talents. "Within the next few days, sir," Rice says, "there is bound to be a staff replacement arriving who could handle this investigation without anyone's career being jeopardized."

"Lieutenant," Rambridge retorts, "I have a job which needs doing right now, and you happen to be here right now. Like being in the wrong place at the wrong time and catching a bullet. You're a casualty. Now, do I call a medical corpsman or can you see your way to the door through your fears?"

Rice eventually discovers that Eckles acted out of jealousy, not sociopathology: He caught his newlywed wife making love to the corporal. But out of pride he refuses to acknowledge the mitigating circumstances that would undoubtedly reduce a twenty-five-year prison term. To resolve the case, Rice requires the assistance of a young woman he meets on the beach, Lane Bishop, who is "no more than twenty but with a face suggesting a high degree of intelligence. She's unusually mature and poised, also unusually lovely." This ranks as one of Roddenberry's tamer script descriptions of women, who will most often in the future be introduced by the size of their breasts and their smoldering but noticeable passion for the leading man. It is Lane who tips off Rice that sex lies at the heart of the intrigue.

The plot of "A Very Private Affair" seems to have been suggested by autobiography. Roddenberry himself had just begun a barely secret affair with Majel Barrett, an aspiring—and ambitious—actress in her mid-twenties. At the time, he had been married for twenty years to the former Eileen Rexroat, whom he'd met when she was still a sixteen-year-old Hollywood High School student. The couple had two daughters, fifteen-year-old Darleen and five-year-old Dawn. Frequently unfaithful to Eileen, even during the earliest years of their marriage, Roddenberry had usually confined himself to one-night stands or brief liaisons.

In the script's denouement, Private Eckles, though he knows otherwise, insists to Rice that his wife's actions with the corporal amounted to no more than "just a thank-you kiss, something you did all the time back home with someone who you've danced with."

"And supposing that wasn't it at all," the wife coos. "Suppose I was so lonely and scared and tired [of being home alone every night, while he slept in the barracks], I did make a mistake. Would you still love me, Johnny?"

As written by Roddenberry and budgeted by Felton, *The Lieutenant* appeared to be prohibitively expensive. The only way to bring the show in, Felton believed, was with the help of the Marines at Camp Pendleton, located on the southern California coast between Los Angeles and San Diego. In exchange for supplies, uniforms, and even Marine extras, the Marines got veto power over scripts.

Soon after production on the pilot began in the spring of 1963, Felton received an early morning call from assistant director Erich von Stroheim, Jr., at Camp Pendleton. In a frantic voice, he explained that the company had come to a standstill; a hundred Marine extras in a mock-up of an Asian village were doing nothing.

Felton wondered why the show's producer had not resolved the situation. "What about Roddenberry?" he asked. Von Stroheim laughed, and the line went dead. Felton jumped into his car. Passing through Pendleton's security checkpoint two hours later, he stopped to pick up Lt. Colonel Clement J. Stadler, the officer assigned by the Marines as a liaison to the producers. Stadler nervously confirmed the stoppage and said that the camp commandant had just driven out to the location.

Escorted to one of Pendleton's distant corners, Felton saw the scene that von Stroheim had described: Amid a hundred Marines milling around aimlessly, the nearly apoplectic director, Buzz Kulik, was able only to utter the sentiment that Felton should fire von Stroheim—who was nowhere to be found. The director of photography, shrugging his shoulders and throwing up his hands, pointed Felton toward Roddenberry—standing some distance away next to the camp commandant, both of them grinning for the unit photographer.

Roddenberry's posed smile disappeared as soon as he saw Felton. To cover his embarrassment, he insisted that Felton's picture be taken with the commandant.

"You're a producer, so produce," Felton told him before rectifying the situation himself. The problem was that three fighter-bombers had been sent from the El Toro air station, carrying enough fuel for only two runs over the village where the Marines were to stage combat exercises for the camera. If the shot could not be captured in those takes, the jets would have to be sent back for refueling, costing the production time and money. But the ground personnel had not been ready on the first pass, resulting in friction between director Kulik and von Stroheim that gridlocked the production. It was the producer's dilemma to solve, and Roddenberry had not even tried.

Kulik, whose directing career reaches back to the early days of live television, says that Roddenberry had passively abdicated his role. "He was really out of it, to a great extent, because of his drinking and his personal problems."

Eileen Roddenberry had joined her husband on location, as had Kulik's wife, Lorraine, the two couples staying in adjoining rooms in an Oceanside hotel outside of Camp Pendleton. Every night, the Kuliks could clearly overhear the Roddenberrys screaming and fighting, their angry voices passing through the thin wall that separated their suites. During the day, while their husbands worked, the two women became friendly enough for Eileen to confide in Lorraine about how her husband was mistreating her. Forced to overhear the nightly arguments, Lorraine had no reason not to believe the charges—some of them including physical abuse.

Kulik's impression was that Roddenberry remained drunk throughout the location shooting. "I did not get along with him," Kulik says. "He was a very abrasive man, abrasive to just about everyone. I suspected he was covering up his personal problems."

By the time principal photography on *The Lieutenant* pilot had been completed, the networks were already locking down their fall schedules. To meet the rigid deadline, an editor worked nearly around the clock, as did the other postproduction craftsmen. Within two weeks, Felton boarded an airplane for New York, the cans of film on his lap.

Weitman scheduled three separate screenings, several hours apart, in the MGM screening room—one for each set of network executives. By noon the following day, NBC had committed to the show. Felton called Roddenberry with the news that turned him from a wannabe into a television series producer.

When Felton stepped off the plane on his return to Los Angeles, he was met on the tarmac by a dozen or so men and women from the production staffs of *Dr. Kildare, Eleventh Hour,* and the series pilot. Wearing Marine caps and assembled into military formation, they were led through mock drills by Roddenberry, much to Felton's delight and amusement.

Soon thereafter, Roddenberry, Felton, and Camp Pendleton's

liaison, Colonel Stadler, traveled to the Department of Defense in Washington, D.C., to work out details of what was and was not permissible to say about Marine life. Conflict being the engine of drama, good stories demanded controversy, contests, and contentiousness. But army colonel Joseph Daugherty, the Pentagon's final arbiter, presented the producers with a long list of objectionable material. In essence, if *The Lieutenant* wanted to use the facilities and personnel of the Corps—and to re-create the Marine seal at the end of the show—almost anything that portrayed the Corps as less than a military utopia was to be avoided. Roddenberry and Felton protested but to little avail; without the Marines imprimatur, which could be withheld or withdrawn at any time, the production would become untenable.

For Roddenberry and Stadler, however, the trip was not all work. They shared a mutual love of good times, which translated to booze and female companionship.

Back in Los Angeles, Roddenberry began hiring a production staff. For story editor he chose Del Reisman, whose credits included *The Twilight Zone*. Reisman had known Roddenberry when he was still a cop frequenting the Cock 'n Bull.

Roddenberry told Reisman that he'd chosen Rice as the protagonist's name in order to make a statement about what he saw as America's inevitable alliance with the Pacific countries. "Rice conjured up an image for him," says Reisman. "He knew no one else would pick up on it, but he thought of it as something."

From the beginning, Roddenberry was hazy on the overall direction the series should take. He gravitated toward new situations and characters each week. But for *The Lieutenant* to be a ratings success, the stories had to sell Gary Lockwood, the actor, as William Rice, the Marine lieutenant. (Capt. Rambridge was played by Robert Vaughan.) Stories that did not promote the audience's affection for Lockwood would not kindle their devotion to seeing him in action every Saturday night.

Felton wanted Roddenberry to turn out something akin to "Lieutenant Kildare," with Camp Pendleton substituting for Blair General Hospital. Roddenberry pointed out that *Kildare*'s storytelling arena was inherently soft, while *The Lieutenant*'s took place against the harshness of Marine combat training.

"I think that Gene always saw the show as the maturing of a young man," Reisman says. "Rice's rite of passage was the basic philosophical premise. Here was an officer and a gentleman placed in a leadership position. And yet, what was he leading? What did he know about people? I think that Gene's rite of passage in the business was really parallel in his mind to Lieutenant Bill Rice's."

Rice likely became Roddenberry's fantasy alter ego. Rice was young and handsome, and, with allowances made for youthful exuberance, invariably wise. Brave and bold, he seemed a man's man. His Camp Pendleton was a military summer camp where young men of mettle went in ready to be shaped and came out fully formed—a place where beautiful young women made themselves available for whatever young men of mettle wanted. Always beautiful, always ready to serve our lieutenant, these young women were as smart and as savvy as he needed them to be, never more. Most importantly, they understood him, and by understanding his needs, his wants, his moods, they acceded to them: the man's man and his woman's woman.

Now that he'd become a producer, not just a writer, Roddenberry set out to remake himself sartorially, to change his image of a sloven in ill-fitting pants, an old sweater, or misbuttoned shirts. He instigated an arrangement with a men's clothing manufacturer in downtown Los Angeles's garment center, and began wearing suits or sport coats, a different one, every day. Unfortunately, many of them were made of then primitive synthetic fabrics, and the producer sometimes looked more like a cheap pimp than a Beau Brummell. "There were times," Reisman says, "when Gene resembled the advance man for a circus."

Roddenberry set up screenings of the pilot and invited writers, some of whom then came into the offices and pitched stories. Based on gut instinct, he handed out assignments, insisting on the usual outline as a first step. When outlines began to arrive a few weeks later, he complained to Felton about their poor quality. On his way up the steel stairway to Roddenberry's second-floor office,

Felton once saw him throw an outline across the room. "I have to rewrite everything. Everything!" he bellowed.

Felton bought him a dart board and encouraged him, when enraged or despairing, to pick up the darts. Each time the two men played, Felton was careful to let him win.

Early in the writing cycle, when first drafts of full scripts began coming in, Reisman handed one to Roddenberry. "I like it," he said, "but I don't want to say anything to the writer until you read it first. I have some concerns, but I don't want to tip you off. You should read it fresh."

Roddenberry took it home.

Early the next morning, he called Reisman into his office. "I want to have a real talk with you," he said, shutting the door for privacy. "I started reading this thing; got to the end of the first act, page fifteen. It was all mixed up. It wasn't what we thought, not the outline at all. I got so angry, I started to rewrite it. I rewrote and rewrote and rewrote. Then I realized, halfway through the script— the writer's script—that he simply replaced information. Instead of in the first act, it was in the second act. So now what've we got?"

Reisman suggested that they try to combine the versions, culling what was best from both. He called the writer, who responded angrily but came in anyway. Reisman handed him notes that he'd made, instructions on what to keep from each draft. The writer returned some days later with the new draft, which Roddenberry promptly rewrote in its entirety.

There was his way, and the wrong way. But being the producer, that was his prerogative. With the exception of the pilot and the final episode of the series, Roddenberry didn't write, he rewrote. Writers complained to Felton that Roddenberry was impossible to please. After their scripts were shot, they rarely heard from him again. The twenty-nine episodes employed nineteen different writers and seventeen directors.

The Lieutenant debuted September 14, 1963, against the juggernaut of Jackie Gleason's hour on CBS. Within weeks it had built the highest ratings of any NBC show ever in that Saturday time slot. But Roddenberry, Felton, and Reisman found themselves in repetitive battles over script content with the Department of Defense. The Pentagon's Colonel Daugherty believed that the Marine image was best served by portraying life at Camp Pendleton as though it were an overnight camp for postadolescent males. (After watching several episodes, Daugherty once complained about the "short-skirted chippies" often seen in background scenes. "One of those short-skirted chippies," Roddenberry said defensively, "is my niece." Daugherty backed off. Later, when asked about the niece, Eileen Roddenberry informed the staff that her husband the producer didn't have any nieces.) One script, submitted for consideration, concerned the consequences of not paying attention: A sergeant provides instruction in the proper use of explosives. Because he wasn't paying attention at the time, the platoon jokester is subsequently injured in an explosion. "Nothing ever happens like that," Daugherty said, refusing the script. "We're really careful." Another script in which grenades were to be thrown for practice was nixed because American mothers might have gotten the idea that their young sons could be hurt during military training.

Such preposterous reasoning plagued the production team, which now concluded that its deal with the Marines had been a devil's pact. And yet, they had to accept the evil as a necessity: If the Marines collapsed their tent, the additional costs would bankrupt the show. Of the three men, Roddenberry proved most adept at finessing a compromise position that the DOD could live with and that wouldn't gut the script completely.

By early November, the workday had grown abysmally long, with blood pressures climbing and tempers shortening. Production had fallen behind schedule, not least because of the shortage of approved scripts. Roddenberry announced one morning to Reisman that he would soon be leaving on a three-week cruise through the Panama Canal with his family. He had often confided in Reisman about his marital problems, acknowledging the need for privacy to make difficult phone calls and explaining why he'd have to be off the lot. Reisman asked if Felton had approved the vacation. Roddenberry admitted that he hadn't even broached the subject. He left it to Reisman, who would essentially be functioning as producer in Roddenberry's absence, to inform Felton of Roddenberry's imminent departure.

Felton angrily mounted the staircase to Roddenberry's office. He snatched a dart from the board and aimed it at Roddenberry.

"Don't throw it," Roddenberry pleaded.

When he returned from vacation, he walked into his office to find phony cobwebs covering most surfaces. This was Felton's doing. Roddenberry also found his crew filming an episode on MGM's back lot. The story concerned a recruit who'd died in a training accident. Lieutenant Rice accompanies the young man's casket to his Midwest hometown, there to present the flag to the family.

On the Friday morning of his first week back, while the funeral scene itself was being shot—using Marine buglers playing "Taps"—Roddenberry was in his office, arguing over the phone with Daugherty at the Pentagon over the merits of another script. Reisman, pacing back and forth in front of Roddenberry's desk in anticipation of the argument's outcome, saw Roddenberry go suddenly pale. Placing his hand over the mouthpiece, Roddenberry said, "The president's been shot."

An hour later, after John F. Kennedy's death had been confirmed, Roddenberry closed down the filming of the funeral scene, the echo of "Taps" still in the air.

Early in 1964, MGM chief Weitman phoned Felton. "NBC's calling to say that the Pentagon's not very happy with you guys," he said. "What the hell are you doing, Norm?"

If there was anything the network, in the person of "The General," David Sarnoff, disliked more than poor ratings, it was a government agency displeased with something for which he held ultimate responsibility. In this case, the DOD's hackles had been raised by Roddenberry's refusal to alter a storyline about racial prejudice. "To Set It Right" centered on a black Marine (played by Don Marshall, whose wife was played by Nichelle Nichols) who joins

Rice's platoon and suddenly attacks, apparently without provocation, a white member of the platoon (Dennis Hopper). The two men, in fact, had been classmates in high school, where Hopper's character often joined with other bigots to gang up on blacks. Eventually, the two Marines learn to work together and respect each other, if not for nobility and idealism then for the safety of the platoon.

The Pentagon claimed that racial problems were unknown in the military.

"We're going to do it anyway," Roddenberry insisted. Felton stood behind him.

"It was this story," Felton says, "that lost us the cooperation of the Pentagon."

To make up for not having Camp Pendleton, the crew began filming on MGM back lots two and three, where vestiges of the area's natural brush-covered topography were relatively close to some man-made areas—jungle, a stream, a lake, and decrepit barracks left over from World War II films. To compensate for the loss of Marine extras, Roddenberry hired two former Marine drill instructors, in whose charge were put extras and bit players who'd had military experience. He scavenged two trucks' worth of surplus supplies and weapons that had been in storage at a military base on the outskirts of the Mojave desert. Associate producer George Lehr matched the new props to the old and supervised the creation of scenic backdrops to re-create Pendleton. Instead of filming jet fighters flown for the camera's benefit, he obtained existing footage of land and naval exercises.

Shrewd maneuvering had successfully kept costs manageable, the albatross of Pentagon approval had been eliminated, and ratings held respectably steady all year. But *The Lieutenant* met its maker anyway at the end of that first season, the victim of outside forces that began insinuating themselves into not only the production but all of American society.

The tenor of the news dispatches about American military "advisers" who'd been sent to Vietnam, a tiny country in Southeast Asia, grew bleaker by the day. Americans had been sent to help the South Vietnamese in their civil war against the Communist forces of North Vietnam, but with no readily apparent objective and no conspicuous rewards, the snowballing venture appeared increasingly questionable to many.

An executive at NBC called Felton and danced around his point out of deference to the man who would have, the following fall, another two promising shows on the network, *The Man From U.N.C.L.E.* and *Jericho*. "Norm," he said, "there's a lot of discussion, as you know, about what the army is doing over there in Vietnam. A lot of people don't like it and are not happy with this show of yours now that it doesn't have the Marine seal of approval on it. It's beginning to get, well, inflamed, the way people feel. Believe me, it's not the politics; it has nothing to do with the show's politics."

"I get the idea," Felton said.

"I don't think," the executive concluded, "we're going to renew next year."

In February 1964, knowing that there'd be no tomorrow for *The Lieutenant*, Roddenberry assigned himself the series' swan song, an episode entitled "To Kill a Man," in which Rice is sent to Southeast Asia on a short mission. Though the name Vietnam is never used (fictitious towns with a Vietnamese resonance to them, like Peng Dong, were referenced), the script's descriptions of the country's topography and references to its internal politics suggest the input and assistance of Colonel Stadler. Shot down in a helicopter, Rice and a South Vietnamese army captain become friends as they fend for themselves in the jungle, employing all the survival techniques both men have been taught. It's later revealed, however, that the captain is in fact a rebel—presumably Viet Cong—and intends to obtain the information Rice possesses any way he can, including torture. Through a somewhat improbable turn of events, the men engage in a long dialectic (it lasts much of the fourth act) on the nature of war, freedom, idealism, and friendship. "To fight for different ideas does not mean we must hate," the rebel captain says to Rice, a submachine gun trained on the lieutenant. "The history of war has many cases where men fought each other bravely but still held great respect and affection for the other."

The script—and the series—concluded on an eerily prescient

note: Rice, after finally dispatching the captain with four rounds from his .45-caliber service pistol, sits at a bar, pleased that his request has just been granted. He will not be going home, but rather will serve a tour of duty as an adviser.

The plot of "To Kill a Man" bore some thematic similarities to the unsold pilot Roddenberry had written a year before, "APO 923," which took place on an unnamed Polynesian island in 1943, at the height of the fighting. (The script was based on a concept by executive producer William Sackheim, whose APO number, as a member of the Army Signal Corps during the war, had been 923.) Three soldiers confront the issues of killing in wartime through two interrelated stories. In the first, the army lieutenant is racked by what he calls a "gut full of guilt" for having killed a Japanese soldier; he carries with him a picture of the man's family that he had found on the corpse. (The part was played by Jim Stacy, a teen heartthrob after Shelley Fabares sang "Johnny Angel" to him on *The Donna Reed Show*.) Later, his two friends discover the gravity of his emotional paralysis when he's unable to kill another enemy soldier, even at the risk of his own life.

In the second story, the three friends discover a mountain village on the island that is populated by Chinese innocents who have suffered great cruelties at the hands of the Japanese. They believe, in the words of the village's wise old man, that "the greatest courage is not to kill—even in the face of death." The Americans must convince the villagers that ultimately pacifism can be more costly than a willingness to combat aggression: "Your way is maybe more violent than ours," a captain says. "Just by sitting still and letting it happen you can hurt more people than the rest of us who fight back."

The resolution leads the hamstrung lieutenant to self-realization: "This is the whole war in a nutshell," he says. "You know, it was just like our own country. They bent over backwards trying to avoid it. Finally, there was only one way for them: kill or be killed."

These words had been composed by a man who'd not traipsed through jungles on patrol "or felt the fear of ambush" or seen the corpse of the enemy that he'd shot. But Roddenberry had indeed been acquainted with these jungles. As a B-17 bomber co-pilot, he'd flown several dozen times into South Pacific combat zones to discharge destruction on enemy targets.

Though Roddenberry would later tell interviewers that he'd flown anywhere from 89 to 109 combat missions, the Army Air Corps's records do not support his claim, nor can any members of the 394th bomber squadron, Roddenberry's outfit, confirm those numbers; all believe it's too high. Leon Rockwell, who as a member of the 23rd Bomber Squadron was in the same bomb group as the 394th, flew 80 missions—but remained in the South Pacific for two years, almost three times as long as Roddenberry.

Joe Jacobs, a captain and the navigator on the ten-man crew for which Second Lieutenant Roddenberry flew co-pilot to Captain William L. Ripley's pilot, guesses that they flew no more than twenty-five combat missions together. The distinction, however, may be largely a matter of semantics, for even reconnaissance missions could be dangerous. "There were all kinds of missions," Jacobs says. "Most of them were search missions."

Both Jacobs and James Kyle, the crew's bombardier, had been at Pearl Harbor as members of the Fifth Bomber Group, 23rd squadron, on the day it was attacked by the Japanese, December 7, 1941. Six months later the Fourth Reconnaissance Squadron was redesignated as the 394th Bombardment Squadron—the number being reactivated from World War I—and they were reassigned. When Lt. Gene Roddenberry arrived in early 1943 after completing seven months of flight training school, he wasn't yet twenty-two years old. "He was so young, he did more listening than talking," Jacobs says.

On the island of Espiritu Santo, located in the northwest portion of the New Hebrides, the new 394th was given one day to get its old B-17s—nicknamed "Flying Fortresses," at the time the largest planes in the Air Corps—into shape mechanically. Then they were sent east to Fiji, an important Allied supply point, where they were initially a training squadron before receiving combat orders.

"We did both bombing and surveillance missions," Kyle recalls. "When we weren't flying combat, on our day off, we flew surveillance. That consisted of about twelve hours of missions. You'd fly eight hundred miles out, a hundred miles across, eight hundred miles home. At 160 miles an hour, it took about twelve to thirteen hours to cover that space."

Jacobs remembers that he was initially less than impressed with the rookie piloting skills of both Ripley and Roddenberry. Ripley was often drunk on duty, and neither man held the course he'd charted as well as the pilots Jacobs had known since Pearl Harbor. "Those other guys I worked with, when the navigator gave them a steer, boy, they kept that heading within a degree or so. Old Ripley and Roddenberry, hell, they'd stray eight or ten degrees off the heading sometimes."

In the early days of the war, Japanese air resistance could be fierce, and even the B-17 bombers became targets of Japanese artillery shells, fired in panic. At the battle of Midway (which predated Roddenberry's arrival), one of the planes in Jacobs's squadron took a direct hit on the wing from what appeared to be, judging by the size of the hole—"Big enough for a man to crawl through," Jacobs remembers—a projectile launched from a sixteen-inch gun. It was a measure of the B-17's sturdiness that the plane made it back safely to Oahu for repairs.

Roddenberry's crew endured no attacks of that severity. Rockwell says that most losses after Midway were attributable not to enemy airfire but to poor navigation; their targets were often tiny islands, and the planes had no radio navigation.

"We got shot at a few times," Jacobs says, "but we never really got a man scratched." Their most harrowing adventure came as a complete surprise one day, and was caused by nature.

At the time they believed they had flown into a force-five monsoon, and only later discovered it was a hurricane. "The inside of a hurricane—the eye—is usually oval, almost circular, and it's pretty calm," Jacobs says. "But going in and getting out you have to go through the ring again, where there are all sorts of updrafts and downdrafts, which are dangerous."

The crew had learned that Ripley's fondness for drinking often made him an undependable commander, thus giving Roddenberry more responsibility by default. On this sobering occasion, however, both men were at the controls.

The Air Corps's technical manual had prescribed techniques for flying through such storms, but pilot Ripley, co-pilot Rodden-berry, and navigator Jacobs had not read the manual's instructions. "We went through it doing everything wrong," Jacobs says.

In Roddenberry's recounting of the event, the plane flew into the storm at an altitude of six hundred feet. Ferocious winds batted them about like a shuttlecock, pushing them up to 2,500 feet and then back into the ocean spray, ripping out several wing rivets.[1]

"They sort of had to manhandle the airplane a little more than they would have had to had they known the correct procedure," Jacobs says. "We got out by the grace of God. It was a miracle, to tell you the truth. I guarantee you, after that trip, the three of us got out the tech orders and really studied them."

Many of the crew's missions were in support of the land forces engaged in the bitter jungle battles for control of Guadalcanal. The planes would fly about three hundred nautical miles north to the island of Bougainville, dropping their bombs on the harbor from which Japanese troops often debarked on fast destroyers heading to Guadalcanal as reinforcements.

In July 1943 most members of Roddenberry's crew—at least a few of them Pearl Harbor survivors—were sent back to the United States. New crews were assembled for the 394th. Becoming a first lieutenant, Roddenberry passed the test given by the check pilot, was made a full pilot, and given his own crew. Two days later, on August 2, he sat in the cockpit preparing to fly his first mission out of Espiritu Santo. He checked ahead of him and saw that the coconut trees and foliage at the end of the runway—steel segments laid over coral—had been hacked into stumps standing no higher than two feet.

Elmer Schoggen, the assistant squadron operations officer, was present on the ground. He saw Roddenberry's plane begin down the field. "As he got going," Schoggen says, "he saw that he didn't have an air-speed indicator. For some reason, it wasn't there. He just went straight ahead, through all those trees. He never got off the island." It was the war's only such incident on the island.

Leon Rockwell, who also witnessed the crash, says that Roddenberry realized he didn't have adequate air speed at the two-thirds mark and had to choose whether to brake or chance a takeoff. He hit the brakes, which apparently went out. The plane slammed into the coral and coconut trees, tearing off the nose and badly damaging the undercarriage. All but two of the crew jumped out unscathed. Those two, the bombardier and navigator—a husband and father who'd volunteered to stay for one final mission—had been in the nose and were killed instantly. Its tanks full of gasoline, the plane soon began burning, which set off the ammunition for the thirteen .50-caliber machine guns on board. Soon the Flying Fortress was reduced to charred and twisted pieces of scrap metal.

Roddenberry returned to the United States later that month, after only a few more uneventful missions. In a brief story recounting the airman's reunion with his wife and his parents in their suburban Temple City home, the *Los Angeles Times* reprinted one of five stanzas to a satirical song Roddenberry had written while away. He said that the song was adopted as the theme of the 394th, but was heard being sung all over the South Pacific by Allied soldiers and pilots:

I wanna go home.
I wanna go home.
Time tells us that ack-ack's a beautiful sight.
Life printed a picture of tracers at night.
But the stuff that we see is real.
From up close it loses appeal.
Oh Ma, I'm too young to die
I wanna go home.

CHAPTER THREE

On

the Outskirts

of the

Final

Frontier

ONE SUMMER morning in 1963, Christopher Knopf telephoned Gene Roddenberry at MGM and asked if his old friend was willing to play hooky that afternoon from *The Lieutenant.* Two of the best seats in Dodger Stadium—field box, directly behind home plate—had come into Knopf's possession, and he wanted to share the riches.

Knopf, a successful television writer—and nephew of noted book publisher Alfred Knopf—had been introduced to Roddenberry six years before by *Have Gun, Will Travel* creator Sam Rolfe. They'd worked together briefly, along with Bruce Geller, in late 1959 at Four Star, having been hired to write three anthology scripts each for *The June Allyson Show* in anticipation of a Writers Guild strike that would have halted production had finished scripts not been in the pipeline. Provoked by the sight of their Spartan accommodations in which they were expected to hatch nine brilliant scripts, Roddenberry had instigated a raid on the executive suite, dragging a better class of furniture and several handmade, extravagantly expensive chairs into their own offices. "We can use this stuff better than they can," he'd said.

But after writing only a single script (with Geller), Roddenberry had left Four Star with the explanation that he had "something better to do." On his first day at Screen Gems, where he was to write and produce the "Night Stick" pilot, he decided to show the company's imposing president, Irving Briskin, that he would not be intimidated by him. When Briskin, who was then in his late sixties, rose to greet Roddenberry, Roddenberry put his hands on Briskin's shoulders and forced him into a 360-degree spin.

At the Dodger game, Roddenberry's mind was less on baseball than on work. *The Lieutenant* had not yet made its broadcast debut. No ratings yet, no critics, no network commentary. He was as full of hope and optimism as a manager during spring training, before the season's first ball is thrown out. Knopf, by contrast, had recently completed his contractual relationship with Four Star, after writing the pilot for *The Big Valley*. He felt wonderful having an afternoon to himself.

With the score tied in the late innings, Dodger catcher John Roseboro animated the crowd by tripling. The rattled pitcher paid little attention to Roseboro while facing the next batter. Roseboro increased his lead off third.

Roddenberry chose that moment to ask, "You want to hear an idea for another series?"

"No," Knopf said, eyes on the game.

Undaunted, Roddenberry continued: "I've got another series idea. I'm going to place it at the end of the nineteenth century. There's a dirigible, see? And on this dirigible are all these people of mixed races, and they go from place to place each week, places no one has discovered yet."

Now he had Knopf's attention, so neither of them saw Roseboro steal home. They heard only the roar of thirty thousand people, who were now standing.

"How would you like to write the pilot?" Roddenberry asked.

There are two likely explanations for why Roddenberry would ask another writer to write a pilot for his own idea. He either didn't have the time, since he was producing a weekly series, or he believed he lacked the skill.

"There's no question in my mind," Knopf says, "this idea was absolutely the philosophical forerunner to *Star Trek.* "

Roddenberry and Knopf met with Norman Felton, who warmed to the concept. The untitled show was to have been produced at MGM by Felton's Arena Productions. Presumably, Roddenberry would have been either executive producer or producer, with Knopf's role unknown aside from the writing of the pilot. What derailed the project, in the end, was money. "There wasn't enough to go around," Knopf says.

The following February, with *The Lieutenant* soon to be just a memory and Roddenberry once more a free-lancer, he again approached Felton with the idea, this one set in the future instead of the past, the mode of transport a space vehicle instead of a dirigible.

Roddenberry's agent, Alden Schwimmer, the West Coast head of the Ashley-Famous talent agency and a man with an unerring instinct for hit series, had suggested that he devise a science fiction series. He was sure he could sell it, Schwimmer said. At the time, millions of eyes were looking skyward, as the American Mercury space program appeared to be lagging behind the Soviet Union in the so-called Race for Space.

After they'd batted the idea around for a while and considered some possibilities, Roddenberry went home and composed a six-page outline that summarized the concept and contained brief character sketches of the principals.

Roddenberry presented the outline to Felton. "It's 'Wagon Train in the sky,'" he said.

"You mean, 'Wagon Train in Space'?" Felton prompted.

"Right. 'Wagon Train in Space.' What do you think?"

"I don't think much of it," Felton said. "I wouldn't do it. I don't see how you can. Sure, you're doing *Wagon Train,* but it's one thing to do it on earth and another entirely to go out in space. Where are you going to go? You have to go to different worlds. You're going to have to have scenic backgrounds; all the places can't look alike. And the same with the clothes they wear."

"You don't like it," Roddenberry said.

"It's not that I don't like it, but it's too expensive," Felton said. "You can't do it for television."

Roddenberry had no reason to disbelieve Felton, who was a television veteran and a formidable risk taker. If Felton thought this idea was essentially unfeasible, it probably was. Except for Schwimmer's certainty that much of the prime-time television audience was hungry for science fiction, Roddenberry would have abandoned the project and moved on to the next paycheck without a second thought.

Not long before, Schwimmer's boss, Ted Ashley, had negotiated an unusual (probably unique at the time) deal to make Ashley-Famous the agent for Desilu Studios, which had seen its once-thriving enterprise go mostly bust. In the fifties, when Lucille Ball and Desi Arnaz produced *I Love Lucy* and ran the studio they'd founded, the soundstages had been filled with network productions developed and owned by Desilu. Now, following her divorce from Arnaz, Ball alone owned the studio. If not for *The Lucy Show* and the shows that merely rented space there, Desilu's soundstages would have been silent. Ashley-Famous's task was to revitalize the studio—to begin again producing hit shows for Desilu.

As an incentive to Ball to continue making *The Lucy Show,* which was a huge hit, every year CBS presented her with a sum of money above and beyond the license fee it paid to air the weekly thirty minutes. The $600,000 bonus was ostensibly intended to be used as a development fund for Desilu, but Ball was entitled to spend the money any way she chose. If she had wanted to, she could have pocketed it. She chose to spend it on development, entrusting Ashley—the Michael Ovitz of his era—to restructure the studio hierarchy and to invigorate the development department.

Ashley assigned Schwimmer to carry out the mandate, and for a brief time Schwimmer kept an office at Desilu, abandoning it only to discourage an appearance of a conflict of interest between his clients and the studio. One year later, the fund would be used to commission both the *Mission: Impossible* and *Mannix* pilots. Now some of it was offered to Roddenberry as incentive to expand the science fiction idea into something that weighed a bit more in both thought and expression. (Without the money, Roddenberry may not have written another word, being disinclined, as later memos suggest, to write on speculation.) CBS, which traditionally saw all Desilu projects first, required a more detailed treatment before commissioning a pilot script. Herb Solow, Desilu's executive in charge of film programs, who decided which ideas would be pitched to the networks, worked with Roddenberry on refining and redefining the concept. As Solow saw it, Roddenberry's short treatment essentially described an anthology series, one with new characters every week that would require entirely too much exposition before getting to the meat of the story. Inasmuch as anthology stories had become all but extinct on network television, Solow knew it was a fatal flaw. His remedy: a captain's voice-over that would allow quick exposition by explaining the hows, whys, and wheres of particular situations. "That way, you could cut to the chase," Solow says. (Later, in a letter to Alden Schwimmer, Roddenberry sang Solow's praises: "Solow, whom I worked with most directly and intimately, was enormously helpful. One of the most pleasant and talented men I have ever had the pleasure to work with in this business." Nonetheless, Roddenberry usually credited "my cousin in Ohio" for the innovation.)[1]

Roddenberry would later claim to have been an avid science fiction fan as far back as 1926, with the debut of the magazine *Amazing Stories.* And at least one classmate from Benjamin Franklin High School in Los Angeles, class of Winter 1939, remembers Roddenberry hiding his science fiction reading behind the cover of a textbook. "Gene sat right in front of me," Dean Scurr says. "Roddenberry and Scurr. Alphabetical order. He'd hide them inside the books so the teacher wouldn't know he wasn't studying."

Roddenberry's personality profile in high school does fit a particular stereotype of the eccentric genius of the imagination. "The only thing that sticks in my mind about Gene during high school," says classmate Russell Moody, "was he always wore brown corduroy pants and a white shirt, the pants hanging too low on his hips and the shirttail always out. He carried a ringed notebook most of the time for his homework, but it was a sloppy thing, too. He just never put the papers into rings; he'd just stuff them inside the covers, so they'd be sticking out all over."

For Paulette Spyrell, one school memory of Roddenberry dominates: "There was a place on campus," she says, "where you walked across from the auditorium to the main building, and it had an overhang. It wasn't all that high, just high enough. Gene was just standing on it one day, opening an umbrella. But it wasn't raining. I asked what he was doing. He said, 'I'm going to see if this works like a parachute.' He jumped off and broke his leg. I never forgot it. It's about the only thing I really remember about him.'"

According to a consensus of classmates, Roddenberry was essentially a loner. "He was not the most social cat there was," Scurr says.

"I would say that it's very possible," Moody says, "that he never had close friends."

Eula Lee Geisert believes that Roddenberry dated infrequently, if at all.

"I can't think of anybody that he really actually buddied with," Miriam Nordahl Post adds.

Perhaps paradoxically, Roddenberry was his graduating class's boys' social chairman. He was also one of two senior boys to represent the school in the third annual Southern California High School Debate Tournament held at the University of Southern California two months before he graduated, competing in the oratory and extemporaneous divisions. He'd joined the school's Junto Club, which encouraged forensics by holding oratory contests and debates, as well as the Spanish Club and author's workshop; and attended meetings of the International Forum, Franklin's contribution to the World Friendship Club—"designed to promote better feeling among nations," in the words of Franklin's 1939 yearbook.

Cliff Wynne recalls often seeing Roddenberry in a particular posture at his school desk: slumped low, his long legs sticking out, hands clasped behind his neck as he stared at the ceiling. "I remember thinking, 'I wonder what he's thinking about.' He struck me as pensive. Now that I look back on it, he gave things a lot more thought than a lot of people did. I think he probably had lots of stuff in there." His mind, even then, was on his creative writing. "I think he was writing then pretty much what he wrote later, things of a futuristic nature," Urban Moor says.

Moor and the others may be accurate, but the science fiction professionals and aficionados Roddenberry dealt with soon after beginning work on *Star Trek* knew him to be a neophyte—one with a vision, but still a neophyte.

Needing help with his *Star Trek* treatment, Roddenberry approached his friend of some years, the talented and prolific writer Samuel Peeples, who eventually authored more than two dozen novels and some three hundred scripts. The two men had been introduced by their agents in 1957 when both were up for a Writers Guild of America Award in the best Western category. Peeples was nominated for an episode of *Wanted: Dead or Alive*, the series that starred the young Steve McQueen as a bounty hunter; and Roddenberry for a *Have Gun, Will Travel* script titled "Helen of Abajinian," about an Armenian grape grower. When Roddenberry won the award (it was his first and only major scriptwriting award, despite later assertions to the contrary), he confided to Schwimmer that he'd voted for Peeples's script. Peeples, meanwhile, told his own agent that he'd cast his ballot for the winner.

"I voted for Gene's script," says Peeples, "because I felt that he'd put a lot of humanity in the story. Most Westerns were shoot-'em-ups that lacked any real dramatic structure." Roddenberry's story had a conventional theme of a woman needing rescue, but with an unconventional twist: This woman had the soul of a poet.

Roddenberry knew that Peeples owned one of the largest collections in the world of science fiction and fantasy magazines. His library held every issue of *Amazing Stories,* and through his friendship with noted science fiction writer Robert Bloch, Peeples had become acquainted with nearly everyone of accomplishment in the field.

"I don't think Gene had ever written science fiction before," Peeples says. "He came to my house and looked at my collection several times." While concocting his characters and stories, Roddenberry needed to visualize their physical universe. "He took photos of the covers to get ideas for the spaceship—the *Enterprise* [née S.S. *Yorktown*], as it became. He wanted to know what had been done, and what would constitute science fiction as opposed to fantasy."

As a sort of condensed primary education in the field, Peeples let Roddenberry borrow his copy of Olaf Stapledon's classic science fiction history of the future, *The Last and First Man.*

Correspondence pertaining to Roddenberry's visits with Peeples suggests that the *Star Trek* creator had a limited knowledge of science fiction and its purveyors. A Roddenberry memo of a conversation the two men had over lunch refers to Peeples having told him about *Quartermass*, "a science fiction television series and then later motion pictures done by BBC"; it also mentioned eight notable sci-fi writers, Robert Bloch, Frederic Brown, Nelson Bond, Richard Matheson, Howard Brown, Pohl Anderson, Theodore Sturgeon, and James E. Gunn—at least some of whom would have been known to Roddenberry had he been familiar with science fiction.[2]

A letter from Roddenberry to the Writers Guild written after the lunch asks for the agency contacts of these same men (with the exception of Bloch, who presumably could have been reached through Peeples).[3] A letter to Peeples asks whether "there is in existence any list of SF writers, possibly a 'SF Writers Guild' organization or etc. from which I might ultimately be able to query members re their interest in taking a stab at TV."[4]

At the same time Roddenberry arranged a meeting with writer Jerry Sohl at Nickodell's restaurant on Melrose Avenue, a studio hangout for both Desilu and next-door-neighbor Paramount Pictures employees. The author of twelve science fiction novels as well as a television writer, Sohl had not known Roddenberry, who introduced himself as a former policeman, a *Have Gun, Will Travel* writer, and the soon to be former producer of *The Lieutenant*.

"I found him to be amiable and easy to talk to," Sohl says. "I had no idea what the hell he was trying to do. He didn't seem to know an awful lot about science fiction, and he confessed that he didn't. That's why I was there. He was going to pick my brains and, quite frankly, find out what I thought of this series that he had in mind, and whether I'd be available as a writer."

Roddenberry asked Sohl for the names of science fiction writers on the West Coast. Sohl's impression was that Roddenberry hadn't known the men's work, but the list mostly coincided with the one Roddenberry had culled from Peeples. He suggested William Nolan, Charles Beaumont (for whom Sohl had actually ghost-written *Twilight Zone* scripts when the Alzheimer's disease that later killed him was as yet undiagnosed), George Clayton Johnson, and Harlan Ellison. "My mentioning their names seemed to reaffirm that they would make suitable candidates for at least an interview," Sohl remembers.

Two months later, in August, Roddenberry wrote again to Peeples: "It's time I sent you another note of sincerest thanks for the most helpful information you keep providing on science fiction for my *Star Trek* television series. I don't want to become a burden and hope I'll have opportunities to repay the kindness."[5]

CBS had quickly passed on the project, and Roddenberry had worked energetically toward satisfying the deal Desilu's Solow had made with NBC after pitching it through the network's programming hierarchy. The network had agreed to consider financing a complete pilot script—and then, of course, its production, pending script approval—if offered a choice between three well-developed outlines, each representative of the type of stories *Star Trek* would present. Outlines for "Mudd's Women," "Landru's Paradise," and "The Cage" had been submitted in July, and with them a letter to Schwimmer: "Hope we can get a decision from NBC quickly on them as I'd like to get into pilot script as soon as possible.... While awaiting the *Star Trek* decision, I should get started on something else immediately. Any suggestions?"

Taken together, Roddenberry's three original story outlines may tell us almost as much about their author as they do about his conception of the series he wanted to produce. In "Landru's Paradise," which later mutated into the episode "The Return of the Archons" (Archons was the name of the police club at Los Angeles City College, which Roddenberry briefly attended after graduating high school), he attacked both authority and conformity. An *Enterprise* landing party, visiting "a far-off solar system," finds itself in a sort of fin de siècle midwestern American town in which the residents seem content with their provincial worldview. But as Capt. Robert April (the name of the character whose place is taken by Lieutenant Rice on the mission to Vietnam in the final episode of *The Lieutenant*) soon discovers, the appearance is illusory. In fact, the inhabitants are ignorant and repressed.

"Archon is anything but a paradise," Roddenberry wrote. "What can be seen on the street, the happy friendliness and tranquillity, masks despair, dullness, almost a living death. There are no police, no crime, no jails, because the slightest infraction is stamped out ruthlessly by The Lawgivers."

Roddenberry, says his friend Christopher Knopf, "seemed to distrust high authority—people in power. He liked to tweak authority. As opposed to just nailing them and going to war, he liked to tweak. That was his way of bringing them down. He seemed to have a great affection for people in low places."

The plot resolves when it is revealed that Archon's computer-mandated laws and edicts have not benefited Archon. Forced to answer a direct question with a truthful response, the computer admits to April that "The laws of Landru are destroying Archon's people," and that they have accomplished nothing useful. "Can the computer do anything for Archon?" Only self-destruct, which it soon does in a flash of smoke. This was the first of what would be several *Star Trek* episodes in which man searches for God, finds Him, debunks Him, and lives more happily afterward—or kills Him off metaphorically, thus improving mankind's well-being.

"Gene once explained his view of religion to me," Knopf says. "He felt that when the world was invented, there were only negatives—negative gods who kept us from all types of behavior. You couldn't do this, you couldn't do that. Then, suddenly, man says, 'Wait a minute. Hold it, hold it. Let's have one god. We'll still fear him, but let's make him a positive force.'"

The God that Eugene Wesley Roddenberry had been introduced to as a young boy was the God who, in the words of the "Battle Hymn of the Republic," wielded a "terrible, swift sword"; a God whose wrath was to be feared, and for whom love was less important than respect. This, in many ways, also described his father, Eugene Edward Roddenberry, the product of a strict southern upbringing, and a man holding bigoted and racist views.

It was in the Baptist church in El Paso, Texas, that the senior Roddenberry, a World War I cavalry veteran making a meager living as a lineman for the local electric company, met Caroline Glen

Golemon, an operator with Tri-State Telephone. Caroline, who lived at home with her parents and five siblings, was only sixteen, five years younger than Eugene Roddenberry, when they were married in November 1920 by Burt Bray, a Seventh-Day Adventist minister.

Along with two of Caroline's siblings and the senior Golemons, the newlyweds moved into a tiny house at 1907 East Yandell, located in the so-called Five Points area of El Paso. The tiny red-brick structure had four rooms surrounding a toilet chamber. There were no cabinets in the kitchen, and only one sink for everyone's use, from shaving to dishwashing. Into that cramped misery came Eugene Wesley Roddenberry, born at home, with Dr. Herbert Stevenson attending, on August 19, 1921—nine months and two weeks after his parents' wedding. (Gene's birth certificate contains a number of inaccuracies. His middle name was spelled "Westley," the address was jumbled, and, most galling to his anti-Semitic father, Caroline's maiden name was listed as "Goldman." In the mid-1960s, the elder Roddenberry was introduced to Desilu Studios executive Herb Solow at a social event. "You know," he told Solow, "it wasn't till I first came to see my boy here that I met a Jew." Then after tasting fine champagne that his son had bought to impress him, he said, "Personally, I like Thunderbird.")

When young Gene was two, the financially struggling Roddenberrys moved to the promised land of Los Angeles, where Eugene Edward became an officer with the Los Angeles Police Department—at the time among the most corrupt and poorly run in the country. The former cavalryman, who was said to have ridden out of Fort Bliss into Mexico, in search of Pancho Villa with General Pershing's forces (Fort Bliss, in El Paso, says it has no record of his service), became a mounted officer. "I can still remember age four, riding up there behind him, the ground seeming a hundred feet below as he patrolled our city's then beautiful Lincoln Park, its lake and boats, a huge merry-go-round, the lovely botanical gardens and zoo," Roddenberry once said.[6]

It seems reasonable to assume that a man fitting Big Gene's personality profile would not, in the 1920s, have embraced the sort

of nonsexist tolerance that in the 1990s passes for enlightenment—not when his son was gangly, unathletic, and sickly. Little
Gene most likely disappointed Big Gene's expectations of what the
son of a generally redneck tough guy ought to be.

But whatever unpleasantness Roddenberry may have suffered
at the words, deeds, or attitudes of his father, he typically later
painted the old man in rosy tones. "He had a side to him that was
diffident, quiet," Roddenberry said. "He had an ugly side, too, but
it was, I think, legitimate for him at that time, as I know how he
grew up in the Florida-Georgia backcountry."[7]

In the same romanticized vein, he recounted the time "Father
returned home from LAPD patrol and went to his bedroom and
cried." The elder Roddenberry had walked in on a robbery in
progress, surprising the robber, who panicked and fired several
rounds from a .45 Colt automatic at him, "which caused the suspect to die from a .38-caliber bullet," Roddenberry said. "Only
afterwards did my father learn that the suspect was just sixteen
years old. I like him for attending the boy's funeral despite the anger
he knew must be faced there."[8]

In an interview with *The Humanist*, the magazine devoted to
the philosophy of enlightened self-interest that he espoused (he sat
on the magazine's board of advisers), Roddenberry claimed that
his father was a visionary who predicted both the Los Angeles free-
way system—"Gene," Roddenberry quoted him as saying, "someday they'll rip out whole blocks of the city and put gigantic
highways through here"—and the defeat of the German army precisely at Stalingrad. (Interviewer David Alexander seemed reluctant to challenge Roddenberry's statements, and at one point
himself stated that Roddenberry's father had been the inspiration
behind the character of visionary Edith Keeler in the *Star Trek*
episode "The City on the Edge of Forever." But, in fact, Harlan Ellison wrote that original script, and while Roddenberry later rewrote
it considerably to fit the show's budget and format, Joan Collins's
Keeler showed up essentially as Ellison had created her: a combination, he says, of several women suffragettes and some evange-
lists, including Aimee Semple McPherson. Roddenberry did not

correct Alexander's statement. "I didn't even know Gene Rodden-berry's father," Ellison says. "I didn't know if he'd had a father or whether he'd been issued like a postage stamp.")[9]

"I guess many of my beliefs about ordinary people and what they can do come out of respect for my father," Roddenberry said.[10]

Along with his four years younger brother Bob and five years younger sister Doris, Roddenberry did most of his growing up in Highland Park and Temple City, quiet suburban areas near downtown Los Angeles. The kids sometimes accompanied their parents to evening volleyball games at a nearby grammar school, where one of the other participants was a young policeman named William H. Parker, who later, as its chief, would remake the Los Angeles Police Department in his own image—and deliver speeches written by Roddenberry.

Gene Roddenberry was raised to be a good Baptist, just like his mother. But in his early teens, he began questioning his religious inculcation. "I was around fourteen and emerging as a personality," Roddenberry told *The Humanist*. "I had never really paid much attention to the [church] sermon before. I was more interested in the deacon's daughter and what we might be doing between services. I listened to the sermon, and I remember complete astonishment because what they were talking about were things that were just crazy. It was Communion time, where you eat this wafer and are supposed to be eating the body of Christ and drinking his blood. My first impression was, 'This is a bunch of cannibals they've put me down among.' "[11]

Apparently, Roddenberry hadn't paid very close attention in church to the reasoning behind the Communion ceremony, because he said that he "puzzled" over its origins: "How the hell did Jesus become something to be eaten?"[12]

At that epiphanic moment, Roddenberry continued, he began to equate Jesus with the likes of Santa Claus and chose to ignore "the nonsense," "magic," and "superstition" of religion. Thus freed from the concept of God—"the guy who knows you masturbate"—he tried to extricate himself from shame, guilt, and blame, from contrition or penitence—from any emotion or thought that might undermine the pursuit of pleasure or the quenching of passion.[13]

The second of Roddenberry's three potential pilot stories, "The Women," began as a short synopsis: "Duplicating a page from the 'Old West'; hanky-panky aboard [the *Enterprise*] with a cargo of women destined for a far-off colony." In its next and longer draft, still bearing significant differences from the episode that was later titled "Mudd's Women," the space trader who came to be known as Harry Mudd is named Harry Patton. Patton's job is to supply wives—"most of them beyond their prime, but who undoubtedly look good to lonely men"—to colonists. "Rather plain, colorless females who would normally be inept and shy, they have a strange compelling need for men." Eventually, the ship's doctor, Boyce, and Captain April discover that Patton is using a "hypnotic" drug on the women that somehow enables them to "handle" the colonists. April seizes the drug, which of course dooms the women to become again the "inept shy females" they really are. Having now made everyone miserable in the process, April returns the contraband and allows the men and women their mutually beneficial illusion.

In "Landru's Paradise," Captain April chose to extinguish the inhabitants' ignorant bliss, while in "The Women" he eventually sanctioned it. So, after two pilot stories, the score was one for illusion and one for reality. "The Cage" broke the tie in favor of reality. Evidently, April made arbitrary decisions about which dream was up. Either that, or his reasoning was inscrutable.

In "The Cage," April doggedly refuses to allow the "crablike creatures" (they became the humanoid "Telosians" in the outline's second draft) who hold him captive on the planet Sirius IV to live vicariously through his memories, thoughts, and fantasies. His fellow prisoner, Vina the seductress, attempts to convince him to "relax and go along with the illusion. It's pleasant, isn't it? Everything looks real, feels real, the pleasure can be equally real." The third-person narrator continues: "He can't deny that this is out of his own daydreams. And it's a fine one. The more intelligent the man, the more colorful and more pleasant the variety of his dreams. Imagination is superior to real life, there is no flesh and blood to be hurt. He can even relax and delight in those secret evil things which lurk in the back of every man's mind."

Meanwhile, Mr. Spock and navigator José Tyler try to extricate April by using their "lasser" guns. And when, finally, April does outwit his captors and escape, he acknowledges "that there is nothing lovelier than an illusion. Or more dangerous."

When Roddenberry wrote these three stories, the loveless rift between himself and his wife was irreparable. He confided to friends that each day felt a little more lifeless.

Sam Rolfe attributes the couple's problems to Roddenberry's career change creating situational pressures for young adults whose middle-class upbringing, at least on the surface, had more in common with Norman Rockwell than Salvador Dali. What happens to a policeman and his family when his daily existence of maintaining order in the city's concrete grid becomes the filtered reality of Hollywood? When a casual dinner in the latter costs the equivalent of week's pay in the former? When life and death are measured by lost credits, not lost blood? One day Roddenberry had to play by the rules, and the next day he made them. In some ways, all a policeman and a producer have in common is the air they breathe—certainly not their expectations for tomorrow, or their temptations in the present.

"Suddenly their world opened up because of what he could do," Rolfe says. "And she didn't understand it. Eileen never understood it. She hated Gene's writing career. Well, she loved the money—all the perks—but she couldn't keep up with it. She once told my wife, 'I wish he'd never started writing.' She didn't comprehend the society in which he was moving. Eileen is of a world that's more natural, more middle America. So, increasingly, she got left out of it. Also, let's face it: Gene played around a lot after that. He had all these openings, and he took them."

Like Rolfe, Christopher Knopf met Eileen Roddenberry only after Gene had become a writer and the problems between them had stultified the relationship, after he'd stopped displaying pleasure at her company. They never met the woman he fell in love with. "Her head was always pulled back, like she was tense, very tense," Knopf says. "She seemed very uncomfortable."

Robert Justman, *Star Trek*'s associate producer, conjectures that circumstances conspired against Eileen. "I think she feared the sort of life that Gene was getting into," he says. "I think she feared for their marriage, for her safety, for their family, for their financial future. The people that Gene was now associating with represented an industry that disgusted her and threatened her. That, I think, is what made her cold."

Roddenberry often gave voice to his soured feelings. "From time to time," Justman says, "he would make remarks in front of her, and I would feel terribly embarrassed. There was a lot of heartbreak for her, because he would mess around."

There may have been one other unmendable breach between Mr. and Mrs. Gene Roddenberry, particularly when he began living by the products of his wits and socialized with those of the same ilk. "His mind was so much better than hers," Rolfe says. "He could easily go with the flow. He had an ego that could stretch as far as it went."

Given Roddenberry's marital situation, it's no wonder that all three pilot stories concerned themselves with illusion and reality, or that two of them—"The Cage" and "Landru's Paradise"—addressed what must have occupied Roddenberry's daily ruminations: Just what, precisely, ought to be the nature of man's mate? Is she the temptress, the pleasure provider? Or is she the tormenter, the dream breaker? With Majel Barrett, who lived near the Desilu Studios in order to be near her lover, he found the seductress. "Gene," says Justman, "made no bones about the fact that he was keeping Majel. He even invited me over one evening to the apartment for drinks—you know, sort of a party. I said, 'Gene, I don't want to know about it.' I tried to talk him out of continuing their relationship. She was his mistress. I was afraid that someone would find out. Little did I know that he enjoyed that sort of illicitness."

In his series description, Roddenberry described yeoman J. M. Colt: "With a strip queen figure even a uniform cannot hide, Colt serves as captain's secretary, recorder, bookkeeper, and with surprising efficiency. She undoubtedly dreams of serving Robert April with equal efficiency in more personal departments."[14]

And the man being served so efficiently by this ideal female? "The first and most important impression of April is of a man who might as easily stand at the helm of a naval cruiser in our own day," Roddenberry wrote, giving the year as anywhere from 1995 to 2995. "About thirty-four, lean and capable both mentally and physically." This made him exactly ten years younger and about thirty pounds thinner than his creator.

NBC chose "The Cage" as its pilot script in July 1964. In August, Roddenberry completed the first draft teleplay. Four months and several drafts later, following Herb Solow's preparation of a preliminary shooting budget, the network committed to funding the pilot's production. Roddenberry changed his protagonist's name to Christopher Pike, taking Pike from the last name of the lead in his "APO: 923" pilot, and Christopher, possibly, from Columbus leading his ships into the new world.

The script completed, the thorniest problem now became production design. It would be relatively simple to design the human Telosians, their barren aboveground planet, the "cage" in which Pike was to be held, and the various background locales to which his imagination jettisons him. Not so simple, and of paramount importance to the credibility of the series, was the design of the United Star Ship *Enterprise*.

Walter (Matt) Jefferies had been working on the Desilu lot as the production designer for *Ben Casey* when studio officials asked him to meet with a producer whose name he'd never heard. "I was informed that a man was coming in by the name of Roddenberry who had an idea for a space show," Jefferies remembers. Like Roddenberry, Jefferies had flown B-17s during World War II. The two talked briefly about that experience, then for fifteen minutes Roddenberry described his preliminary parameters: a shirtsleeve environment, quasi-military; a crew of several hundred; a craft not powered by visible rockets or jets, but powerful in appearance nonetheless. Roddenberry showed him the photos he'd taken of the magazine covers belonging to Sam Peeples. Then they went their own separate research ways.

As a member of the Aviation Space Writers Association and a

professional aviation illustrator, Jefferies had access to a library of potential resource materials, and he viewed every available *Buck Rogers* and *Flash Gordon* episode. He returned in two weeks with his first set of sketches, and a revised set a week after that.

In the meantime, Roddenberry was consulting so-called experts who might be able to speculate intelligently about what space travel might look like in the as yet undated future. Through his Pentagon and Marine contacts, he located a colonel at the air force's Weapons Effects and Tests Group in Albuquerque, New Mexico. Through him he found another air force colonel, and a scientist at the RAND Corporation, which is a social science, science, and military think tank in Santa Monica, California. Through him, Roddenberry contacted a physicist, who agreed to participate, Roddenberry said, if "we keep it at least enough in accord with the laws of physics that scientists can enjoy the program too."[15] But having to satisfy scientists in addition to a studio, a network, a production designer, and cinematographers became too burdensome. When the "experts" deemed their designs too far advanced of the most optimistic speculation, Roddenberry concluded that scientific plausibility was less critical than viewer credibility and aesthetics. He embraced pure fiction, not necessarily related to science.

"Eventually," Jefferies says, "we came up with a space ship design that we were both happy with. I really think he knew what he wanted. Of course, I had my own particular practical reasons for what I thought should be in and on the ship. And I knew it had to be photographable—a shape you could pick up under almost any lighting conditions."

Unlike the vehicles seen in *2001: A Space Odyssey* and *Star Wars*, which are covered by equipment-filled nooks and crannies, the starships of the future, Jefferies reasoned, will be smooth. He thought it likely that vital maintenance areas would be accessed through the craft's interior, rather than its exterior. "What man makes to work is going to break sooner or later," Jefferies explains. "So why put people in the most dangerous environment imaginable outside to make repairs? Logic, to me, says the work should be done on the inside."

The *Enterprise* would require an identification number. Jefferies began the notation with the letter *N*, which, under international aviation agreements, has always designated the United States and would therefore imply the U.S. to the cognoscenti. But wanting additional letters as well, and to satisfy Roddenberry's insistence that the vessel be transnational, Jefferies added two *C*'s—not, as some believed, because the Soviet Union's abbreviation in the Cyrillic alphabet was CCCP. "My main concern was that the letters be easily read," he says. For the same reason, from the numerals he immediately eliminated threes, fours, sixes, eights, and nines; viewed from a distance they can too easily be misread. While playing with the remaining permutations, he noticed NC-17740, the notation on his own plane that had been built in 1935 for the Indiana governor's office. A little tinkering and, voilà, NCC-1701—the U.S.S. *Enterprise*.

In early 1965, production began on "The Cage." Months later, Roddenberry solicited comments from crew members and production staff, and compiled them into digest form in preparation for what appeared to be the grind of getting out a weekly television show. "The general consensus is that our crew and departments did a good job," he wrote. "Many did an outstanding job. However, it is generally agreed that bringing in a series of this nature, with quality and on budget, requires an early and highly critical evaluation of all the lessons learned during pilot production."

Most of the comments were technical in nature—such as, spraying the color of the *Enterprise*'s bridge a neutral gray and enlarging the platform on which it stood, muffling the noise on the soundstages, limiting the number of opticals and effects per episode. But one nontechnical comment stands out: "Whenever doing a time-consuming episode, we should limit the use of females. Since other aspects of the show can be very time-consuming, we cannot often afford the forty-five minutes per actress lost each day in hairstyling time."

CHAPTER FOUR

Lost

in

Space

MEMO TO "All Concerned" from Gene Roddenberry: "Per conversations with most concerned,
the problem of too modern hairstyle of male
actors in *Star Trek*, regulars as well as both SAG and SEG, has
been resolved. Rather than requesting altering of the basic contour
favored by the actor, a simple and easily adjustable change is being
made in the sideburns, i.e., pointing the bottom of them rather
than wearing them square across."[1]

In the mythology of *Star Trek*, NBC vetoed "The Cage" as "too cerebral." Roddenberry often spoke sharply of the network's decision,
deriding network executives for their shortsightedness. *Star Trek*
fans were invited to share his contemptuous laughter.

"The first pilot was rejected on the basis of being too intellectual for you slobs out in the television audience," he told a Rochester
Institute of Technology audience in 1976. "It did go on to win the
international Hugo Award, [the award given annually by the World
Science Fiction Convention for excellence] but I suppose many
things turned down by networks would win awards."[2]

Roddenberry's implication was that "The Cage" was an identifiable blueprint for a successful prime-time series, one that would
have appealed to millions of television viewers beyond the hidden
core of science fiction fans, and perhaps it was. But if so, his words
created the densest of ironies: Had "The Cage" been *Star Trek*'s

prototype, there would have been no Kirk or Bones, and a Spock who smiled at vibrating plants.

Roddenberry's account of NBC's decision contained an element of truth, but not the entire truth. And therein lay an essential reality of his personality. When he felt it was necessary to the circumstances, Gene Roddenberry reinvented himself. He was the Mutable Man, defining and redefining his belief system and worldview to accommodate his own foibles. His unifying philosophy was that his desires supported his actions, and his actions were supported by the facts. To remain unencumbered by self-doubt, he continually rationalized his behavior—and padded his résumé. After *Star Trek* finally made it on the air, he credited himself as co-creator of *Have Gun, Will Travel,*[3] when in fact his friend Sam Rolfe had created the series with Herb Meadows. He called himself a multiple Emmy winner, when in fact he never won one.[4] He insisted he was "a charter member of the [Writers] Guild,"[5] when in fact the Screenwriters Guild was founded in 1933—around his twelfth birthday.

In re-creating his past to match what he thought his audience wanted to hear, he turned those who had rejected "The Cage" into villains worthy of more disdain than the Klingons, despite the networks' considerable role—accidental or not—in the success of *Star Trek.*

In the mid-1960s, the three major networks divided the vast majority of the viewing audience. As the greatest advertising vehicle in history, television's raison d'être was to broadcast entertainment programs that reached the largest possible numbers. A program that wasn't welcomed into a sufficient number of living rooms, or was deemed inappropriate by advertisers, was generally replaced. Gene Roddenberry realized that in order to get on the air and stay on the air, *Star Trek* had to attract many more people than just hard-core fans of science fiction. *Star Trek* would have to be a bona fide action-adventure series.

"People want action-adventure, not science dialogue," he wrote to air force colonel Donald Prickett, one of his technical advisers, in May 1964, *before* writing the first pilot.[6] Echoes of that sentiment would later reverberate throughout his correspondence relating to the show. "Although no one has the complete answer [how to entertain the mass television audience], television has learned some things which seem presently vital to any successful drama-action-adventure series," he wrote in an early draft of the *Star Trek* writer-director bible.[7] His letter to Don Durgin, NBC's vice president of sales, written after the series was green-lighted, noted that the network's planned promotional emphasis on "drama-adventure [is] an idea which pleases me greatly." In his commentaries on other writers' scripts, he frequently noted that each show ought to milk every potential moment of "jeopardy" by placing the characters and ship in danger whenever possible. After cutting ten minutes from the first edited version of "The Cage," he said, "The thing which pleases me is that we get down to the planet and into lead character jeopardy sooner."[8] (Desilu executive Herb Solow points out that Roddenberry was unique among producers in trying to correspond directly with network executives: "No other producer of a television series ever wrote to a network vice president. He was trying to insinuate himself into areas he didn't belong. Over the years, NBC used to call me all the time and ask me to get him off their backs.")

Roddenberry's instincts did prove correct—"jeopardy" is what made many *Star Trek* episodes so successful. But his repeated chants of "too cerebral" were disingenuous at best. He protested too much.

When Herb Solow refused to accept NBC's initial rejection of "The Cage" and, pending script approval, got the network to commit to a second pilot ("It was Herb's tenacity and Herb's presentation that sold the series," says Jerry Stanley, then head of NBC's filmed programs), Roddenberry sought creative assistance.

"Gene was very frank with me," Sam Peeples says. "He said that they needed a new approach; some new characterizations. I'd told him before that I thought [the first pilot] was too much of a fantasy, not enough science fiction. He said, 'Evidently NBC agrees.'" (Mort Werner, NBC's programming department chief, later told Solow that he'd chosen "The Cage" because it had been the most difficult of the three submitted scripts to shoot. Since *Star Trek* was the first show Desilu had ever sold to NBC, he explained, and because science fiction was inherently difficult to produce, he wanted to test the studio's capabilities.)

As head of business affairs for NBC, Herb Schlosser negotiated the deals for both pilots with Solow. He recalls sitting with Mort Werner and West Coast programming head Grant Tinker in scheduling meetings in which both men argued strenuously with the sales people, who couldn't foresee mass appeal for *Star Trek*. "It wasn't an easy thing to get on the schedule," Schlosser says. "Both Mort and Grant were strongly for it. They wanted to try something new. Mind you, though, those were the days when there was quite a bit of science fiction around—*Voyage to the Bottom of the Sea*, *Lost in Space*. It wasn't as though science fiction wasn't being done. The big thing was that nobody knew from the [*Star Trek*] pilots what kinds of stories would be generated."

In a slight variation on the first arrangement, the network wanted to choose the second pilot from three finished scripts. Out of that came Roddenberry's own "Omega Glory"; Steven Kandel's "Mudd's Women," which was a much changed and improved version of Roddenberry's "The Women"; and Peeples's "Where No Man Has Gone Before."

After reading Peeples's first draft outline (then called "Star Prime") about a man, Lt. Mitchell, with accelerating cognitive powers, Roddenberry sent the writer a letter that listed his fifteen immediate reactions and suggestions. One of them said that, because NBC was likely to read the completed outline, Peeples ought to come right out and state the show's theme: "absolute power corrupteth absolutely."[9] Another suggestion related to the story's female officer, Elizabeth, who becomes involved with Mitchell. Roddenberry wanted to make her "something less than a 'swinger,' a little overly intelligent and inhibited." (In the script that was finally filmed, Mitchell refers to her as a "walking freezer unit.")

"Let me repeat now, Sam, that these are only suggestions and even ones you agree with might better appear in script than in outline," Roddenberry reiterated parenthetically near the letter's end.

"The decision is yours." He closed by calling Peeples's first draft "a hell of an exciting outline."[10]

It is an indisputable fact that Peeples played a critically important role in the genesis and development of *Star Trek*. Without him, NBC most probably would not have picked up the series. Kandel's "Mudd's Women," an otherwise enjoyable episode (after it was later rewritten), didn't begin to hint at the breadth of the show's possibilities, while Roddenberry's "The Omega Glory" was clumsy. It concluded, after an improbable cat-and-mouse chase, with Spock getting fried by a laser beam, which allowed the captain to dispatch the villainous turncoat. "The Captain hurries to Spock whom we find lying on his face, his body glowing strangely," it read. But Spock's not dead, because "his home planet is a place of volcanoes and fire...lovely, lovely heat which sustains and heals but never destroys those who are born there."[11]

Of the three, only "Where No Man" was a genuine pilot script, which was why NBC chose it. Significantly, Peeples's script refined the vision of the *Star Trek* universe in ways that would prove consequential to the show's development. Though neither Uhura nor McCoy were introduced, the sharp dialogue, the interplay of characters, and emphasis on pure science fiction that would mark the best episodes are first seen here. "You should have killed me when you could," Mitchell tells the captain. "Command and compassion is a fool's mixture."

Peeples had accepted Roddenberry's request to write the pilot strictly out of friendship. "It was a favor to Gene," he admits. At the time he was writing a pilot at MGM for *The Girl From U.N.C.L.E.*, and two pilots at Twentieth Century-Fox, *Lancer* and *Custer*—all of which were paying him considerably more than the $5,000 Roddenberry offered for "Where No Man Has Gone Before."

Except for the changes picked up in Roddenberry's script notes, "'Where No Man Has Gone Before' is completely mine," Peeples says. Beyond helping to sell the series, his monumental contribution to *Star Trek* may have been the episode's title. "Where no man has gone before" became the thematic hook that clarified the "Wagon

Train in space" (which turned into "Wagon Train to the stars") sales pitch. Later, the fans adapted the phrase as a recognizable refrain.

"When Gene did the first pilot," Peeples says, "the mission of the *Enterprise* was to check up on established colonies, the way *Wagon Train* would go from this point to that point, delivering new settlers and bringing in supplies. We felt to really branch out in this thing, we should take off into the unknown."

"*Enterprise* log, Capt. James Kirk commanding," Peeples's shooting script began, reflecting the change that would soon be made in the series lead. "We are leaving the vast cloud of stars and planets which we call our galaxy. Behind us, Earth, Mars, Venus— even our Sun—are specks of dust. The question: What is out there in the black void beyond? Until now, our mission has been that of space law regulation; contact with Earth colonies and investigation of alien life. But now, a new task—a probe out into where no man has gone before."

For the starship captain's log entry narrations, Roddenberry wanted to devise a futuristic measurement of time reference. He called Peeples. The two men had a few drinks while brainstorming, and soon began chuckling over their imaginative "stardate" computations. "We tried to set up a system that would be unidentifiable unless you knew how we did it," Peeples says.

They marked off sections on a pictorial depiction of the known universe and extrapolated how much earth time would elapse when traveling between given points, taking into account that the *Enterprise*'s warp engines would be violating Einstein's theory that nothing could exceed the speed of light. They concluded that the "time continuum" would therefore vary from place to place, and that earth time may actually be lost in travel. "So the stardate on Earth would be one thing, but the stardate on Alpha Centauri would be different," Peeples says. "We thought this was hilarious, because everyone would say, 'How come this date is before that date when this show is after that show?' The answer was because you were in a different sector of the universe."

Though his contributions to the show have gone largely unrecognized, Peeples is content to remain a footnote in *Star Trek* history. "When you're working in Hollywood, creating a television series," he says, "you really can't afford to bend over backwards giving everyone credit. You stand center stage in the spotlight and take your bows."

In *Star Trek* mythology, it has become an article of faith that NBC refused to have a woman as first officer of the *Enterprise*. The network's position, Roddenberry said, was that viewers would not buy a female second-in-command, even in the future. "We would like you to take out the female because we don't believe her in command of anything," he quoted NBC executives as saying. "To show you the intelligence behind that remark, they said, 'And while you're at it, get rid of the guy with the ears.' It seemed to me that we were having so many arguments at this time that I couldn't save them both, and so I decided to save the alien character...."[12]

His explanation accounts for why Majel Barrett, who played the character of Number One in "The Cage," was not seen in "Where No Man Has Gone Before." But NBC executives deny that the role's gender even crossed their minds. The decision, apparently, was made because Barrett's acting did not appeal to either network or studio executives.

Barrett, a native of Columbus, Ohio, had grown up in Cleveland. After graduation from Shaker Heights High School and the University of Miami in Florida, she briefly attended law school and then took up acting. Her credits included several stage productions and half a dozen small parts in feature films. By the time Roddenberry cast her as his Number One (both professionally and privately), she'd made about twenty television appearances on such shows as *Dr. Kildare, Bonanza, Leave It to Beaver*, and *The Lieutenant.*

"No one liked her acting," says Herb Solow. "The decision that she not be in the second pilot had nothing to do with her being female. She was a nice woman, but the reality was, she couldn't act. She got the part because she was Roddenberry's woman. When she later showed up as [nurse Christine Chapel, a recurring but small role for which she wore a blond wig], the network still didn't like her."

The fact that Roddenberry, a year after the first pilot's rejection, listed "a female Executive Officer" as one of the *Enterprise*'s continuing characters, would seem to corroborate Solow's explanation.[13] His compulsion to continue demonizing the network on this issue undermines his credibility. But Barrett's acting skills and nepotistic casting aside, the truth is that Roddenberry did indeed envision a command scenario that appears far more plausible in the 1990s than it did in the 1960s, when a female commander really did smack of science fiction. It it interesting that he couldn't accept credit without assigning blame, though one may find it admirable that he tried to protect the woman he loved from slings and arrows.

One other major cast change was made for the second pilot. Roddenberry later claimed that Jeffrey Hunter, the actor who'd portrayed Captain Pike, "was very disappointed when" NBC turned down "The Cage." In fact, Hunter asked to be excused from further participation.[14] Best known for playing Jesus Christ in *King of Kings,* Hunter was recognized as a movie star, despite his recent forays in television. Roddenberry and Desilu considered themselves lucky that he'd consented to appear on their small-screen show, something motion picture actors in the early 1960s did rarely if ever.

In an effort to change Hunter's mind, Desilu arranged a screening of the pilot for his wife. As his de facto manager, she was in a position of influence. But after watching "The Cage," she stood up and told Solow, "Jeffrey's not going to get anything out of this."

Roddenberry tried to persuade Hunter to return for one or two extra days of filming, at the rate of a thousand dollars per, in order to shoot "an additional action opening which can result in a fast, tightly cut, exciting film release"—that is, a motion picture.[15] This was an idea he'd broached with Norman Felton at the conclusion of *The Lieutenant.* With a theatrical release in mind, he'd written an hour's worth of follow-up that he hoped to tack on to his Vietnam episode. In the case of *Star Trek*, however, Roddenberry had no authority to offer a thousand dollars a day, or even a dollar a day. His authority to spend money, as series producer, extended only to the assignment of scripts.

Hunter's agent did not formally request his release from the upcoming filming of *Star Trek*'s second pilot until two weeks after his six-month exclusivity to the project ended on the first of June (1965). By then, Roddenberry and Desilu had rejected *Stoney Burke* star Jack Lord—"Jack takes his name too seriously," Roddenberry quipped[16]—and made a tentative deal with William Shatner to portray the *Enterprise*'s new captain, James Tiberius Kirk. (Kirk shared the same middle name as *The Lieutenant*'s William T. Rice—Tiberius, the Roman emperor from A.D. 14 to 37.) Since Hunter's first grumblings in April, Desilu had pursued Shatner, an accomplished stage actor who was also familiar to American television audiences from such shows as *Twilight Zone* and *Playhouse 90*; Shatner was represented by Ashley-Famous, the same agency that represented the studio. Though Roddenberry later claimed that he designed *Star Trek* to be an ensemble show in which all the actors had lead roles, one early letter to Shatner refers to planned stories that would highlight Kirk as "the dominant central character." The stories were conceived, he wrote, "to combine believability with great personal jeopardy—a way, it seemed to me, to firmly establish the man."[17] An early draft of the writer-director guidelines, written by Roddenberry, later described the show as being "built around a central lead role," and it describes Mr. Spock's character under the heading "Principal Supporting Role."[18]

That lead role was to differ significantly from its predecessor, Captain Pike. "An unusually strong and colorful personality" is the way Roddenberry labeled his new captain once he knew it would be Shatner. Correctly perceiving that the character's personality would have to mesh with Shatner's, Roddenberry rethought his "prisoner of *Angst*" approach. Thus, Kirk became less intellectually tortured, more the traditional appealing hero. Shatner's Kirk would be quicker to make love to a woman than Hunter's Pike, whose Capt. Horatio Hornblower persona was to have been tempered by a touch of doubting Hamlet.[19] As such, Kirk's perfect dramatic counterbalance would be a half-human machine of pure reason. Spock.

NBC, as Roddenberry noted, was initially displeased with the

Spock character. In *Star Trek* lore, the story of an NBC executive ordering the network's art department to airbrush Spock's pointed ears out of early publicity photos is well known. Roddenberry had to fight long and valiantly to keep Spock, whom he claimed to have based on his former boss, LAPD police chief William Parker.[20] ("I regret that so many people are surprised to learn that...Spock... was suggested by several Bill Parker philosophies that I heard in those days," he said.)[21] "Among our crew of familiar human faces," Roddenberry pointed out to the network, "Spock helps keep our broad space potential alive for us."[22]

His first and only choice for the role was Leonard Nimoy. Dorothy Fontana, who worked as a secretary in *The Lieutenant* offices, recalls the day in early 1964 that Roddenberry handed her the original *Star Trek* outline. "I have only one question," she told him after reading it. "Who's going to play Mr. Spock?"

Roddenberry pulled an eight-by-ten glossy from his drawer and pushed it across the desk toward Fontana. The photo was of Leonard Nimoy, who had guest-starred earlier that season as a movie producer on an episode of *The Lieutenant* (with Majel Barrett portraying an actress), and who, coincidentally, had been in the first script Fontana ever sold, a 1960 episode of *The Tall Man* with Barry Sullivan, produced by Sam Peeples.

During the preproduction and filming of Nimoy's *The Lieutenant* episode, Roddenberry had been on his Panama Canal cruise/sabbatical. Nimoy, cast by the show's director, Marc Daniels, had never met Roddenberry until he was summoned to the studio to discuss what his agent called "a science fiction pilot."

"I went in thinking I was auditioning," Nimoy says. "Once I was there I got the feeling that I was really being sold on the idea of doing the job. Gene, I guess, had made up his mind and was showing me the various phases of preproduction—what was happening in the wardrobe department and prop department, for example. We talked about the characters, and I was hired."

(During the filming of "The Cage," Roddenberry approached Nimoy between takes of a scene in which Spock was to dash across an exterior landscape. Advising Nimoy to run with a limp, Roddenberry said, "We want to play this as though Spock has been injured on a previous mission; as though these are ongoing missions. This isn't just a one-mission movie we're making here." The notion that Spock's leg injury from a previous escapade would still be bothering him on a different stardate is intriguing—and ahead of its time. More than a decade later, *Hill Street Blues* and *St. Elsewhere*, though not soap operas, treated their characters like real people whose lives don't begin anew as blank slates every week. But because there was neither contextual foundation nor direct reference to the injury, people still ask Nimoy why he was limping in "The Cage.")

Spock had not hatched in Roddenberry's imagination with the characteristics that later endeared him to million of fans worldwide. He'd been devised as one of several characters supporting the captain's lead (Nimoy signed for $1,250 per episode, in contrast to Shatner's $5,000 per), and was described only as being in self-conflict—with "a red-hued satanic look and surprisingly gentle manners."[23] His home planet of Vulcan (the Roman god of fire and metalworking) was conceived much later .

"The character was not nailed down well enough for the pilot," Nimoy says. "We were fishing. There was no dictum that the logical shall hold sway ninety-five percent of the time, which was what we finally went for."

When Roddenberry lost Number One, he folded her personality traits into Spock, whose presence had been intended primarily as a weekly reminder of space travel's efficacy in meeting other life forms. "I decided I couldn't make this without having at least one alien aboard," he said, "and so the woman had to go and I kept Spock on. [I] later married the woman."[24]

"Where No Man Has Gone Before" reveals that Spock absorbed Number One's detached, emotionless cool. However, not until they shot the first episode, "The Corbomite Maneuver" (aired two months after the series premiere), did Nimoy feel that he'd locked down the character. For that he credits director Joseph Sargent— who'd originally resisted the job.

Sargent's name had appeared on a short list of directors, highly recommended by story editor John D. F. Black, who'd worked with him. "I'm going on vacation," Sargent had told Black on the phone. "I'm not doing any segment television."

"But Joe," Black had insisted, "it's an important thing, the first show of the series."

"No, I'm going to Hawaii with my wife. We haven't had a vacation in five years."

Putting him on hold, Black consulted with associate producer Robert Justman. Then he told Sargent, "Graduation day, Joe. I just got your price kicked up."

"You son of a bitch, you owe me," Sargent said before hanging up.

In Jerry Sohl's "The Corbomite Maneuver," the *Enterprise* is confronted by a strange object that has the ability to block the ship's path. This causes consternation on the bridge, evoking great anxiety and fear. "Fascinating" is the only utterance given to Spock.

"When I rehearsed it," Nimoy remembers, "I said it in the same heat-of-excitement tone as everyone else. Joe told me, 'Be different. Do it cooler. Do it with curiosity. Be detached.' So I said it as he suggested and we shot it that way. It gave me a whole handle that then became the spine of the character."

NBC ordered its first batch of *Star Trek* episodes on the sixth of March 1966. Shortly thereafter, Gene Roddenberry stood before a gathering of writers in the boardroom of the Writers Guild— writers whom he hoped would attend one of several pilot screenings that he'd scheduled and, perhaps, submit stories. It was time to buy scripts, which is difficult in Hollywood only if you insist on consistent quality—and he wanted *Twilight Zone*, not *Gilligan's Island*. Had Rod Serling or Reginald Rose been standing there to introduce a new series, his name and reputation alone would have sent the best writers running to their muse for a chance to participate. But Roddenberry was not, at age forty-four, one of Hollywood's better-known or more respected writer-producers. "It's Roddenberry, like rotten berry" is the way he introduced himself, providing a mnemonic device that had in fact been his high school nickname.

He was outfitted as usual in a suit that appeared to belong to someone else, although it came from a collection that had actually been made for him in Hong Kong. After *The Lieutenant* he periodically sent a favorite suit to a tailor there and received in return several replicas in different colors and fabrics. "Good fabrics or bad, how could you tell?" says John D. F. Black, *Star Trek*'s first story editor. "With Gene, you wouldn't have noticed if he was wearing a crown on his head." Bruce Geller, the creator and producer of *Mission: Impossible*, which filmed at Desilu on soundstages adjacent to *Star Trek*, once speculated that the suits arrived from Hong Kong complete with cigarette holes and ashes in the same spots. "Somebody said you could dress Gene in a tailored suit and in five minutes he'd look like a saggy, baggy elephant," Dorothy Fontana says. "I don't know if it was the way clothes hung on him or the clothes themselves."

In front of a crowd, Roddenberry came alive. Articulate and bright, he often held court at parties and in social situations, his knowledge born of reading and experience—war, policing, piloting. He was a born schmoozer who excelled at telling everyone what they wanted to hear—an asset for a television producer. That afternoon at the Writers Guild they wanted to hear that *Star Trek* would let them write to the limits of their craft and their art.

The job of selling both himself and the show was made infinitely easier by his feeling of self-confidence. He felt full of piss and vinegar, having good reason to think he'd moved up on the Hollywood food chain. Not only would *Star Trek* debut in the fall for a minimum of thirteen episodes, but "Police Story," another pilot he'd written and produced in 1965, remained under consideration for NBC's fall lineup. "Police Story", starring Steve Ihnat, was a thirty-minute-long action-adventure cop drama about three special investigators working for the police commissioner. Though ultimately rejected, it bears some retrospective noteworthiness for three reasons: one of the investigators was played by Rafer Johnson, the 1960 Olympic decathlon champion; his partner, played by Gary Clark, was named Questor, which years later became the title of another of Roddenberry's failed pilots; and the show's two guest stars were DeForest Kelley and Grace Lee Whitney—eventually to be *Star Trek*'s Dr. McCoy and Yeoman Janice Rand.

(Roddenberry had also produced a third pilot, one written by his friend Sam Rolfe, for ABC. "The Long Hunt of April Savage" was a Western about a man hunting his family's six murderers; Rolfe's idea was that April Savage would catch up with one man per season. In a dispute at the time with his agents and the network, and anxious to get out of Dodge for a sabbatical after almost twenty prolific years, Rolfe had left the script behind at Desilu while he moved his family to England. Reluctantly, the project was given by Herb Solow to Roddenberry, who cast Robert Lansing—later to guest star in the *Star Trek* episode "Assignment: Earth"—as Savage and took a crew to Big Bear, a mountainous area of southern California, for a ten-day shoot in the fall of 1965. Roddenberry had known that the job was strictly work for hire, that Rolfe would return to produce the series should the pilot be bought. As a consequence, he'd comported himself with less political graciousness than in his dealings with NBC, which held his immediate future in its hands. Complaining about "network interference," he'd ordered his associate producer, Robert Justman, to banish from the location set ABC's visiting executive, who'd driven out to check on the network's investment. In a consummate example of it's-a-small-world-and-what-goes-around-comes-around, that representative was Harve Bennett, who fifteen years later replaced Roddenberry as producer of the *Star Trek* motion pictures. Roddenberry's cavalier behavior, which permeated the pilot, was the cause of a rift between him and Rolfe that lasted many years.)

Despite his later assertions, Roddenberry's actions do not constitute a portrait of one who'd grown weary of television's editorial restrictions and was planning to make this science fiction series a last-ditch effort in the medium before moving on to less censored and more creative pastures. "I just decided I had to get out of television, so I could write something from my heart and my mind," he explained. "That, after all, is what art is all about. Artists comment. And when you can't comment, you dry up. I thought I'd take one more chance with some things, and I thought of Jonathan Swift, who faced the same problem with his century."[25]

In truth, Roddenberry had every enthusiastic intention of becoming, like Norman Felton, a major supplier of television series—whether they were *Gulliver's Travels* or *Dragnet*. Once he got *Star Trek* on the air, Herb Solow says, he was anxious to move on to another show, and then another and another.

"The first pilot really began with the fact that TV in the days when I began was so severely censored... I thought maybe if I did what Swift did, and used far-off polka-dotted people on far-off planets, I could get away with it," Roddenberry said, sounding a great deal like Rod Serling before him.[26] Serling had created *The Twilight Zone* in 1959 partly as a metaphorical soapbox after losing a dozen well-publicized battles with the networks over controversial and provocative material. Tackling racism and lynchings in the South, as he tried to do in *Playhouse 90*'s "A Town Has Turned to Dust" (starring William Shatner), was forbidden. The same subject, however, was fair game for any of *Twilight Zone*'s parallel universes. Unlike Serling, however, Roddenberry had never displayed any notable inclination to dramatize society's most divisive issues.

Roddenberry introduced himself to the Writers Guild audience through a self-deprecating—and apocryphal—anecdote intended to establish, in an off-handed way, his credibility: Long ago, when he was just a novice producer, he said, he'd been forced to cast a part in which some beautiful actress would have to bare her bosom for the camera. Of course, this called for him to audition each beautiful breast right there in his office. Shy, timid, and not a little embarrassed, he called the actresses in one at a time and with tedious care offered an apologetic explanation of why he required them to show him the goods.

"Thank you, that's fine," he quoted himself as saying.

Then the next actress would arrive and receive the full treatment before she, too, willingly auditioned.

After several prospects had come and gone, their qualifications duly noted, Roddenberry realized that at the present rate he'd have spent the better part of a week interviewing applicants. A light went off over his head. With the next woman he affected a tone of ennui and, eschewing apologia, said, "All right, let's see 'em"—whereupon she showed 'em, as did every subsequent actress.

It doesn't matter that the story wasn't true. The point Roddenberry was making with a twinkle in his eye was that he was a producer; he knew what he wanted and what he wanted was the best they had to offer. The audience's laughter at the story's punchline confirmed that they were all professionals who'd matriculated through the ranks—that they were peers and he deserved their respect and trust.

When the laughter died down, he was ready to pitch *Star Trek*.

"While we want strong themes and intelligent writing, our category of science fiction must not trap us into violating proven entertainment techniques," he said, taking his cues directly from the first writer's bible. "We'll be competing with other television series for a mass audience on an adventure-drama-action basis. That audience will sit out there, as ever, with a hand poised over the control knob—beer, potato chips, and a dozen other distractions around them. Perhaps the fact that we're science fiction and therefore somewhat suspect, we may need even more than average attention to a story which starts fast, poses growing peril to highly identifiable people with identifiable problems, and with more than the average number of hooks at act breaks." In short, he said, you don't have to think of yourself as a science fiction writer to write for *Star Trek*. It was the fiction, not the science, he intended to emphasize. ("Contrary to popular belief, science fiction writers do not necessarily make good *Star Trek* writers," the writer's bible for the third and final year of the series said. "The problem seems to be the fact that science fiction writers can't really write science fiction very well either.")

Roddenberry spoke passionately, his ardor for *Star Trek* obvious—and, judging by the numbers of top writers who eventually viewed the pilot, contagious. Ernest Kinoy, Theodore Sturgeon, Harlan Ellison, John W. Campbell, Shimon Wincelberg, A. E. van Vogt, Barry Trivers, George Clayton Johnson, and Richard Matheson were among several dozen top writers attending screenings. "His talk was delightful," Jerry Sohl remembers.

The story editor–associate producer with whom free-lance scriptwriters would be dealing was John D. F. Black, a writer whose my-word-is-my-bond type of integrity was well known in the industry. Black had gotten the job, his first staff position, on March 24, the day after he'd won a Writers Guild Award in the episodic drama category for his *Mr. Novak* script "With a Hammer in His Hands, Lord, Lord."

Amidst the congratulatory tumult following the presentations, Roddenberry had managed to break through the concentric rings of well-wishers surrounding Black and introduce himself as the producer of an upcoming science fiction series for NBC. Two weeks before, he'd assigned a script to Harlan Ellison, who that night took home the anthology award for his *Outer Limits* script "Demon with a Glass Hand." Ellison would be writing a script titled "The City on the Edge of Forever."

"I'd like to talk to you about my show," Roddenberry told Black. "Why don't you come over to my house tonight. I'm having a party."

"I got the Writers Guild Award at ten P.M., and by midnight the pitch was in," Black says. "He took me into the den and said he wanted me to come on the show. And I didn't know that I wanted to be there. I was very happy being a free-lance writer." Never having written science fiction, Black didn't understand why Roddenberry had wanted him as the man who would deal with writers of renown and distinction in a field he knew little about. "I told him, 'The people that you want on *Star Trek* are esteemed writers. I don't know the genre yet, but I know that these are important people in it.'"

Pinning *Star Trek*'s success on getting great scripts, Roddenberry may have thought that Black's reputation as a straight shooter would soothe their trepidation. These writers—their stories and expertise—were to be the real stars of *Star Trek*. He'd known that from the beginning and paid them twice the Writers Guild minimum—nearly as much per show as William Shatner. In some cases, though, they'd be science fiction writers who'd never written for television. Then, Black's solid craftsmanship would prove invaluable.

"My deal was this," Black says: "If I rewrote, if I was compelled to rewrite anything, I wouldn't take credit on it. Because in free-lancing, credit is everything."

According to the Writers Guild rule, a contracted writer could deliver an original story outline, a script, a complete rewrite, and a polish; the producer could not ask for more unless he offered additional money. After that, a producer or staff writer who substantially rewrote the script had to submit the work to the Writers Guild arbitration committee for a ruling on the credit. At stake was prestige, pride, and a residual.

Presuming that top writers would not want their scripts rewritten willy-nilly, Black extracted a promise from Roddenberry that the free-lancers could, if they were willing, be responsible for their own work as long as the stories conformed to the *Star Trek* universe and were delivered on a reasonable schedule. If a script got to the point where the writer's best efforts weren't going to be good enough or production was being held up, then Black was obliged to let the writer off softly, and either he or Roddenberry would rewrite. But neither of them, Roddenberry had promised, would usurp credit.

Just as Black was responsible primarily to the script, Robert Justman, the show's other associate producer, devoted himself to the actualization of the script in production. In reality, however, with only the three of them (and Dorothy Fontana, then Roddenberry's secretary), the job descriptions tended to meld; Justman became well known for his detailed and often funny script and story memos.

Justman had been called in by Roddenberry before the filming of "The Cage" to interview as its associate producer. At the time he was an assistant director on *The Outer Limits,* where he worked with, among other directors, James Goldstone, who'd recommended him to Roddenberry.

Roddenberry impressed Justman. "Gene was a large man, tall, but he wasn't too heavy yet," he says. "He had marvelously graceful hands, with long, almost exquisite, fingers. When he talked he held his cigarette in a way I'd never seen before"—at the fingertips instead of between them—"and he'd take a deep drag and let it go and say, 'Bob, don't you think...' He seemed very graceful, the way he did that. And he always did that."

After hearing that Roddenberry needed an associate producer with experience in opticals and special effects, Justman had politely declined the job. "I said, 'Thank you, I really do want to move up,'" Justman remembers, "'but I don't feel that I have the requisite knowledge to do what you need to be done.'" He recommended Byron Haskin, with whom he had worked on *The Outer Limits*. Haskin had also directed the movie *Robinson Crusoe on Mars*, which impressed Roddenberry.

Walking to the Desilu parking lot, Justman had coincidentally passed Haskin on his way to meet Roddenberry. Haskin got the job. But Justman ended up working with Roddenberry anyway on "The Cage" when Herb Solow arranged to borrow him from *The Outer Limits* as assistant director.

Months later, Justman received another call. "We're shooting a second pilot," Roddenberry told him, "and this time I want you to be the associate producer." Roddenberry hadn't gotten on with the crusty Haskin.

This time Justman took the job. "I felt I knew enough," he explains. "In the meantime I'd learned a lot about opticals and special effects that I hadn't known."

Reunited with director Goldstone, Justman became both associate producer and assistant director on "Where No Man Has Gone Before." Roddenberry interviewed no one else for the series job.

Nearly six months later, on August 1, 1966, five weeks before the show's broadcast premiere, Justman sent Roddenberry an urgent memo and gave a copy to Black. He wrote, "It is important that you compose, without delay, our standard opening narration for Bill Shatner to record. It should run about fifteen seconds in length, as we discussed earlier." Shatner's opening recitation in "Where No Man Has Gone Before," about the magnitude of our galaxy within the "untold billions" of galaxies, would not do for the series. Besides being too long, it failed to give the adventures a sense of purpose from week to week.

The next day generated a flurry of memos on the topic, each man copying the other two with a carbon of his ideas. First, Roddenberry wrote: "This is the story of the United Space Ship *Enterprise*. Assigned a five-year patrol of our galaxy, the giant starship visits Earth colonies, regulates commerce, and explores strange new worlds and civilizations. These are its voyages...and its adventures."

Justman wrote: "This is the story of the Starship *Enterprise*. Its mission: to advance knowledge, contact alien life and enforce intergalactic law...to explore the strange new worlds where no man has gone before."

Black, noting that the narration needed "more drama," offered two versions, the first estimated to run eleven and a half seconds: "The U.S.S. *Enterprise*...star ship...its mission...a five-year patrol to seek out and contact alien life...to explore the infinite frontier of space...where no man has gone before...a STAR TREK."

He timed the second version at fifteen to seventeen seconds: "Space...the final frontier...endless...silent...waiting. This is the story of the United Space Ship *Enterprise*...its mission...a five-year patrol of the galaxy...to seek out and contact all alien life...to explore...to travel the vast galaxy where no man has gone before...a STAR TREK."

The *Enterprise*'s five-year mission was a wish fulfillment order from agent Alden Schwimmer. After five years on the air, he said, there'd be enough episodes for syndication.

CHAPTER FIVE

Impractical

Jokes

O N JOHN D. F. BLACK's first day at work, April 19, 1966, the Desilu offices of *Star Trek* hadn't yet completed their renovation and refurbishing. For this one day, when there wouldn't be much to do anyway, Black and his secretary, Mary Stilwell (later to marry Black and become a writer herself), occupied a temporary office. Located in a converted prop storehouse on the second floor, the rooms were accessible only by an iron staircase. The austere space, at some distance from the rest of the staff, was theirs alone.

Story treatments solicited by Roddenberry had begun arriving. Black was reading one of them when Roddenberry called and asked him to interview an actress for a small role. "I don't have the time," Roddenberry said, "and it's not part of Justman's job description. You might as well break in doing this sort of thing right now."

A while later an attractive blond woman in her mid- to late twenties climbed the stairs and identified herself to Stilwell as the actress whom Black was to interview. Stilwell buzzed Black on the intercom and announced the candidate. "Send her in," Black replied.

"Mr. Black is expecting you," Stilwell said in her best Ann Sothern voice.

The actress entered Black's office and closed the door behind her.

"Would you please sit down," Black said, already uncomfortable with the task that faced him. A former actor, he'd quit the profession at twenty-three after appearing in the film *Lonely Hearts* with Montgomery Clift, in part because he'd really only wanted to learn to write through acting, and in part because of the potential humiliation all but the top actors face in just such situations as these.

Black tried to phrase his first question delicately, hoping not to let on that he was entirely unfamiliar with her work. "You're supposed to know them," he says. "I mean, the actor's whole thing is the self. And if you mention that you don't recognize them or don't know who they are, that's not much fun for them."

Instead of asking, What have you done? or, Tell me about yourself, Black said, "Did you work with Gene Roddenberry on *The Lieutenant*?"

"No," she said demurely.

"Well, do you know Gene Roddenberry?"

The actress gushed out a breathless explanation that she'd only met him recently and that he'd offered a job interview but instead she'd been diverted to Black, and, oh, she really wanted to work, wanted it so bad she could taste it, had wanted it her whole life, wanted it more than anything in the world.

"There's nothing I wouldn't do to get this job," she said, standing up and beginning to undress.

"Please," Black said, not quite stammering yet. "This isn't anything you should do, and it's certainly nothing that I expect you to do." More horrified than amused, Black, a married man, watched her strip down to bra and bikini panties.

The situation had been engineered by Roddenberry as Black's initiation, and in Stilwell's office the rest of the *Star Trek* staff, including the producer himself, had gathered. They crouched by the door, listening to the exchange between Black and Majel Barrett.

After they finally burst in, amid shrieks of laughter and surprise and welcome-to-the-club pats on the back, everyone stood around awkwardly. At last came a buzz from Black's intercom and Stilwell's voice, loud and deadpan: "Mr. Black, your wife is on the phone." The joke went unrecognized by the assemblage, who amid giggles and twitters quickly cleared the room.

Over the following months, the story of Black losing his *Star Trek* virginity was told often around the watercooler (minus Stilwell's kicker), and eventually became a fixture in the show's lore. Its meaning always resided in the context of what wild and wacky days those were, and while that may have been true for some, the anecdote expresses a peculiar, *Rashomon*-like quality that was typical of the *Star Trek* working experience when viewed through eyes other than those of the show's creator.

Roddenberry may have chosen to haze Black not because he was a rookie, but for the stuff he was made of. Black flashed his principles and ideals in neon. His acceptance speech after winning the Writers Guild Award a few weeks before had reflected the deeply humble gratitude of a young man who'd just been recognized by his peers and was seriously exhilarated. "His speech was so naive I was almost embarrassed by it," Stilwell remembers. "He'd just won the award for a very clean, wonderful script, and his acceptance speech sounded about as naive as anybody could possibly hear." And it was Roddenberry's introduction to the man.

His second contact with Black was through contract negotiations. Black hadn't demanded more money, nor a bigger office, nor better billing. His only deal-breaking condition was that free-lance writers were to control the integrity of their own scripts, and that the producer stand behind him on this. Such devotion must have seemed almost quaint to Roddenberry.

"We are, in many ways, I've often thought, two people," Roddenberry later said. "As long as the inner person believes and admits that decency is good, the outer person who has to deal with the world—a world that is not always fair—is allowed to slip from time to time. I suppose that I have thought all my life that the only real person was the inner me."[1]

Older, more cynical, and far less romantic, Roddenberry may have found Black's rectitude irresistible for tweaking. Black represented the sort of fresh-faced standards that he'd long before abandoned to "reason." "The presumption may have been that this was going to be one of those great practical jokes in which the guy is caught, literally, with his pants down," Stilwell says. "I really think Gene believed that he would find John ready to jump onto Majel."

"Men," Roddenberry often said, quoting madam Polly Adler, "come to women like little boys with their pants down."[2] In his view, sex was a weapon and all temptations were equal.

Roddenberry, Black says, "was prone to orient everything to sex." References to prurient titillation and to the female anatomy occur throughout Roddenberry's work, both on the screen and behind the scenes, as an unflagging constant. No single other subject is mentioned with the same frequency.

Sex was where *Star Trek* began its journey, says Leonard Nimoy, who in decoding "The Cage" discovered a story about sexual fantasies: Aliens holding captive a male humanoid must entice him to mate with an attractive young woman in order to extend their race. "How can we arouse this guy? That's what it was about," Nimoy says. "A series of sexual fantasies they created from what they picked up in his unconscious. All very Jungian, these various archetypal, sexual fantasy situations: the pastoral scene with the pretty young girl and the horse and the picnic in the hills on the grass, a dragon lady dancing for him semi-nude giving him pain and pleasure. What would arouse? That was the question."

Commenting on an early draft of Robert Bloch's "Wolf in the Fold" script, Roddenberry wrote: "Let's establish that the nature of this place keeps women eternally young, beautiful, and remarkably busty. Perhaps hormones work better here. At any rate, let's cast and clothe in that direction with a vengeance. This place is remarkably peaceful because the women are beautiful and they screw a lot. Isn't that logical? Or if we can't be logical, let's at least be provocative."[3]

In his script notes on Gene Coon's first draft of "Space Seed," Roddenberry wrote, "In the case of Marla, she is so sophomoric, I doubt if any of us could stand her even today…except, possibly, as an extremely shapely immoral actress, of which, unfortunately due to gross negligence on the part of the casting department, we get too few of on this series."[4]

When an interviewer once asked him for an example of the network censorship that he claimed had almost driven him out of television, Roddenberry did not allude to politics, race, or religion. "You could not have visible nipples," was his answer. "How much skin was permitted to show used to be almost a matter of geometry and measurement."[5]

In another interview, with ABC radio's Tom Snyder, Roddenberry noted that "a great deal of the censorship was sexual censorship. They would actually measure the cleavage on a girl. They would keep threatening you, 'If you do any open-mouth kissing, we're not going to keep the scene in.' "[6]

Roddenberry even injected sexual innuendo into Dorothy Fontana's script for the episode "Charlie X." Having finished the script before a European vacation, Fontana returned to find that Roddenberry had substituted raging hormone–type lust for the naiveté of the young male character who sees a woman for the first time. "Sex always got into Gene's work," she says.

One particularly telling Roddenberry line—an oxymoron—comes from an early writer-director set of guidelines, in which he describes the then nameless captain's yeoman, a female, as "uncomfortably lovely."[7] Webster defines uncomfortable as "causing discomfort or distress; painful; irritating." That a woman's loveliness could cause Roddenberry distress suggests that he was out of control in her presence, and that her good looks threatened him. He was that little boy, pants down at his knees.

Surely, Roddenberry decided, Black would find Barrett as "uncomfortably lovely" as he did.

Some months after the Black-Barrett incident, Roddenberry got seven-foot actor Ted Cassidy to impersonate him in order to test the mettle of a male job applicant. Cassidy, who was on the lot filming the episode "What Are Little Girls Made Of?," sat behind Roddenberry's desk, identified himself as Roddenberry, and conducted the interview while wearing a bald cap and ghastly makeup. Months later, when the same episode was being dubbed, Roddenberry played a practical joke on Robert Justman, who was then taking an exhaustion-inspired vacation in Hawaii. He sent a series of cryptic telegrams that alluded to production problems about which Justman had been particularly concerned.

But Roddenberry was not the type to invite reciprocation of his practical jokes. Though Black and Stilwell took part in several stunts during their six months on the *Star Trek* staff—as both joker and jokee—not one was directed at Roddenberry. "G.R. was a tight ass," Black says. "It wasn't something you did to him."

Roddenberry seemed unapproachable. Amid the rubble of his marriage, he was busily reconstructing himself behind ever-higher emotional and intellectual barriers, hidden from scrutiny. "There were walls," Stilwell says, "and walls beyond walls." The metaphor extended to his physical universe. "He had his office, and his inner sanctum"—an interior room in which he would tryst with Barrett and others. "One was always careful not to step over into his domain."

For the first thirteen episodes of *Star Trek,* Gene Roddenberry held the title of producer. When producer Gene Coon came aboard, Roddenberry became executive producer. (Years later, Roddenberry told his friend, the comedian and actor Howard Stevens, that Coon had beat out several other producers after passing a test: Like the young man who had faced Ted Cassidy posing as Gene Roddenberry, Coon had played it nonchalantly in Roddenberry's office when confronted by beautiful Nichelle Nichols—with whom he was having an affair—wearing only a knit sweater.)

In fact, neither Coon nor Roddenberry produced the show, at least not as the position is normally understood. That job belonged to associate producer Robert Justman. Working with the respective department heads, Justman supervised everything from choice of director, to casting, wardrobe selection, and set design, as well as all facets of postproduction, including editing, special effects, and dubbing; he also had input into story and script, as his long, detailed memos attest. Roddenberry certainly wielded veto power; other staff members often saw Justman walking out of Roddenberry's office, chewing his mustache nervously. But for the most part, Roddenberry remained behind closed doors, devoting himself to the scripts. It was the scripts, not the production itself, that he believed were the most important element. They, not great matte paintings or splashy opticals, would make the audience suspend disbelief. And he knew that the audience wanted to suspend disbelief; just give them a good story, and they would.

"I rewrote or heavily polished the first thirteen episodes," Roddenberry often said.[8] (Coon, according to consensus, also concentrated on the scripts and left the production details to Justman.)

Roddenberry intended to construct a cohesive universe, but since the raw materials he worked with were other people's scripts—all thirteen of them—he was left to mold their creations into shapes that coincided with his own vision. He cherry-picked ideas until, slowly, script by script, the *Star Trek* universe began to assemble, its laws of physics qualified and quantified, its history and future part of an ever-emerging mosaic. Does it work; does it make sense? Those were the criteria by which scripts and ideas were judged before becoming elements in the world of *Star Trek*.

With the exception of Spock's logical mind, which at the beginning was far from fully developed, the *Star Trek* that existed at the end of seventy-nine episodes bore little in common with Roddenberry's prototype. *Star Trek* the child grew over a period of three years (though primarily the first two) through the influence of many talented contributors. The Vulcan nerve pinch used by Spock throughout the series to disable enemies was a Leonard Nimoy suggestion choreographed by writer Richard Matheson, who had conceived of a nonviolent maneuver for "The Enemy Within." Conversely, in "The Man Trap," written by George Clayton Johnson, Kirk seeks to hunt and kill an alien creature, about whom little was known, without considering its point of view; this would later have been a violation of *Star Trek*'s ethical and moral code. Writer Paul Schneider's "Balance of Terror" introduced the durable Romulans, soon to be a constant in *Star Trek*. The Vulcan mind meld, which was used by Spock to determine thoughts, debuted courtesy of Shimon Wincelberg in "Dagger of the Mind." In "Miri," by Adrian Spies, the term "space central" rather than "Starfleet Command" was used. Spock's parents, as well as the Andorians, the Tellarites, and the Vulcan death hold were all created by Dorothy Fontana. As for the villainous Klingons, they showed up near the end of the first season in "Errand of Mercy," the brainchild of Gene Coon. And it was Coon who expanded the mind meld to include nonhuman life forms in "The Devil in the Dark," about an apparent monster that was actually a mother protecting her young.

Even the characters' backgrounds usually came from other writers. Theodore Sturgeon's second *Star Trek* script, "Amok Time," for example, described the history and customs of the planet Vulcan that, until then, hadn't existed.

"Over the years a lot of people have swallowed the line that Gene Roddenberry was the sole creator of *Star Trek*," Dorothy Fontana says. "And it's not true. If you look at the development of the scripts along the way, you see all the elements that were contributed by other writers. The base was there, the bones were there, the skeleton was there; maybe even the flesh. All the rest, the laying on of the weight and the muscle, was done by others."

While the "Wagon Train in space" concept accommodated the density of detail that made *Star Trek* so successful, the series *Lost in Space*, for example, was similarly devised with a sharp concept—Swiss Family Robinson in outer space; what it lacked were the brilliant contributions of top-notch writers to make its universe appealing.

Roddenberry's real accomplishments were constructing *Star Trek*'s parameters, selling the series, seeking quality writers, and often recognizing brilliance when he saw it. He also insisted on a multiracial, multiethnic supporting cast, holding firm even when some stations in the South opposed the idea of a black woman, Nichelle Nichols, on the bridge of the *Enterprise*, and threatened not to broadcast the show.

Those accomplishments alone entitle him to the lion's share of credit for *Star Trek*. But it is also inarguable that he acted in concert with many talented people, all of whom deserved recognition and praise for their contributions. For a show as big and as popular as *Star Trek*, he might have given thanks where deserved at no detriment to himself. But as the years passed, Roddenberry increasingly assumed credit that belonged to others. On his own *Star Trek: The 25th Anniversary* tribute show, he did not convey gratitude to a single writer.[9] At around the same time, during a speech to *Star Trek* fans, he claimed that Gene Coon's idea of making the "Horta" monster a mother in "The Devil in the Dark" had been his. "When I suggested it," he declared, "everyone said, 'Are you sure we could do that?'"[10] And in a newspaper interview he once said, "Had to tell the writers the difference between a galaxy and a solar system."[11]

"Bullshit," Fontana replies. "These were people like Richard Matheson, Harlan Ellison, Theodore Sturgeon, Jerry Sohl, Jerome Bixby, George Clayton Johnson, Robert Bloch"—men whose reputations in science fiction long preceded his. "Give me a break. He'd say that to make himself look bigger and make them smaller. But it was bullshit."

Vanity and insecurity had long before led Roddenberry to conclude that "great writers are great rewriters."[12] In that regard, he had his admirers.

"I remember very specifically a script we were having trouble with," Leonard Nimoy says. "I went to do a scene with [DeForest Kelley] and there were some new pages in it. We started to play it, and it was a pleasure to play. We looked at each other and said, 'This is Gene.' Gene had rewritten this scene. You could tell the difference. He had an attack, he had a use of language, he had a subtextual approach. When he was on his game, he was brilliant."

Robert Justman notes that Roddenberry often rewrote scripts at night without going home, night after night. Trying to get a jump on preproduction, Justman would read the pages as they came in. "Gene's first act would be brilliant," he says. "Second act, very good. Third act, good. Fourth act used to be just a mess, because by that time he'd been up, say, two or three nights and was wasted. After some sleep he'd come back and write the fourth act and it would be fine. He wrote beautiful dialogue, and he had ideas." ("I find it well nigh incredible that you managed to do this complete rewrite in the space of one single night," Justman wrote in a memo to Roddenberry regarding the script for "Space Seed." "And I also find it practically astounding that you have managed to clean up the story and straightline it into its present shootable condition.")[13]

Fontana recalls several times when she and Coon would become stuck on a particular logic or plot point and go to Roddenberry for successful resolution. Such a case, she says, occurred during the second season, while she was assigned to rewrite Jerome Bixby's "By Any Other Name." In the story, a few aliens in human form commandeer the *Enterprise*. The problem Fontana faced was one of plausibility: How would just a few entities overcome 430?

As she explained her dilemma to him, Roddenberry began playing with a paperweight on his desk; she had bought him the piece of onyx carved into a decahedron two years before in Mexico. Pushing it around by one finger, he said, "Suppose they have a device that changes people into something like this. It's the essence of the person. And that's what they do to the crew of the *Enterprise* to get them out of the way. They just leave alive or functional the people who they need to run the ship. Obviously, they can bring the others back if they need them."

It worked. And it made sense, within the logic of *Star Trek*. In the opening teaser segment, Fontana immediately established the aliens' transmutation abilities.

Roddenberry's memos reveal a sure sense of the show, its characters, its direction, and its dramatic possibilities. Responding to Richard Matheson's "The Enemy Within," a story in which the *Enterprise* captain splits into a good Kirk and an evil Kirk, he wrote that Dr. McCoy was coming off too much like the doctor on *Gunsmoke*: "He should be much more the 'H. L. Mencken,' the curmudgeon, the sharp-tongued individualist." Later he added, "Lose the order for women to lock themselves in their cabins. We're playing women crewmen as equal to men, including equally well-trained and with equal responsibilities."[14]

A letter to writer Don Mankiewicz regarding the first draft of "Court Martial" sums up as well as any single document Roddenberry's sense of the show's direction. Chiding the writer's "pessimistic view of the future" (but admitting "I often feel the same way"), Roddenberry insisted that the audience will care for the show and its characters only if the twenty-third century—and all its institutions—seems appealing to a twentieth-century spectator.

...when you add up the following things, it is hard to have much feeling or respect for *Star Trek*'s century, the Earth, and the military service it represents. Things such as a harbormaster prejudiced against Kirk for the "simple" reason that Kirk still holds flight command; the use of a computer instead of reasoned judgment for legal questions; thus an implied assumption that computers are constantly photographing and recording all aspects of life, personal and professional; ugly antagonism from what seems an unreasoning group of individuals on the base, developing almost to physical violence; and the placing of a man of the rank of Starship Captain in jail even when a trial has not yet been concluded. Not leaning on you, Don, but want you to see the direction in which the sum of all these things would be taking *Star Trek* as a series.[15]

After reading Carey Wilbur's "Space Seed"—about a "sleeper ship" of crewmen, led by the evil Khan, awakened by Kirk from a state of deep-space sleep—Roddenberry sent a memo to Gene Coon that detailed ways to replace the script's "shaky logic" with "believable ideas."

Worse than any of the preceding, our Starship Commander must wait on "higher command" to make a quite ordinary and human decision whether or not to revive a group of people who are presently in suspended animation. God help us if we've come no further than this in three more centuries! In fact, God help us if the Captain of the cruiser, U.S.S. *Los Angeles*, would wait for higher command in the Pentagon or State Department to make a simple decision like that. There seems to be a compulsion among writers to picture the future as totally computerized, inhumanly authoritarian, and coldly big-brotherish. I know none of us wants to go that direction, but God help *Star Trek* if our writers push us that-a-way.[16]

Gene Coon received Roddenberry's script notes on Margaret Armen's "The Gamesters of Triskelion" (then called "The Gamesters of Pentathlon"), a story about Kirk and crew being made into gladiators for the amusement of planet Triskelion's "Providers." Though incisive, the comments appear to reflect aspects of Roddenberry's personal life as well.

91

Seems to me we give away too early the fact that athletic competition is the primary diversion of the Providers. And, incidentally, we should develop in greater detail later *why* these rulers of the planet need diversion. The best answer that suggests itself is that since they have lost their power of physical locomotion, the joy of challenge, since they have "evolved" too far down a blind alley, they now just provide themselves action and adventure in a vicarious way. In other words, they have "improved" their species past a point of no return, discovered too late that brains and intellectual power is not enough, that life needs movement and challenge. Having gone too far to turn back, they had to find action and excitement through other species. Just as in today's world, many of our males find themselves prisoners of marriage, children, mortgage payments and so on, find *their* action and adventure vicariously through the Saturday afternoon sports programs on television. Really, the two situations are quite similar...

It's going to be a little difficult to like Kirk when he "knocks her out deftly." Maybe it will work, but we'll have to be convinced it is quite necessary, since they have begun to have a quite friendly relationship just before this happens. Not that girls don't like to be knocked around a bit. My friends tell me they rather enjoy it. Is this true, Gene, or am I being lied to by my friends? One finds so few persons one can trust nowadays.[17]

Theodore Sturgeon, the most anthologized writer in the English language but one who'd never written for television before *Star Trek*, received several long letters and memos from Roddenberry. His reaction to Sturgeon's first draft of "Shore Leave" (then called "Finagle's Planet"), about a planet on which fantasies become real, emphasized that each show was not an anthology drama complete onto itself but rather another installment of the entire series. *Star Trek*, he said, was an episodic situation drama with continuing characters whom the audience would come to know through each week's story. As such, he defined the boundaries of the characters' relationships:

When Kirk is fatigued, tired, desperately needs a rest, doesn't this create a need for a scene between the Captain and McCoy? After all, McCoy is the ship's surgeon and Kirk's confidant in these matters. Or, at least, there should have been some discussion between the two on this subject, even if it is only referred to. In the Kirk-Spock exchange in the cabin, we find Spock cast somewhat in the role we had planned for the ship's doctor. McCoy is Kirk's confidant in areas of fatigue, sex, loneliness, etc.; Science Officer Spock is Kirk's confidant in matters of ship operation, logic, science, records, etc.[18]

When the first draft of "Miri" came in suffering from a bad case of technobabble, Roddenberry wrote to its author, Adrian Spies, suggesting that he abandon thinking of *Star Trek* as science fiction and begin conceiving of the episode's locale—a planet deadly to anyone but children, who are its only inhabitants—as earth in the 1920s. In this way, Roddenberry said, Spies could concentrate on the situation's human drama:

> Mister Spock? To make our parallel work, let's say he's a half-Chinese scientist, second in command, an expert on all things scientific, perhaps more of an expert on Earth's 1920 era than most non-aliens. Now if we're playing him as indicated in pilot and format, a highly logical and curious kind of bird, he would already be operating as the scientist he is, perceiving a little more than the others, theorizing, and commenting...
>
> More importantly, keeping Kirk in mind again as a Twentieth Century Naval captain, the central character upon which a series will rise or fall, does your review of your script satisfy you that the job he is doing, his attitudes and lines, the decisions we thrust upon him and his handling of them, are what you would have written in a non-sf script?

Roddenberry was the keeper and arbiter of the unique *Star Trek* logic. He knew what was possible, what worked, what made sense. In time, certainly, others did, too. But at the beginning, he trusted only himself. Unlike *The Lieutenant*, which was Norman Felton's show no matter what it said on the screen or in his contract, *Star Trek* belonged to Gene Roddenberry.

"It was not unusual when we were working on the first thirteen episodes for me to be there until two or three in the morning, typing Gene's changes on a script so that the typing company could pick it up, retype it in proper form, and have it to the set in the morning," says Fontana, who was still at the time Roddenberry's secretary.

He rewrote those thirteen compulsively. Until the cameras actually recorded the actors saying the lines, no words were etched in stone. This did not endear him to some writers—in particular, John D. F. Black, whose contractual agreement, sense of ethics, and dramatic instincts these actions violated.

Black remembers seeing the rewriting on the wall when the first script came in, several weeks after he began work. By prior agreement, the script was duplicated on an early model Xerox machine and copies given to Roddenberry and Justman. Roddenberry left for home with his copy at four that afternoon, Justman with his an hour later. Black stayed to work for a few hours on his original script for "Naked Time" before going home to read the submitted script. He returned at ten the next morning and handed his rough notes to Mary Stilwell for typing. He planned to circulate them to Roddenberry and Justman before passing them along to the writer, who'd then be expected to incorporate them into the second draft

"Dorothy put G.R.'s script notes on your desk," Stilwell told him.

Sitting down in his chair, Black picked up the script folder. Inside were not rough notes but rewritten script pages, typed on Roddenberry's recognizable IBM Selectric, and some barely legible handwritten addenda—Roddenberry's.

"G.R. had rewritten the first draft, which we had agreed he was not going to do," Black says. "I did not blow my stack. I went in and talked to him about it. And he said that it was his show and he had a right to do with it as he pleased."

Black threatened to quit but was convinced to remain by assurances that this had been a onetime-only event.

Soon Shimon Wincelberg's "Dagger of the Mind" arrived. Black read the script cursorily and dictated preliminary notes to Stilwell, anticipating a thorough reading later and a chance to expand his verbal shorthand into something more meaningful and incisive. Stilwell, as usual, also made notes, meant for Black's eyes only; they were full of playfully sarcastic comments. Commenting on the scene in which Wincelberg had Dr. McCoy crying out in alarm that a character was trying to swallow his tongue, she wrote, "I've been sitting here for the past forty-five minutes trying to swallow my own tongue. It can't be done."

When Black arrived in Roddenberry's office to discuss the script, he was surprised to see Wincelberg there. Roddenberry, who'd not yet read the script, snatched Stilwell's notes from Black's hand and gave them to Wincelberg.

Black was mortified. He admired and respected Shimon, who was a Broadway playwright, renowned fiction writer, and veteran writer of at least one hundred teleplays; in fact, Black didn't believe he was qualified to sharpen the man's pencils, let alone critique his work. Any comments he'd have passed along to Wincelberg about script problems should have been handled far more delicately and tactfully than that embarrassing sledgehammer. A few days later, Wincelberg mailed a note to Black, who shuddered when it landed on his desk. Gracious and without rancor, Wincelberg said that Black possessed "a rare capacity" to be harsh without being vicious. As for the proposed tongue swallowing, "it just goes to show," he deadpanned, "how inadequate the younger generation of writers is."

For the six months and thirteen scripts that he remained as *Star Trek*'s story editor–associate producer, Black had the repeatedly unpleasant task of informing free-lance writers that their creativity had been usurped. Roddenberry's rewrites led Wincelberg, and other *Star Trek* writers, to seek pseudonymous screen credit. It is, of course, a matter of opinion whether the original scripts were better or worse than Roddenberry's versions. All writers maintain a congenital aversion to being rewritten.

Viewed from the historical perspective, success is difficult to contest; any adulation and affection accruing to those thirteen episodes would seem to endorse Roddenberry's vision. But here again, opinion is notoriously unobjective. David Gerrold attributes the popularity of a fan-favored *Star Trek* episode, his own "The Trouble with Tribbles," to its humor. In it, the fuzzy, fast-multiplying creatures called Tribbles create consequences and problems for

Kirk and the *Enterprise*. "We didn't set out for it to be a comedy," Gerrold says. "As the script went through a number of drafts, we started putting in more and more jokes." And as the director and cast began playing with it, its comedic undertones were pushed to the fore. "Everybody was saying, 'Let's have fun.'"

Significantly, Gerrold had worked on the script with Coon and story editor Dorothy Fontana. Roddenberry was out of town on vacation for the rewrites and, because problems with other scripts accelerated the schedule, the show's production, as well; by the time he returned, the show was in the can. "I'm sure when he got back he was upset," Gerrold says. "Gene didn't have a sense of humor, and here his characters are telling jokes. They're clowning around. They're having fun. Nobody was ever allowed to tell jokes. God forbid somebody should tell a joke."

In *Star Trek* lore, the story of how Roddenberry drastically rewrote Harlan Ellison's script for "The City on the Edge of Forever," about the *Enterprise* crew's trip back to 1930s earth to change the course of history, has achieved nearly mythical status. Their ongoing feud, kept alive mostly by Ellison, often played itself out in public. Ellison, angry and defiant, entered his original script for a Writers Guild Award and won, while Roddenberry's version earned a Nebula and is generally cited as the most popular episode. Roddenberry, while acknowledging the brilliance of Ellison's original script, insisted that the changes had been necessary because, one, the show as written would have been a budget buster; and two, Ellison's script was many things, all of them good, but some of them distinctly un–*Star Trek*–like. Though that may have been substantially true, Roddenberry stated numerous times that Ellison had turned Scotty into a "drug pusher," which he had not. Taking his bows for the show, Roddenberry did not acknowledge the substantial contributions of Gene Coon and Dorothy Fontana, both of whom had rewritten drafts of the script before Roddenberry's final version—which contained much of the material they'd created.

"Anybody who had to deal with Roddenberry on a daily basis was driven crazy," Ellison says. "And then, whatever came of it that was good—boom!—he was out on the goddamned stump circuit in fifteen minutes taking credit for it. He could barely write. I mean, he could really barely write."

In John D. F. Black's opinion, Roddenberry's rewrites rarely improved on the original drafts. "He took the writing out of the scripts," Black says. But what bothered him more was that Roddenberry had broken his pledge, which in turn called into question his own credibility. "I'd given the writers my word that they could rewrite themselves. They knew I'd given my word, and they knew the word was violated. They also knew I wasn't responsible."

Black stayed as long as he did because Roddenberry's explanation that the writers couldn't possibly have understood *Star Trek* yct—not the ship, nor the relationships, nor the universe's capabilities—seemed plausible. "That's where I kept holding onto hope," he says. But when he turned in his own script for "The Naked Time," he abandoned hope.

The finished product was Xeroxed and distributed on June 24, a Friday afternoon. On Monday morning Stilwell arrived at nine, an hour before Black, to find Fontana looking grave. "Mary," Fontana said, "G.R. rewrote 'Naked Time' and said he wants all the secretaries to copy [portions of] it."

Stilwell had never been asked to copy anything for anyone but Black; Roddenberry employed Fontana, and Justman had his own secretary. By tacit decree, one did not make such requests. She refused, believing Roddenberry wanted to make her a party to treachery. She told Fontana that she would not participate, and Fontana agreed to cover her. "He was intentionally trying to humiliate me," Stilwell says. "He liked to see things in a ferment as much as possible. There was a constant sense around the office that he wanted to see people stirred up. Not necessarily upset or angry, but energized, popping."

"Agitated," Black says. "He really enjoyed it. The more agitation going on, the better he liked it."

When Black arrived later that morning, he was prepared to receive Roddenberry's and Justman's script notes, but not to find a wholesale rewrite. He visited Roddenberry's office.

"For God's sake, Gene," he said. "I can maybe—maybe!— understand it for somebody who doesn't know the show. But I'm the story executive. I work here. I know the show. And you know I know it." There had been the time, for instance, when James Doohan, who portrayed Chief Engineer Scott, asked Black what a lithium crystal (as it was then called, before being changed to "dilithium" when someone discovered that lithium was a real element) looked like. Black, who shared rock-cutting as a hobby with Roddenberry and Alden Schwimmer, spontaneously picked up a piece of cut quartz from his desk and offered it to Doohan—voilà, the *Enterprise*'s power source.

"Well," Roddenberry replied, "I want it the way I want it, and that's it, and that's the rewrite."

Roddenberry stood there, Black says, wearing a "shit-eating, that's-the-way-it-is-and-up-yours grin," and Black began making plans to leave his employ.

Production on the first *Star Trek* episode, "The Corbomite Maneuver," was scheduled to begin May 24, 1966. Early in the month, designer Walter Jefferies put the finishing touches on the sets that comprised the U.S.S. *Enterprise*. He called the staff down to the soundstage to tour his final standing set, McCoy's sick bay. Everyone was impressed, particularly by the space-age-looking beds and the twenty-third-century medical tools, which were in fact a pair of Swedish salt and pepper shakers.

As it happened, that same week Los Angeles played host to a medical convention; among the conferees were doctors who worked for NASA and the air force, as well as trauma surgeons. Roddenberry, who'd read about the convention in the newspaper, smelled the possibility of prebroadcast publicity that *Star Trek* could use. He got NBC to invite about fifty of the doctors, and members of the press, to a guided tour of the *Enterprise*'s sick bay—and while they were at it, the other sets as well.

Shortly before noon on the appointed day, the group of doctors, reporters, and NBC executives arrived on the Desilu lot. They were ushered first to the commissary, where they were plied with food. Roddenberry moved among them, talking up the show; its attention, wherever possible, to scientific veracity; its view of a future made hopeful by technology.

When stomachs were full, Roddenberry led them to the sets, guiding them through one by one. Last was sick bay. With Roddenberry at the head of the line, they filed in and began wandering around. Mostly, there was silence.

"We'd really like to know what you think about it," Roddenberry said.

After a pause, one doctor spoke up. "It's really a shame," he said, "that you couldn't get one of the newer beds."

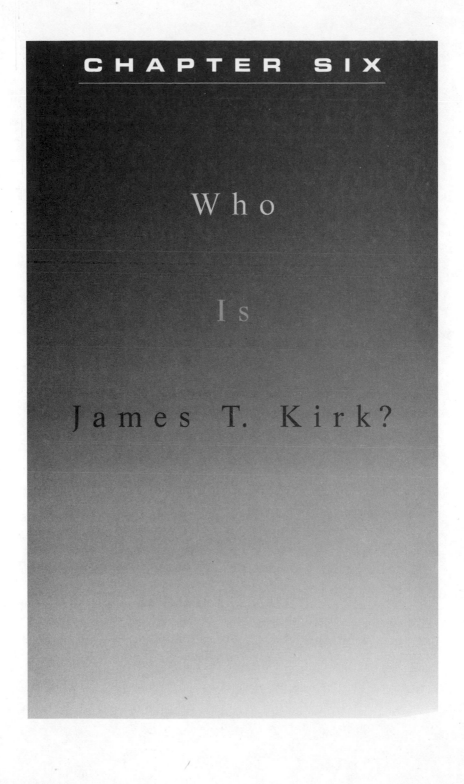

CHAPTER SIX

Who

Is

James T. Kirk?

EVERAL WEEKS before *Star Trek* debuted in the fall of 1966, Gene Roddenberry took Majel Barrett and Jerry Sohl out for a celebratory evening. Though George Clayton Johnson's "Man Trap" was to be the premiere episode shown on September 8, Sohl's "Corbomite Maneuver" had been the first episode filmed and would be broadcast in November. In the meantime, Sohl was at work on another *Star Trek* script and was considered an integral part of the *Star Trek* family of writers—one who should be made to feel welcome and happy.

They met after work for drinks at Barrett's apartment near Desilu Studios. Judging by the arrangement and the couple's obvious coziness, Sohl believed that Roddenberry was either in the process of divorcing his wife or had already done so. It was his distinct impression that Roddenberry was paying Barrett's rent and bills.

Many, many more drinks were consumed at a Beverly Hills restaurant, and the fun escalated in direct proportion to the alcohol. All three were reasonably looped when Roddenberry confided in Sohl: Just days before his forty-fifth birthday, and weeks before the launch of what he hoped would be both *Star Trek*'s five-year mission and himself as a major player in television, Roddenberry was pretty damn pleased with the way things were going. And now that he was at the top, he told Sohl, he was going to make everybody under him crawl the way he'd had to crawl on the way up.

Those words may have been compelled by the alcohol, but they lodged in Sohl's memory.

Over Labor Day weekend, less than a week before *Star Trek*'s broadcast premiere, Sohl accompanied Roddenberry to the Twenty-fourth World Science Fiction Convention, held that year in Cleveland. Roddenberry, a convention virgin, planned to show both pilots as a way of building word-of-mouth among the faithful; if they liked it, he felt, the rest of America might follow. He brought along Sohl, whose novels and *Twilight Zone* scripts were known by many attendees, to offer additional credibility. The producer of *Star Trek*, after all, was unknown to them.

Roddenberry's wife, not Majel Barrett, accompanied him to Cleveland. When a reservations mix-up at the fully booked hotel left Sohl stranded, Roddenberry volunteered to have a cot placed in his and Eileen's room. Lacking an alternative, Sohl accepted. "I kept wondering how in the hell he could be so jovial and friendly with his wife," Sohl recalls, "after he'd just been with Majel like that." In fact, Roddenberry moved between the two with ease. He would soon surprise Eileen with a trip to Hawaii, a twenty-fifth anniversary celebration that had little celebrating in it.

Roddenberry was not met with open arms at the convention. Its co-chairman Ted White, among many in attendance, had little respect for Hollywood. Science fiction had had a checkered history in film. In the past only a handful of movies—*The Day the Earth Stood Still*, *War of the Worlds*, *The Time Machine*, and *Forbidden Planet*, for example—had been treated with the intelligence and care the subject deserved. And television had fared even worse. There hadn't been a single worthy series, not one that could be classified as serious adult science fiction. While *The Outer Limits*, *One Step Beyond*, and *The Twilight Zone* had science fiction elements in them, all three more correctly fell into the category of speculative or imaginative fiction. Television's conception of the genre was insipid fare like *Voyage to the Bottom of the Sea* and *Lost in Space*. It was no wonder that the annual World Science Fiction Convention mostly honored the written medium, and no wonder that Gene Roddenberry was treated with such skepticism.

Before presenting "The Cage" and "Where No Man Has Gone Before," Roddenberry sought to showcase some *Star Trek* costumes in the convention's futuristic fashion show. But Bjo Trimble, who ran the fashion show with her husband, John, refused on grounds that the contest had always been a showcase for essentially amateur, though not necessarily amateurish, talents; to introduce the work of professional designers seemed unfair. Besides, the show had already been timed down to the second, and as a virtually lifelong science fiction fan (she attended her first convention in 1952), she just didn't trust Mr. Slick on general principles. "There's no way I'm gonna let this damned Hollywood producer stick a couple of his damned costumes into my fashion show," she said.

Given the news, Roddenberry invited Trimble to have a drink at the bar with him. She accepted, firm in her conviction that his costumes would not be seen on stage. "Then Gene turned on all of his Irish charm," John Trimble recalls, and the *Star Trek* costumes were accommodated in the show.

It was at the convention that Roddenberry met Isaac Asimov, with whom he began a long relationship, mostly through letters and phone calls. Asimov was in Cleveland with his friend Harlan Ellison, performing the first of what would be many joint appearances, the two of them on stage discussing any and all topics in an unrehearsed and frequently hilarious exchange of wit. Some months later, Asimov knocked *Star Trek* in a *TV Guide* article, mostly on grounds of its presenting scientific inaccuracies. Offended by the king of science fiction's words, Roddenberry wrote to Asimov to provide a brief education on the inherent limitations of television production, and assured him of the show's dedication to credibility. *Star Trek* may not have been perfect, Roddenberry said, but it was the best science fiction ever available on the tube; and in exposing millions of viewers who'd never even heard of Asimov's *I, Robot*, he pointed out, *Star Trek* was vastly enlarging the potential science fiction market—that is, the book-buying public.

Apparently impressed, Asimov reconsidered his criticism. The following spring he wrote another *TV Guide* article, this one in praise of Spock particularly and the show in general. In a thank-you letter, Roddenberry solicited Asimov's creative guidance. After twenty-seven episodes of *Star Trek*, Roddenberry said, the role of

Capt. James. T. Kirk still seemed unfulfilled. He asked for suggestions to fill out the role.

It's easy to give good situations and good lines to Spock. And to a lesser extent the same is true of the irascible Dr. McCoy....And yet *Star Trek* needs a strong lead, an Earth lead. Without diminishing the importance of the secondary continuing characters. But the problem we generally find is this—if we play Kirk as a true ship commander, strong and hard, devoted to career and service, it too often makes him seem unlikeable. On the other hand, if we play him too warm-hearted, friendly and so on, the attitude often is "how did a guy like that get to be a ship commander?" Sort of a damned if he does and damned if he doesn't situation.[1]

Interestingly, Roddenberry confuses Kirk with William Shatner. "Actually, although it is missed by the general audience," the letter continued, "it is Kirk's fine handling of a most difficult role that permits Spock and the others to come off as well as they do. But Kirk does deserve more and so does the actor who plays him. I am in something of a quandary about it. Got any ideas?"[2]

In Roddenberry's mind, the actor and the character had merged into one. A simple Freudian slip of the Dictaphone or not (he dictated letters to a secretary), Roddenberry did indeed project a strong psychic association with Kirk. First as producer and then as executive producer, Roddenberry saw himself as the ship's captain, and his analysis of Kirk's tightrope walk between geniality and forcefulness applied equally well to him: "if we play him too warm-hearted, friendly and so on, the attitude often is 'how did a guy like that get to be a ship commander?'"[3] Even if the episodes began as other writers' tales of Kirk, they were also Roddenberry's fantasies.

In this regard Roddenberry was no different from, say, Dashiell Hammett, C. S. Forester, and Ian Fleming. All fiction writers project their fantasies onto their heroic creations; that's what storytelling is about. Kirk shared with Nick Charles, Horatio Hornblower, and James Bond the trait of being their creator's perfect leader of men, the one they'd wish to be.

Kirk's author did in fact make at least two Kirk-like decisions off the screen that first year of *Star Trek,* showing not physical courage but ethical leadership. In the spring of 1966, NBC had hired Stanley Robertson as an executive, one of several that the networks employ to work with studios and series producers as a way of ensuring that the network gets the type of show for which it contracted. Robertson, as it happens, was black—the first black television executive in the industry's two-decade-plus history. His mentors were Mort Werner and Grant Tinker, both of whom had been adamantly in favor of integrating the executive suite. (Perhaps in an effort to curry favor, Roddenberry told Nichelle Nichols that he had to fight NBC to keep her, a black woman, on the show. But NBC executives had long been in favor of integrating network television. Long before *Star Trek* aired, Werner had sent a letter to the producers of every NBC show, encouraging them to cast their shows with more nonwhite faces.)[4] They could have unilaterally assigned their Jackie Robinson the stewardship of several shows, but they wanted to avoid throwing him to the wolves. Some producers, they knew, would find the newness of the situation offputting. The subject had to be broached gently. After all, it was Robertson who'd have to approve or disapprove story outlines and scripts, and work with the producers to improve the product. Then Roddenberry called Werner. "I understand you have a new Negro executive," he said. "I'd like to have him work on my show."

"Gene knew it would be a sensitive time for me and the network," Robertson says.

In the mid-1960s, the idea of equality among the races was still more resisted than accepted. Robertson recalls his first visit to WMAQ, the NBC affiliate station in Chicago; the entire staff came out to gawk at the executive, simply because he was black. "People didn't know what the problems were at networks then," he says. "Unless you were inside, you couldn't know. There were a lot of people in the NBC hierarchy who said, 'Aren't you moving a little too fast, guys?'"

Over the course of his year as *Star Trek*'s network liaison, Robertson had several conversations with Roddenberry about race and police brutality—topics of much concern only twelve months after the Watts riots of August 1965, particularly for two men with backgrounds vested in the events. Robertson, like many blacks who grew up in the 1950s in South Central Los Angeles, had hated the police. Roddenberry, the son of a racist cop, had been a cop himself and written speeches for the most hated cop of all, Chief William Parker. "Gene was a redneck white kid, the son of a raging racist," Robertson says. "He admitted, 'I should have been a racist, too.' I give Gene Roddenberry a lot of credit."

Roddenberry's second courageous stand came late in 1966, when he hired Dorothy Fontana as *Star Trek*'s story editor.

In late September, Fontana quit as Roddenberry's secretary to pursue her free-lance writing career. Roddenberry called her to do a rewrite on Jerry Sohl's "The Way of the Spores," which in her typewriter became "This Side of Paradise." He needed the rewrite quickly, because Steven Carabatsos, who'd taken over John D. F. Black's job, would soon be leaving. "If you can do the rewrite fast enough and good enough to please the network and the studio, I will back you as my story editor," she remembers him saying.

Having been with the show since its inception—and having written the excellent "Charlie X" and "Tomorrow Is Yesterday" episodes—Fontana knew the series intimately and was a natural choice. The only misaligned peg was her gender. "To have a woman story editor on an action-adventure show, that was unheard-of," she says.

On the twenty-third-century *Enterprise*, neither Roddenberry's choice of Fontana nor his relationship to Robertson would have been remarkable. And though the years since may seem to have diminished the importance of each victory, it must be remembered that in the United States of America, 1966, both were worthy of Capt. James T. Kirk.

From the beginning, Roddenberry drew Kirk to be Capt. Christopher Pike of "The Cage," minus his over-the-top angst. But no matter how Kirk's character changed in the development of *Star Trek*, what remained constant in Roddenberry's guidelines were references to his new captain's imperfections. Kirk made mistakes. He let his passions overtake him. He wasn't infallible. Yet his weaknesses didn't endanger the safety of the beings under his command or the *Enterprise*. Kirk was always the best starship commander in the galaxy. His faults, whatever they were, paled in the light of his leadership. In fact, his faults were appealing.

Two decades later, things changed considerably. Kirk's progeny, Capt. Jean-Luc Picard of *Star Trek: The Next Generation*, appeared to have sprung forth from Zeus's skull in a state of perfection. Picard was a fully-evolved creature—Kirk reincarnated, having assimilated the lessons of past lives, able to avoid pitfalls and mistakes.

"He identified with his captains," says Dorothy Fontana. "There's no question about that."

June 18, 1947, was a typically hot and humid day in Karachi, soon to be the capital of the new country of Pakistan. At 3:37 in the afternoon, Pan American Airways flight number 121 departed for Istanbul on the next leg of a tedious westward journey that had originated in Calcutta and would eventually arrive in New York, which was home base for its American crew.[5] In the cockpit were Capt. Joe Hart, flight engineer Robert Donnelly, and first officer Robert McCoy.

Third officer Gene Roddenberry, without flight responsibilities on this 2200-mile leg, sat in the rear of the passenger compartment with twenty six British and Indian passengers. He'd flown this route often in the year since becoming a Pan Am pilot and always found it unexciting, but at least now he could eat, drink, and sleep as much as he chose. There was no way around the fact that flying for a living was boring—more boring, probably, than driving a bus. That's what he considered himself, he said, a glorified bus driver. In later years he would brag to friends that on transatlantic flights he'd sometimes put the craft on automatic pilot, passing the hours with several drinks and a nap. He even noted that the airline, facing an emergency manpower shortage, had once called him at home to pilot the next flight to London. Drunk at the time, he said, he had promptly shown up at the airport and assumed his duties.[6]

Roddenberry, like the other members of the cockpit crew, was a World War II flying veteran who had grabbed the opportunity to use his skills in an employment market saturated with veterans. For a short time after returning from the South Pacific, he'd been an air corps investigator, searching for crash causes. Once he got the Pan Am job, flying on a six-week rotation out of New York, he and Eileen had relocated to nearby New Jersey. Harboring visions of someday becoming a writer, he took extension writing classes at Columbia University in his spare time.

Roddenberry was asleep five hours into the flight, when the number one engine malfunctioned over Iraq. To reduce wind resistance, Captain Hart feathered the engine's propeller. There didn't seem to be reason for worry; such things happened with frequency. Anyway, no airfield before Istanbul was equipped with spare parts for a Lockheed Constellation. Contacting Istanbul, Hart ordered an engine cylinder to be ready for their arrival. After a quick fitting, the plane would be ready to continue and a long delay averted. He knew every one of the ten-member crew, not least himself, was anxious to get home as soon as possible.

Sometime later, the thrust bearing on the number two engine failed, inhibiting the flow of oil from the feathering motor to the propeller dome. It soon became apparent that the remaining engines could not provide sufficient airspeed to cool themselves. Hart reduced engine power and descended from 18,000 feet to a lower altitude. He decided to make an emergency landing, but could not reach any local airfields. Finally, he radioed Pan Am in Karachi. "Will you inform the civilian airfields in this area that I am flying on three engines," he said. "I departed from Karachi. My destination is Istanbul. My approximate position is over Baghdad; height ten thousand feet. Have been trying to contact Baghdad airfield without success."

The controller responded that all airfields in the area were closed until dawn, about six hours hence, and suggested that he proceed forty miles due west to the Royal Air Force field at Habbaniya, Iraq, near the Euphrates River. He would inform Habbaniya, he said, of the imminent emergency landing.

From Habbaniya, the duty officer soon radioed Hart detailed information about the field's facilities. But Hart had again changed his mind. Damascus, four hundred miles farther west, had an excellent Pan Am service base; Habbaniya did not. "I intend to make for Istanbul," he said. "If unable to do so I shall land at Damascus, providing I have sufficient fuel and height to clear high ground en route." Establishing an open emergency frequency, the captain promised he would return to Habbaniya if at any point further trouble arose that would keep them from reaching Damascus.

Some minutes later Habbaniya informed Hart that the airfield at Damascus would remain closed until four A.M., long after the plotted arrival time, and proposed again that he make his emergency landing at Habbaniya. "Thank you," Hart replied. "Will try to make Istanbul and will stand by on this channel. If I have any more trouble I will turn back to Habbaniya."

While Pan Am flight 121 continued for Istanbul, officials worked to open Damascus airfield. Hart was instructed to maintain contact on the emergency frequency and provide his bearings and altitude every thirty minutes. By eleven o'clock, when he reported his position as being seventy-five miles northwest of Habbaniya, Damascus had relented: The facilities were open, it awaited the landing.

Half an hour later, steward Tony Volpe, who was seated slightly ahead of the sleeping Roddenberry in the cabin, noticed that the "fasten seat belt—no smoking" light had just come on. He jumped to his feet and began awakening the passengers, instructing them to put on their seat belts. At that moment, Hart was frantically radioing Habbaniya. "Number two on fire," he said. That was all the ground crew heard, except for a sustained note, like a continually depressed Morse key.

Within moments, the entire cabin was illuminated by an eerie and terrifying light from the flames on the left wing that had engulfed the engine. Descending rapidly, Hart planned to make a controlled crash landing. It was nearly two in the morning. They were still about three hundred miles northwest of Damascus, near Mayadine, Syria. For six eternal minutes, while the plane headed unsteadily toward the ground, Volpe and stewardess Jane Bray instructed the passengers in crash-landing procedures and tried to calm their fears. There was, in fact, reason to believe that they would survive the impact. A veteran of almost thirteen thousand commercial air hours, and countless more combat hours, Captain Hart had undoubtedly made successful crash landings before.

Still seated in the rear compartment, Roddenberry cinched his seat belt tight and prepared for the worst.

The flaming number two engine dropped off a minute before impact on a treeless, grassless, gently rolling plain of clay and hard-packed sand. Fed by leaking oil and gasoline, the wing continued burning, as did the wheels and tires.

Doing his best to fight the unbalanced and nearly uncontrollable craft, and effect a belly-first landing, Hart was lucky to touch down as gently as he did. Investigators would later guess from the depth of the ground impressions that the force had been severe. First to hit was the left wing tip, then its propeller, then its nacelle and engine. The entire wing, torn from its base, came to a halt 225 feet forward of the first contact point. Momentum sent the plane into a violent ground loop. The craft turned 180 degrees on its longitudinal axis. Then, after skidding backward for more than two hundred feet, it finally came to rest four hundred feet from initial impact.

The fuselage had separated into two clear openings, the right side's ten feet wide, the left's four feet wide. It had also parted laterally along the back edge of the right wing. Flames immediately devoured the cockpit area and the forward section of the passenger compartment, killing seven crew members and seven front passengers, their seated bodies still buckled by seat belts.

Even as their less lucky counterparts were burning to death, passengers at the rear jumped to safety. Despite a broken ankle, Bray led the escape brigade, later receiving unanimous praise for her heroism from the nineteen passengers and two other surviving crew members.

With the burning wreckage behind them seeming like a giant campfire against the desert blackness, Roddenberry, Bray, Volpe, and the eight slightly injured passengers huddled together and gave whatever comfort they could to the eleven whose injuries were more severe. Attracted by the flames, a band of marauding nomads rode up on horses and carried off all unburned personal belongings and salvageable baggage.

One of the few to be fully ambulatory, Roddenberry set out across the plain for the nearest phone, five miles to the west in Mayadine, which he said he found by following telephone lines. At a little after seven in the morning, he telephoned Deir-ez-Zor and reported the situation. The British garrison commander there dispatched an army airplane and ambulance, several jeeps, a number of medical personnel, and military police. A Syrian air force captain made two mercy flights into the area, carrying additional medical personnel and supplies.

It took four hours to evacuate the seriously injured survivors to the Presbyterian mission hospital at Deir-ez-Zor. Roddenberry and Volpe joined the eight other survivors on a flight to Damascus.

A diplomat from the American embassy in Damascus arrived at the crash site that afternoon with a reverend from the Presbyterian mission. Intending to return with the corpses, they learned that gendarmes had already buried the fourteen dead in two common graves. There was absolutely no reason, the gendarmes assured them, to exhume the bodies. Like the wreckage of the plane, all had been burned beyond identification. With the debris still smoking behind him, the reverend held a short graveside service.

Less than a year later, shortly after the birth of his firstborn daughter, Gene Roddenberry quit flying. In years to come he often recounted the incident—not for dramatic effect, but as proof of his atheism. Even when it had appeared that only a precious few seconds of his twenty-six years remained to him, he said, he did not invoke the name of the deity in either a plea for mercy or out of fear. What use was there in begging someone or something that wasn't there?

In July 1967, while the second season of *Star Trek* was beginning production, Isaac Asimov replied to Roddenberry's request for help in making Kirk more appealing. "It seems to me that the only thing one can lead from is strength," Asimov wrote. "Mr. Shatner is a versatile and talented actor and perhaps this should be made plain by giving him a chance at a variety of roles. In other words, an effort should be made to work up story plots in which Mr. Shatner has an opportunity to put on disguises or take over roles of unusual nature. A bravura display of his versatility would be more impressive indeed and would probably make the whole deal a great deal more fun for Mr. Shatner."[7]

Asimov theorized that Kirk could be made more attractive by having Spock save his life in an episode and by having him and Spock team up more closely. "The idea of this," he wrote, "would be to get people to think of Kirk when they think of Spock."[8]

If one believes that Roddenberry identified psychically with his starship captain, there is vivid irony in Asimov's suggestion that Kirk be fleshed out through Spock, who'd been a hit from the beginning and was a popular phenomenon by the third year. Roddenberry spread his name across the *Star Trek* landscape like a Johnny Appleseed, sowing future fruit. "Gene Roddenberry" appeared twice in the opening credits, on two separate cards—either producer or executive producer, and "created by." If he'd been so inclined, both credits could have fit on a single card. But that would have missed an opportunity.

Behind the scenes, too, he made certain that every piece of in-house literature, like the show's bible and scripts, and any reference that would be seen by others, noted that he'd been the creator. "Gene had his name all over the place," Herb Solow says. "He was always scheming." In the second and third years, publicity blurbs written by *Star Trek* staff with studio and network editors referred to Roddenberry as the "series creator," and he insisted that the dust sleeve to an album of music from *Star Trek* say "'created by Gene Roddenberry' on as much of this as possible."[9]

Royalties from this album were to be split fifty-fifty between Alexander Courage, the show's composer, and Roddenberry. Courage's original 1965 contract with Desilu had given Roddenberry the option to compose lyrics for the theme music and continuity music.[10] If he chose to—and he did—Roddenberry was entitled to receive one-half the composer's share of the BMI royalties, whether or not his lyrics were ever heard. His nine lines about "my love wandering in star flight" were never recorded or broadcast, but they entitled him to take home half the music profits.

When these royalties were divided in 1967, Courage protested the inequity, his complaint based on ethicality, not legality. In a letter defending his honor, Roddenberry reminded Courage of the afternoon that they'd met in 1965 in Roddenberry's bungalow office on the Desilu lot to discuss both the kind of music Roddenberry anticipated and the deal itself. Courage, he said, had of course preferred not to give away half his royalty, and credit. But without that acquiescence there would have been no *Star Trek* contract and, later, no *Police Story*—on which Roddenberry "did not ask for a similar arrangement since I had no strong notions about that music and did not expect to work as closely with you on it."[11]

It was likewise within Roddenberry's contractual rights to receive the same royalty on a Mr. Spock album recorded by Leonard Nimoy in late 1966, if the album contained any music. It did, and he did. He also insisted on his right, inasmuch as Spock "is a creation of mine," to exercise editorial authority over the album—and to take a piece of the profit action for the same reason.[12] (Eventually titled *Mr. Spock's Music From Outer Space*, the album was conceived when Desilu business affairs head Ed Perlstein came to Nimoy on the set and informed him that his Spock visage was soon to adorn the cover of an album of space-themed music, released on Dot Records. Nimoy suggested that he ought to have an editorial voice on any album that bore his face on the cover, and the producer gladly invited him to New York. Nimoy spent two days rehearsing before a five-hour session in which he recorded talk pieces that had been written for him and some songs, including Kurt Weill's "Lost in the Stars" and a politically correct ditty called "Visit to a Sad Planet" that became something of a hit. So pleased with the sales was Dot that Nimoy released five more Spock albums on the label over the following three years.)

Roddenberry promoted himself tirelessly. "He was an expert at self-promotion," Solow says. And in the headiness of the times, when his acceptance as Mr. *Star Trek* accumulated a critical mass of recognition, Roddenberry must have lost his bearings. (He once claimed that, in the history of television, no other producer had brought as much personally to a show as he had to *Star Trek.* "Certain qualities," he called it. "I don't know that anyone else has ever tried that. Rod Serling may have come close at one time with his *Twilight Zone,* but I don't think as close as I've come."[13] Of *Twilight Zone*'s 156 episodes, Serling wrote 92; Roddenberry received writing credit on 8 *Star Trek*s, some of them for story only. Serling, on the other hand, never rewrote scripts submitted by other writers.)

A case in point was his attitude toward his own "The Omega Glory," which began as a potential *Star Trek* pilot but was withheld for several reasons, including story implausibility. After a number of rewrites, two by Tina and Les Pine and another by Roddenberry, and a polish by Fontana, it eventually aired March 1, 1968. A heavy-handed parable about war between the Yangs (Yankees) and the Kohms (Communists), "The Omega Glory" is not considered in the top ten best or most popular episodes, and many fans consider it among the show's worst. Yet Roddenberry promoted it at the expense of other noteworthy stories.[14]

In a memo to NBC written ten days before the broadcast, Roddenberry proposed that the network postpone the scheduled March 1 airing in favor of opening the third season with it. "One of the great problems of all shows is to have a smasheroo opening episode and we've really got one here!" he wrote.[15] That same day, which was three days before the airdate of the arguably more worthy "By Any Other Name," credited to Fontana and Jerome Bixby, he wrote an internal business affairs memo suggesting that the studio buy full-page Emmy announcements in the Hollywood trade papers, calling the attention of Television Academy members to "The Omega Glory."[16]

As March 1 drew closer, Roddenberry turned up the heat. On February 26, he wrote to Hank Grant, columnist for *The Hollywood Reporter*, talking up the episode "which many think is a rather unique piece"; and to NBC again, noting that although "it's hard for me to be objective" about the episode, "several others here think it is deserving of a bit of promotion...."

The previous year, Roddenberry and Desilu mounted a campaign for *Star Trek*'s recognition with the Academy of Television Arts and Sciences that paid off with the show winning five Emmy nominations—three in technical categories, one for Nimoy as best supporting dramatic actor, and one for outstanding dramatic series. What galled Roddenberry was that Gene Coon's name, not his, had been attached to the outstanding drama nomination; in those days, only the producer of record was so rewarded, and as the executive producer, he would have had to watch silently if Coon had mounted the dais to accept the award. So he convinced both Coon and Herb Solow, the show's executive in charge of production, to write letters to the Academy on his behalf, and the nomination was reissued to include his name as well as Coon's. (Over its three-year run, *Star Trek* earned thirteen Emmy nominations, eight of them in technical categories, three for Nimoy as best supporting dramatic actor, and outstanding drama for the first two years. Not one of the thirteen turned up in the winner's envelope.)

Roddenberry's thirst for recognition often placed the show's welfare behind his own. When representatives of the Twenty-fifth World Science Fiction Convention notified him, in November 1966, that *Star Trek* was eligible for a Hugo Award but that only specific episodes could be nominated, Roddenberry protested. He stated for the record his belief that it was "a serious mistake to nominate science fiction series on the basis of single episodes," a practice akin to judging "individual chapters of a novel." He reasoned that, while most fans would be familiar with the whole series, the odds were against them seeing that particular episode.[17]

His trepidation having been stated clearly for the record, he entered an episode for consideration—not "Where No Man Has Gone Before," which had been so warmly received at the convention in Cleveland; nor Richard Matheson's "The Enemy Within," nor Theodore Sturgeon's "Shore Leave." He nominated the only episode that whole first season of *Star Trek* whose script was credited to him, "The Menagerie," the two-parter that hadn't yet aired.

"The Menagerie" had its origins in economics, not science fiction. After NBC had green-lighted the series, Desilu and Roddenberry realized that meeting the stringent scheduling requirements given the $190,000 (give or take a few) average budget per episode was inherently problematic, which is to say back-breaking—the equivalent, Roddenberry liked to point out, of shooting half a feature film every six days. It therefore made sense to find a way to incorporate the seventy-five minutes of "The Cage" into a Captain Kirk–led *Star Trek* scenario—to place "The Cage" into a type of "envelope" that fit the new format. Only four additional production days would yield a two-part episode, thus saving more than $200,000 and, more importantly, eight days. Of even more significance, it would yield the two full hours without which, Justman knew, the delivery schedule could not have been met.

The story of Spock abducting the scarred and crippled Capt. Christopher Pike and returning him to live out his life in rich fantasy on Talos IV, the planet on which he'd been imprisoned in the original pilot, was originally devised by John D. F. Black. After Black left the *Star Trek* staff, Roddenberry rewrote the script and put his name on it. As a matter of course, because the script was rewritten by a staff member who wanted credit, the matter was referred to the Writers Guild arbitration board. Naive to the end, Black did not file a statement in his own behalf, detailing why he deserved to be co-credited with Roddenberry, who'd written "The Cage." He maintained that the Guild members adjudging the drafts would surely see his script as the source of the additional footage. He had already witnessed several arguments, engendered by Roddenberry's choosing to pursue credit, resolved in favor of the freelancers. But they'd put up a fight.

The board ruled for Roddenberry, and gave him sole credit. "I never again trusted blindly in the process," Black says. "I never again trusted that the truth would win out by itself."

Roddenberry apparently wanted the Hugo badly enough to pursue it. Some months after "The Menagerie" aired in mid-

November, he repeated his complaints about the nominating system; this time they were forwarded to Ted White, the convention's co-chair.[18] It wasn't fair, Roddenberry said, to pit a single episode of a whole series against feature films that enjoyed ten times his budget and more than ten times his number of shooting days.

White's acidic reply is a marvel of the I'm-putting-you-in-your-place genre. With understated condescension and invective, he reminded Roddenberry that he was still a novice who hadn't yet made his sf bones. "I'm sure it must be disappointing to you," White's letter began, "to find that you are in competition with *Fantastic Voyage* [a movie, not a TV series] and *Fahrenheit 451* for the Hugo Award this year, but unfortunately the Hugo Awards are not geared for your exclusive set of interests, nor will they be."

White agreed that there was indeed a fairness imbalance—in Roddenberry's favor. For a series that was broadcast every week to compete against a movie that may or may not have been seen during its limited engagement at the neighborhood theater seemed distinctly unfair, he said. "There is no question in my mind that if we allowed *Star Trek* to be voted as a series, it would easily win the Drama Hugo. Indeed, if *Star Trek* were not on the air, it might even be that *Time Tunnel* could win on that basis. This places motion-picture sf at a considerable disadvantage, and I think you can understand the point." He accused Roddenberry of "shamefully" exploiting the Cleveland convention. "The dignity of the convention was compromised last year. It will not be this year."

The letter drew to a close with White's observation that Roddenberry seemed "to wish full credit for not only the conception of the series as a whole, but for each episode as well. Perhaps I am uninformed on the subject, but that strikes me as presumptuous"; and it concluded with an offer to buy him a drink should Roddenberry decide to attend.[19]

Bewildered by the letter's tone and content, Roddenberry wrote letters of inquiry to acquaintances in the science fiction community, wondering what he'd done to deserve such a lashing. Fearing possible "humiliation," he told Isaac Asimov, he did not attend the world convention in New York over Labor Day weekend, two weeks before the second season of *Star Trek* began with the airing of "Amok Time." [20]

One of the convention's major events was a benefit auction, the proceeds from which would be used to bring a Japanese science fiction fan (Takumi Shibano) to the United States for a visit and tour. Bjo and John Trimble, who headed the auction committee, had asked Roddenberry to donate some *Star Trek* memorabilia to include in the auction. When the Trimbles arrived at the convention hotel, they found a number of boxes waiting for them. Inside were items like the torn shirt Kirk wore in "Amok Time," several pairs of Spock ears, the original treatment for *Star Trek*, and a copy of the writer's bible. On one box was handwritten the word "Tribbles." The Trimbles, who'd several times visited the *Star Trek* set and met Roddenberry through friends Harlan Ellison, Robert Bloch, Ted Sturgeon, and Jerome Bixby, wondered how Roddenberry's secretary, Penny Unger, could have misspelled their name so badly. When they opened the box, they discovered fuzzy little creatures that seemed to have no connection to *Star Trek*. At the time, "The Trouble with Tribbles" hadn't yet aired, and if not for a copy of David Gerrold's script that Unger had included, they wouldn't have known how to pitch them for auction.

John Trimble credits the Roddenberry-donated items for making the auction "the biggest draw at the convention outside of the Hugo awards. We packed the room." With conventioneers forming combines to bid on the merchandise, he says, the $5,000 needed to bring Shibano to America was raised within two and a half hours.

More significantly, the auction became that galvanizing moment in *Star Trek* history: "It was when *Star Trek* fandom first came together and became a force in and of itself," Trimble says. "People who met each other at the convention went off and started producing fanzines and formed clubs."

"The Menagerie" did indeed win a Hugo. A surprised Roddenberry heard about it from Asimov, who had attended the presentation. For some reason, no one on the convention committee bothered to notify the winner officially. Roddenberry was left to inquire himself whether Asimov had been correct and, if so, how he was to go about picking up his award.

It was late September 1966. *Star Trek* had been on the air for three weeks. The ratings may not have been all that everyone would have liked, but already Mr. Spock was well on his way to folk-hero status. Through his agent, Leonard Nimoy received offers almost daily to make personal appearances at amusement parks, car dealerships, trade shows—virtually anywhere that could benefit from an increase in public traffic. Even when Nimoy made clear that he would not appear in Spock makeup and ears—that he was an actor portraying a character, not the character—the offers continued to pour in. Ears or no ears, the public clearly wanted to be near him. And for a few hours of answering questions, shaking hands, telling stories, or singing a song or two, he'd earn a couple of thousand dollars—more than his *Star Trek* contract paid him for six days of work.

Nimoy's agent had just relayed a $2,000 offer from a Connecticut amusement park operator who wanted the actor to make a personal appearance at the park the following Saturday morning. Had there been a flight to New York later than six o'clock the Friday night before, Nimoy would not have had to ask permission to leave the Desilu lot at five. But coast-to-coast flights in those days were not as plentiful as they later became. So on Monday he broached the subject with the production department, believing that they would be, if not anxious to help, at least accommodating. When on Tuesday he hadn't received a response, he checked back. Time was running out on the offer. He had to let the park operator know whether he was going to be able to accept the job.

On Wednesday he was called to Roddenberry's office. Roddenberry said that he'd been told Nimoy had requested permission to finish his day of shooting a couple of hours early that Friday night. Nimoy confirmed and explained why. In fact, he said, he'd been virtually inundated with personal appearance offers and wanted to keep as many of them as possible. Besides, he added, it was wonderful p.r. for the series.

After listening intently, Roddenberry replied that he'd always known Spock would take America by storm, which was one reason he'd fought so hard to keep him on the series when the network wanted him excised. Then he began talking about a business venture that he and Majel Barrett had discussed founding, something called "Lincoln Enterprises." One of its functions would be to represent *Star Trek* talent for personal appearances, and he wanted Lincoln's first client to be the actor who portrayed Spock.

Nimoy noted that he already had an agent and didn't need someone else taking another twenty percent.

"The difference between your agent and Lincoln Enterprises," Roddenberry said, "is that Lincoln can get you off the lot at five P.M. every Friday."

"Gene," Nimoy said, "I already have the job. I'm asking if you can help me out of here so I can pick up two thousand dollars this weekend."

"The problem with you," Roddenberry said, "is that you have to learn to bow down and say 'Master.'"

For the first two years of the series, Desilu (then Desilu-Paramount, then Paramount) entrusted the licensing of merchandise like models of the *Enterprise* to the Licensing Corporation of America, which regularly sent profit-participation checks to the studio and Roddenberry. Roddenberry, however, did not believe that the checks were as large as they could have been. In 1966, even before the first contracts were concluded, he complained in a letter to Alden Schwimmer that his contributions to the art department (helping to sketch out "a rather unique three-stage phaser hand weapon-pistol-rifle, one convertible into another") as well as to the costuming department ("improving the basic design") seemed to be above and beyond the call of writer-creator-producer duty. "I absolutely am not content," he wrote, "to see Desilu and others getting from this profits off the top while I have to wait for a profit-loss statement on the entire show."[21] Yet when AMT corporation, the maker of a plastic model *Enterprise*—licensed through LCA—sold almost one million units in 1967, Roddenberry declined to pay Walter Jefferies, the *Enterprise*'s designer, even a penny in (courtesy) royalties; he was not contractually obligated to do so.

In early 1968, Roddenberry began Lincoln Enterprises with an unethical kickstart. His marriage to Eileen clearly headed for a future date in divorce court, he conceived of Lincoln as a gift to Majel Barrett. With the company in her name, profits would not be considered community assets and subject to divorce litigation. At the same time, worried that Lincoln's initial merchandising line would be sparse if he played strictly by the rules, he asked his attorney whether LCA could sue Lincoln "in the event we inadvertently or otherwise trespass into a field licensed to some other manufacturer or distributor by LCA."[22] He also asked for a ruling on selling photocopies of other writers' scripts. (His attorney, Leonard Maizlish, was considered exceptionally capable and clever by most who had professional dealings with him, and in later years came to be Roddenberry's legal and personal point man.)

To inaugurate Lincoln, Roddenberry hired science fiction fans Bjo and John Trimble. The couple had just helped save *Star Trek* from cancellation through an innovative letter-writing campaign and Roddenberry was quite impressed with their organizational capabilities. Recently moved from Oakland, California, the Trimbles had worked for a Hollywood script-typing service before agreeing to throw their entrepreneurial enthusiasm into Lincoln. Out of Sunset Boulevard offices, they answered fan mail and sold copies of scripts, copies of the writer's guide, Tribbles (Roddenberry promised Gerrold a portion of the proceeds but never delivered), and frames of 35mm film that Barrett had rescued from Paramount's editing room trash. Most importantly, they put together a mail-order catalogue that formed the basis for the company's future success.

After less than nine months, the Trimbles were summarily fired. Their replacement was Stephen Whitfield, who'd met Roddenberry as the national advertising and promotion director for AMT, the company that had been so successful at selling model *Enterprise*s.

"We had some disagreement over merchandising direction," John Trimble says of their dismissal by Roddenberry. "That's all." With no equity stake in the company, the Trimbles were owed nothing.

Documentary evidence suggests that Roddenberry had long intended to replace the Trimbles with Whitfield, and that he waited to fire them until they'd erected Lincoln's infrastructure. In February 1968, Whitfield had moved from AMT's Phoenix, Arizona, offices to an office directly adjoining the Lincoln office occupied by the Trimbles, for the ostensible purpose of writing and researching a book that later became *The Making of Star Trek* (with Roddenberry sharing authorship credit, though Whitfield in fact wrote the entire manuscript). Considering the proximity of the two offices, it is reasonable to conclude that Roddenberry was paying for Whitfield's office as well as the Trimbles'.

Letters Roddenberry wrote to both parties on the same day, April 22, 1968, indicate that the Trimbles were doing the grunt work at essentially entry-level compensation, while the more expensive Whitfield, who was still (based on the letter's honorifics) on AMT's payroll as national advertising and promotion director, planned Lincoln's future strategies. In one letter, Roddenberry asked the Trimbles for copies of every Lincoln file photograph along with a cost sheet. Another letter to them offered Roddenberry's proposed changes on their first-draft sales copy for the catalogue, as well as thoughts on revising the ordering card. His suggestions on the latter demonstrate noticeable business acumen, despite his lack of hands-on experience.

The more vivid example of Roddenberry's *joie de business* can be seen in his letter to Whitfield, marked "personal and confidential," which reflects an innate shrewdness. Articulating some proposed maneuvering for a deal with Paramount that would establish Lincoln in LCA's former position, he referred to himself, Whitfield, and Lincoln collectively as "we." The letter suggests that Roddenberry wanted Lincoln to usurp a "handshake agreement" Paramount had with a third company, United Fan Mail, to handle fan mail. Lincoln would then get United's share of the fifty-fifty split with Paramount on the proceeds from any resulting sales of *Star Trek* fan kits (photos, etc.).

To realize his scheme and to get the best deal possible from the studio, he planned to first point out to Paramount the declining profits on these fan kits, in contrast to the high cost of United's services. Then, acting the part of white knight, he'd propose to have Lincoln handle the fan mail for six months for less than United's fee; after six months, the fee would be zero. "This may have an immediate budget cutting appeal to [the studio]," he wrote, "and it certainly has been my experience with the Paramount group that they are inclined to grab for pennies and forget dollars." While making it appear that Paramount was saving money by employing Lincoln, he could construct a cheap but direct link to young fans who were the most likely purchasers of his line.

Armed with inside information on the actual size of United's business as opposed to its reported receipts, Roddenberry apparently intended to mislead the studio on the potential profits so as to make his proposal more attractive; the market was larger than either United or Roddenberry chose to admit. "And we can certainly let Paramount know...that the kit business is already dwindling down to almost nothing," he wrote.

This type of wheeling and dealing illustrates why, twenty-five years later, Eileen Roddenberry successfully sued Gene Roddenberry's estate for several million dollars in profits from *Star Trek* and its ancillary products—profits that he had denied or hidden. And it explains the reaction of those who transacted business with Roddenberry.

"My business dealings with him were always miserable," Leonard Nimoy says. "Gene always had an agenda—his own. I didn't see him step up to bat and be the decent honorable humanist that he portrayed himself to be, and that always disappointed me."

Nimoy had to fight Roddenberry over the unauthorized sale of his image (and, by extrapolation, of all the other *Star Trek* actors' images) when Roddenberry began charging admission to see a montage of *Star Trek* bloopers filmed on the set. He also tried to prevent Roddenberry from selling film trims in which he appeared.

"Gene was a pretty sharp character," John Trimble says. "He had his eye out for the main chance. He was looking to make money."

January 7, 1968; 8:00 P.M. On an unusually cold night a group of five hundred students from the California Institute of Technology and other southern California colleges rendezvoused at a Burbank park. Lighting torches, raising handmade signs, and chanting slogans, they fell into parade formation. In an orderly and peaceful fashion, they began their several blocks-long protest march. Members of the Burbank Police Department, complying with the group's parade permit, stopped vehicular traffic for them at intersections.

At last the students reached their destination—not a defense contractor's plant manufacturing weapons for the Vietnam War, but the West Coast Headquarters of NBC. Their mission: to save the low-rated *Star Trek* from cancellation. "We know Spock doesn't have a heart—but don't you, General Sarnoff?" read one placard. "*Star Trek*...sí. Nielsen...no!" read another. And, "Mr. Spock for President."

From an anonymous distance across the street, wearing an outfit of black leather, his visage obscured by a helmet, Roddenberry sat astride his motorcycle, watching the festivities.

Star Trek had suffered ratings problems since the beginning. Though it garnered a rabid following, the network judged the success of a series almost purely by the viewing habits of the Nielsen families across America. The Nielsen Company's projection, based on those twelve hundred families, was that about sixteen million viewers watched *Star Trek* each week, which placed the series closer to the bottom of the list than the top. Knowing this, in November 1966, after fewer than a dozen shows had been broadcast, Harlan Ellison organized the so-called Committee of science fiction writers, which included Richard Matheson and Poul Anderson, to save *Star Trek*. In letters, they implored known science fiction fans to bombard NBC with letters and postcards. Roddenberry had compiled the list after asking Howard DeVore, the associate chairman of the World Science Fiction Convention in

Cleveland, for a roster of attendees; DeVore also included a thousand additional names.

A year later, the ax having been thus far avoided, Bjo and John Trimble organized a more elaborately aggressive "Save *Star Trek*" letter-writing campaign. Out of their home in Oakland, California, the Trimbles sent off hundreds of letters, each encouraging the recipient to send, first, a letter to NBC expressing affection for the series, and then ten more letters to friends and relatives, urging that they do the same—in essence, a "Save *Star Trek*" chain letter.

When letters came directly to the *Star Trek* offices, a Xeroxed copy of preferable protocol was mailed in reply. "Dear loyal *Star Trek* fan interested in saving *Star Trek* from oblivion!" it began.

> I don't want *Star Trek* canceled EITHER!!!!!!!
>
> And if I had a name other than "loyal *Star Trek* fan interested in saving *Star Trek* from oblivion" YOU too could be a member of Star Fleet Command!!!
>
> So there!!
>
> Don't send petitions to me, send them to NBC, that's where they will do the most good.
>
> Seriously, my deepest thanks for what you are doing for *Star Trek*, and on the behalf of myself and the rest of the *Star Trek* gang: "WE LOVE YOU."

It was signed with "sincerest regards" by Roddenberry.

According to Roddenberry, the show had been canceled in late 1967, only to be renewed after a steady increase in the number of fan letters. In a thank-you note to free-lance writer John Stanley for his highly complimentary article on *Star Trek* that had run in the *Miami Herald* Sunday section, Roddenberry wrote that, before granting renewal, NBC had formed a committee of six vice presidents to investigate whether the letters were authentic or an inside job.[23]

To be successful, the "Save *Star Trek*" campaign had to maintain an aura of legitimacy. The network could not suspect that Roddenberry or any member of the *Star Trek* staff—or anyone connected to the studio—had been involved with what appeared to be a spontaneous outpouring of public devotion that cut across all segments of the viewing public. The network executives having investigated the source of the letters to their satisfaction, "we began to reappear on the schedule again," Roddenberry wrote.[24]

But Roddenberry *had* been involved in the campaign.

Two days after the march and candlelight vigil held by the Caltech students, every car in the NBC executive parking lot in Burbank had been plastered with a "Mr. Spock for President" bumper sticker. Roddenberry himself had just paid $303.52 for five thousand of those bumper stickers, according to a memo he wrote to the studio's business affairs department, requesting reimbursement.[25]

Some weeks later, on January 24, two college students who identified themselves as members of the "Committee to Save *Star Trek*" picketed NBC headquarters in New York City and handed out bumper stickers to passersby. One of the two, Devra Langsam, a Brooklyn College student, had arrived at the RCA Building by subway. The other, a Caltech student named Wanda Kendall, had flown in from California. She was representing her classmates, who'd taken up a collection for her airfare, hotel, and incidental living expenses, she told the *New York Post*.

"Mr. Nielsen never asks us," the paper quoted her as saying.

Not Mr. Nielsen, perhaps, but certainly Mr. Roddenberry. It was he, not the Caltech students, who'd sent Kendall to New York. It cost him $350.[26]

As for the story of the six network vice presidents investigating the letters and then putting *Star Trek* back on the air, Grant Tinker maintains that Roddenberry's claim doesn't jibe with the corporate reality. NBC, he asserts, did not take shows off the schedule and put them back again as though they were trying on shirts. Further: "In those days," he says, "vice presidents were relatively rare. If you'd had such a committee, it would have had to include me, and the head of research, and probably sales. But I never heard of anybody doing that. It doesn't mean that networks don't reconsider shows. But they don't do it quite that neatly."

By some accounts, more than a million letters arrived at NBC;

though over the years the estimated number was revised substantially downward—by last count to a mere 150,000. In any event, enough letters arrived that Herb Solow recalls NBC calling him often, "complaining bitterly" about the letter-writing campaign and asking that it be stopped. No one ever traced the campaign to either the studio or Roddenberry.

Star Trek was saved for a third season, and while aficionados agree that the show's last year was largely composed of improbable and silly episodes, those final twenty-four are in fact what allowed *Star Trek* to live long and prosper, first in syndication, then in feature films, and finally in *The Next Generation* and *Star Trek: Deep Space Nine*. Without those episodes, only fifty-five *Star Treks* would have existed, not nearly enough for Paramount to offer a viable syndication package. And without that package, there would have been no groundswell of popular support engendering *Star Trek*'s resurrection.

Before the third year, Roddenberry had told the network that he would return to the series as its hands-on creative producer, as he'd been the first half of the first season, if the show were granted a prime-time slot more in keeping with the viewing habits of its core audience—that is, early in the week, early in the night. Young people, he reasoned, were out and about on dates and the like on weekend nights, and some of them weren't allowed to stay up late on weeknights. In a pitch for renewal sent to Herb Schlosser, NBC vice president of programming, Roddenberry promised that the series would buy scripts only from established *Star Trek* writers. Gene Coon, he said, was committed to providing six scripts, Dorothy Fontana the same number, and he eight scripts.[27] (How he could have written eight scripts from scratch while overseeing sixteen others is a mystery, given his complaints about the work schedule in the show's first season, when he wrote no scripts.)

One day before he wrote that letter to Schlosser, "Assignment: Earth" had begun the first of its six days of filming as a *Star Trek* episode. For three months, Roddenberry had been trying to sell NBC a spinoff series about Gary (né Anthony) Seven, sent to 1968 Earth as a Superman–James Bond adventurer capable of straightening out the myriad social and political problems that threatened the world's safety. The previous July, he'd been told by Alden Schwimmer that NBC chief Mort Werner was in the market for science fiction shows. Immediately contacting Coon, he'd contended that they would be missing a "golden opportunity" by not getting "a spin-off or two on the air."[28] Coon, who'd already departed as *Star Trek* producer (replaced by John Meredyth Lucas), declined, and Roddenberry turned to Art Wallace as a partner.

The new pilot concept was a combination of an unsold pilot called "Assignment: Earth" that Roddenberry had written for Desilu in late 1966, after the first thirteen *Star Trek* episodes had been completed, and writer Wallace's speculative pilot précis titled "Space Cop." When Roddenberry's quickly sketched series outline failed to move NBC, he pleaded with Schlosser, trying to make up for the outline's shortcomings by selling himself as the creator and writer of quality television, one who could deliver the goods. He noted, for example, that he'd been the "head writer" on *Have Gun, Will Travel*.[29] And, guaranteeing the quality of the as yet unwritten script, he later told Werner, "Please do not ask me to prove again to NBC that I am a writer."[30] But when the opportunity to get another show on the air appeared, Roddenberry had first sought out Gene Coon as a creative partner, then Art Wallace—just as he'd contacted Sam Peeples to write the second *Star Trek* pilot. It was Wallace, not he, who wrote the "Assignment: Earth" script.

After NBC scheduled *Star Trek*'s third year for Friday night at ten P.M., Roddenberry, who claimed he was promised Monday nights at eight, opposite *Gunsmoke*, or Tuesdays at seven-thirty, opposite *Lancer* and *Mod Squad*, two new shows, felt betrayed. He concluded that the network had put the show in a graveyard purposefully: with almost certainly miserable ratings, there would be no debate and no second-guessing the inevitable cancellation—no matter how many articulate and reasoned letters might be sent on the show's behalf.

Using the only leverage he believed he had, Roddenberry reneged on his commitment to produce the show. "I couldn't get them to back down," he said. "And I felt at the time that I had to stick by my statement, since I would have to bargain with them at other times."[31]

Roddenberry used the time away from *Star Trek* to write a screen adaptation of Edgar Rice Burroughs's *Tarzan* for the National General Corporation. In a fourteen-page letter to NGC's Sy Weintraub, who owned the *Tarzan* rights and was himself a client of Alden Schwimmer, Roddenberry noted that he'd been screening and studying an assortment of *Tarzan* films from various eras and had decided that "a new approach" would be valuable. "I always felt similar about Burroughs and *Tarzan* as I did about science fiction at the beginning of *Star Trek*: I'd seen all of the *Tarzan* films, but I'd never seen Tarzan on the screen," he told a student audience at the University of California at Berkeley in 1968.[32]

Before writing his version of *Tarzan*, he did as he'd done when writing *Star Trek*: He approached his friend Sam Peeples, a lifelong fan of Edgar Rice Burroughs, who owned a comprehensive Burroughs collection. Peeples's impression was that Roddenberry was not intimately familiar with the literary Tarzan. "I don't think Gene was widely read," he says.

Roddenberry told the assembly in Berkeley that he was committed "to try and do Tarzan as Edgar Rice Burroughs conceived him. There will, of course, be some changes. The screen inherently has certain limitations."[33] Roddenberry's Tarzan was a stud, the sight of whose "splendidly muscled nakedness" sent Amazon women, who made him a sexual slave, into heat. This was not the author's conception, says Peeples, who for years corresponded with Burroughs.

In his absence from *Star Trek*, Roddenberry hired Fred Freiberger as producer, breaking a promise he'd made to Robert Justman during the first season. Justman, who was named co-producer, dismissed the bad news by rationalizing that the studio would not have accepted a line producer instead of a creative writer–producer as the man responsible for overall product. But the case could have been made, if Roddenberry had been inclined, that over the previous two years Justman had written hundreds of pages of often incisive script memos. What he hadn't done, of course, was write scripts, but Roddenberry had known that score when he made the promise.

"I guess he figured co-producer was enough," Justman says. "Gene was a wonderful friend, but he was never someone who would fight for someone else."

Freiberger, who'd known Roddenberry somewhat from the fifties when both wrote scripts for Ziv studios (*Highway Patrol, West Point*), says that he was interviewed in 1966 for the *Star Trek* producer's job, but when he could not begin work immediately because of a family vacation, the job went to Gene Coon. He saw little of Roddenberry during that final year.

"Gene was hardly around at all," Freiberger says. "If I called him and needed something, he was there. Fortunately, I didn't have to call him very often."

It was at this time that Roddenberry began a public display of petulance toward NBC that lasted the rest of his life. He accused the network's executives of stupidity, shortsightedness, pettiness, and even perfidy in canceling the series. From a more objective viewpoint, however, it's clear that NBC handled *Star Trek* with kid gloves, giving it every opportunity to succeed.

"It always irritated me that, over the years, Roddenberry would go out of his way to criticize NBC," Grant Tinker says. "We certainly made a good effort to make it successful, if for no other reason than self-interest."

With few exceptions, there had been remarkably little interference with scripts. "One of the problems we had," says Jerry Stanley, NBC manager of film programs, "was in trying to talk him out of some of his sexual fantasies that would come to life in the scripts. Some of the scenes he would describe were totally unacceptable."

"Why would NBC want to kill a money-maker?" Stanley Robertson says. "It makes no sense." In fact, *Star Trek* had not been a money-maker. The show lost money on two fronts. The first: because advertisers only bought time if the network would guarantee a twenty-share; if the show didn't garner a high enough rating, NBC was obliged to either refund the fee or offer free airtime.

The second: the network often charged ad rates according to the average of the entire prime-time lineup. A low-rated show, like *Star Trek*, pulled down the overall average, costing money throughout the schedule.

There was also a third, less tangible, reason. In the days before channel-surfing, when only a few people had remote control, television viewing on any given night was often a matter of laziness. A viewer tuned to his favorite show at seven-thirty and, unwilling to rise from the easy chair in which he was comfortably ensconced, often left the channel selector untouched throughout the night. This explains why NBC could not schedule *Star Trek* at seven-thirty, and why it moved the show to ten o'clock in its final year: At that hour, it couldn't hurt the show(s) behind it.

As Robertson points out, other NBC series of the same era earning even higher ratings, like *The Magician* and *My World and Welcome to It*, were canceled after only a single season. "*Star Trek* was not performing well," he says. "It was a difficult show to sell, and it skewed very young. It probably should have been canceled after the second year."

Star Trek went off the air not because the network wanted to kill a golden goose, but because after three years, it was still a money-losing proposition. And despite the letters and Roddenberry's promises, in the end, the quality had declined. What, exactly, would be saved, even if another "million" letters bought a reprieve? If it were more shows like "Turnabout Intruder," the series swan song, then, in the opinion of many fans who kept waiting for the consistent week-to-week quality of the first and second seasons, *Star Trek* wasn't worth saving.

"Turnabout Intruder," with a script by story editor Arthur H. Singer, from a story by Roddenberry, featured a female psyche inhabiting Kirk's body. In a pat, stereotypical ending more worthy of 1868 than 1968, the intruder is betrayed by emotions that she can't control.

If Roddenberry felt compelled to blame someone for *Star Trek*'s cancellation, he would have been more correct to look to Paramount. In 1967, Desilu disappeared under the Paramount aegis after both studios had been sold to the giant Gulf & Western Corporation. The two adjacent properties were united to expand Paramount's physical facilities. Desilu's television shows—including *Star Trek*, *Mannix*, and *Mission: Impossible*—appeared to bottom line–minded Paramount as monetary black holes. The studio's vice president in charge of television, John Reynolds, hired Douglas Cramer as executive in charge of production to replace Herb Solow, who'd departed for greener pastures at MGM. Reynolds handed Cramer a mandate to cut costs.

"All three of these so-called successful series were losing a ton of money," Cramer says. "They all cost much more to produce than their networks were paying for them." Down from an average cost per episode of $192,000 the first year, the third year's shows, as per Paramount's edict, were made for less than $180,000—and, as Freiberger points out, that $180,000 had to include substantial raises for the principal actors.

"Roddenberry seemed to me like a slightly quirky, slightly eccentric college professor," says Cramer, who'd once been a college instructor himself. "Just the sort of hero who was off teaching advanced geophysics. He seemed very much in his own kind of little world, and very un-Hollywood." (Cramer recalls the evening that Roddenberry came to dinner at his home. At the time he was married to powerful Hollywood columnist Joyce Haber. "Joyce," he says, "said she thought he was one of the most boring men she'd ever met. It took a Lew Wasserman or Barry Diller for her not to be bored.")

Most of Cramer's conversations with Roddenberry and the production staff were about trying to make the show profitable, he says: "Ways to cut down on the sets, to do fewer special effects, which is where the money really went. And at one point, I think, we even talked about trying to shoot the show in one day less."

Paramount's determination to lower production costs, thus making a profit on the NBC license fee, conflicted badly with NBC's repeated plea to get the series regulars off the *Enterprise* and onto another planet. For three years, Schlosser recalls, "We wanted to open up the show more. Of course, that posed a problem for the production company." Sets designed and built for this week's planet couldn't be reused on next week's planet. Since one of the studio's most effective budget benders was the amortization of set costs over the life of the series, an inordinate number of episodes took place entirely on the *Enterprise*, the set of which, divided by seventy-eight episodes, turned out to be something of a bargain.

With no money for location shooting or imaginative sets, there was a lot less action and a lot more talking. The result—in Justman's words—was "a radio show."

Shortly after Roddenberry received the cancellation notice, he spoke with Jerry Stanley. "We were on the phone," Stanley says, "so I can't say for sure how furious he really was. But he told me that he would never, ever again write anything for television. The next thing I saw was a film he'd written, *Pretty Maids All in a Row*, which was one of the worst pictures I ever saw."

CHAPTER SEVEN

A View

to the

Pantheon

N 1968, GENE Roddenberry left his wife and moved in with Majel Barrett. The terms of the divorce required that their home be sold, with equity split between the former spouses. Eileen Roddenberry received custody of their teenage daughter, Dawn (eighteen-year-old Darlene had entered college), and 50 percent of any *Star Trek* profits, which at the time was half of nothing.

Before *Trek* ended its network run the following year, Roddenberry was paid $100,000 by MGM's vice president of production Herb Solow to adapt Francis Pollini's novel *Pretty Maids All in a Row* for the big screen. "It was a favor to Gene; he was out of work," Solow says. "But he was also perfect for the material"—it was a story about a handsome teacher who beds his female students. "He loved young girls."

Before writing the *Pretty Maids* script, Roddenberry traveled to Japan on MGM's dime. Officially the trip was made to scout locations. But in truth, Solow says, "He told me he wanted to marry Majel in Japan. So I sent him." In those days movie studios had a terrible time getting monies owed to them from foreign exhibitors. In place of cash, a type of barter system was arranged that allowed studio personnel, even whole productions, to travel or film in that country on the captive profits that should have been paid directly. Roddenberry was in Japan spending some of MGM's credit.

Solow's account of the Japan trip differs from Roddenberry's, with Solow's being the more romantic version. In Roddenberry's recounting, he began to miss Barrett while passing the time in Tokyo with several prostitutes. After sending for her, they were married in a Shinto ceremony, both of them wearing silk robes.[1]

Why, with his wounds still raw and knowing how quickly I-do's can sour and how financially devastating a failed marriage could be, was he marrying again so soon? And then there were his obvious problems with monogamy, one of marriage's theoretical underpinnings. (Soon after the ceremony, he bragged to friends, he had a sexual encounter with a masseuse.) With all that weighing against retying the knot, one wonders what compelled him. "I've been married most of my life," he told Kevin Ryan, senior editor of Pocket Books, months before his death. "I can't imagine living any other way."

Roddenberry produced, as well as wrote, the Roger Vadim–directed *Pretty Maids*. An adult male fantasy—one postulated by a forty-eight-year-old writer-producer as an articulation of the relaxed social mores of the 1960s—it was reviled by critics and ignored by moviegoers. To earn a second chance at the big screen, he'd needed a box-office success or critical acclaim.

The experience left Roddenberry chastened. And when he turned back he found the world of television offering little enthusiasm. His unkind words aimed at NBC—and, by inference, all networks—had torched some bridges he now needed to cross. Pushing fifty and essentially unemployable in the six-figure manner to which he'd grown accustomed, he now earned his income from lectures on the college circuit, where *Star Trek* fandom had begun to take hold. "I remember one of my first speeches," he said. "I got all of six hundred or seven hundred dollars, which included the cost of the trip. I felt lucky to net the four hundred or five hundred dollars that they paid me."[2]

Perhaps the seminal event of Gene Roddenberry's final twenty years came in January 1972.

For the previous year, Joan Winston, Devra Langsam, and Elyse Rosenstein had been planning the first *Star Trek* convention. (Langsam was the Brooklyn College student who, in 1968, had joined the visiting Caltech student to lobby NBC executives for *Star*

The extended Roddenberry and Golemon families, El Paso, Texas, 1923. Squatting in the front row center, Eugene Edward Roddenberry holds his two-year-old son Eugene Wesley; his wife, Catherine Golemon Roddenberry, is to his immediate left.

(Photo courtesy of The March of Dimes)

Roddenberry in high school, c. 1935.

(Photo courtesy of The March of Dimes)

Roddenberry (in the middle of the front row)
posing with other members of the Archons,
the police club at Los Angeles City College, 1940.
(Photo courtesy of The March of Dimes)

Roddenberry at his home in Temple City,
a suburb of Los Angeles, shortly after becoming
a member of the Los Angeles Police Department.
(Photo courtesy of The March of Dimes)

At the U.S. Air Force Officers Club on Nandi in the
Fiji islands, 1943. Gene Roddenberry is standing,
second from the left. (Photo courtesy of Leon Rockwell)

The wreckage of Lieutenant Roddenberry's B-17 bomber that crashed on take-off from the island of Espiritu Santo in 1943. Most of the damage was attributable to burning fuel and exploding ammunition after the crash, which killed his bombardier and navigator. (Photo courtesy of Leon Rockwell)

Roddenberry on the streets of New York City, after World War II, when he was a Pan American Airways pilot. (Photo courtesy of The March of Dimes)

Gene Roddenberry on the set of *Star Trek* in the summer of 1966, shortly before the show's debut. (Photo courtesy of The March of Dimes)

Roddenberry posing with Angelique Pettyjohn and the Hugo he received in 1967 for "The Menagerie," the two-part episode of *Star Trek* that aired during the show's first season. Pettyjohn played Shana in "The Gamesters of Triskelion," which was being filmed when the award arrived. (Photo courtesy of The March of Dimes)

For a brief time after *Star Trek*'s cancellation in 1969, Roddenberry spent much of his free time on the golf course. Here he holds aloft a tournament trophy. (Photo courtesy of The March of Dimes)

Roddenberry on the set
of *Genesis II*, 1972.
(Photo courtesy of Susan Sackett)

Roddenberry in his home office, before
moving back to Paramount and trying
to give new life to *Star Trek* in 1975.
(Photo courtesy of Susan Sackett)

Roddenberry with fan Eric Stillwell,
who was later to be a production assistant
on *The Next Generation*, at a *Star Trek*
convention, c.1976.
(Photo courtesy of Eric Stillwell)

Roddenberry, left, talking with production designer Walter Jefferies, in 1977, before the decision to turn *Star Trek II* from a proposed television series into a feature film.

(Photo courtesy of Susan Sackett)

Roddenberry and Susan Sackett at the 1979 Washington, D.C., premiere of *Star Trek: The Motion Picture*. (Photo courtesy of Susan Sackett)

Roddenberry relaxing in his backyard, 1985.

(Photo courtesy of The March of Dimes)

Roddenberry on the set of
Star Trek: The Motion Picture.
(Photo courtesy of Susan Sackett)

Roddenberry at the dedication of his star
on the Hollywood Walk of Fame, September 4,
1985. He is said to be the first writer to receive
such a star. (Photo courtesy of Susan Sackett)

Roddenberry on the set of
Star Trek: The Next Generation, 1989.
(Photo by Richard Barnett)

Roddenberry and William Shatner at the dedication of "The Gene Roddenberry Building" on the Paramount lot, June 6, 1991. (Photo by Richard Barnett)

Roddenberry wears a straw hat as protection against the Caribbean sun on "Sea Trek," a cruise for the show's fans and principals, June 1991. Majel Barrett sits to his right.
(Photo by Richard Barnett)

Trek's survival.) They booked a ballroom at the Statler-Hilton in New York City and put up posters announcing the event in high schools, colleges, store windows, and science fiction conventions. Admission for the entire three-day affair was to be $2.50 in advance and $3.50 at the door. For that price, conventioneers could mingle with fellow fans and view the twenty episodes that Paramount had somewhat bemusedly agreed to send along and that the organizers planned to run continuously; and, among other speakers, they would hear *Star Trek* creator Gene Roddenberry waxing philosophic. He'd agreed to come in exchange for airfare, hotel, food—and an invitation to Barrett, which was gladly extended.

The organizers didn't expect more than six hundred attendees, but by November 1971, three hundred had already registered. Then *Trek* expert Allan Asherman and Rosenstein held an informal *Trek* seminar at Brooklyn College, where seven hundred people jammed into a room designed for half that number. Soon requests for tickets began arriving from as far away as the Midwest and Canada (a representative from a group of forty in Montreal that was planning to charter a bus to New York City asked to receive a group discount). Prompted by a Paramount executive, Winston, who was an executive at CBS, called *Variety* editor Les Brown a week before the convention in the hopes of placing a two- or three-inch story. Even after a reporter made a dutiful visit to her office, Winston had no reason to believe the mention would be granted any prominence. But two days before the convention the paper's front-page headline that accompanied a three-column story screamed, "Star Trek Conclave in N.Y. Looms as Mix of Campy Set and Sci-fi Buffs."

At two-thirty that first Friday afternoon, visitors arriving by elevator at the hotel's penthouse were flabbergasted at the size of the gathering. More than three thousand happy fans were squeezed into a space meant for twelve hundred, and rather than complaining about the discomfort, they rejoiced in the knowledge that there were so many kindred spirits.

Roddenberry spoke about *Star Trek* to the exuberant throng each of the three days. At night, to whomever might be gathered around the hotel suite, he told "tall tales," Winston says, of his air corps days and early show business travails. He was inducted as a member of the "Dinosaurs," the prominent science fiction society, and he renewed his acquaintanceship with Isaac Asimov.

"Gene enjoyed the living daylights out of himself," Winston says. Even Barrett, as the only representative of the show's on-screen talent, was mobbed. "She was so thrilled. The morning after the first night, when they woke up in the hotel room, Gene reached over to kiss her and she said, 'Don't touch me. I'm a star.'"

As he stood before his fans, the Gene Roddenberry who had exhibited such a sure sense of marketing potential four years before could not have failed to realize what those thousands of faces, focused on him in rapt attention, represented.

You could get a contact high from the room's euphoria. Here was the Great Bird of the Galaxy, his image and message evoking instantaneous memories of something grand and wonderful that had beamed into their living rooms for three years; the vision of a future worth living for. He had no choice but to play the role of "Star Trek creator." Anything less would have been cheating them. Listening to stories of Robert Justman or John D. F. Black or Dorothy Fontana or Sam Peeples or Gene Coon or any of two dozen others would have seemed like watching the full moon on television instead of standing beneath the night sky. He became, before their eyes, a visionary. And why not? What could be the harm? It was the mythology of Star Trek that they adored, he believed, and myth was more interesting than truth.

"Some people have good pitch when it comes to music," Roddenberry once said. "I have good pitch about the future."[3] Whether he did or didn't is open to interpretation. But given his penchant for reinventing the past to suit the present, the biographical claims he made after Star Trek should be viewed with skepticism. A case in point is his statement that he'd moved to Los Angeles in 1948 from New York, where he'd flown for Pan Am, because he had gazed knowingly into his crystal ball and seen television remaking American society: "I just saw this thing with the seven-inch screen and I said, 'This is the future.'"[4]

Maybe he really had envisioned what was to come in home

entertainment, via the cathode-ray tube. If so, he was far ahead of the medium's professional broadcasters—and the programmers themselves. "In New York [in 1948]," he said, "television was a little advanced over Los Angeles…. In California, [I thought,] they'll put it in these motion picture studios which are standing empty. And so I made a fast trip to Los Angeles and found that I was ahead of my time…. So I had to wait until television caught up."[5]

If, in 1948, Roddenberry had felt himself capable of writing for television, why didn't he remain in New York, where virtually every television program was being produced live? At the time, and for most of the next ten years, any neophyte with a typewriter and the mildest hint of an idea received a welcoming hug from producers who were having trouble attracting established screenwriters and playwrights. Ambitious amateurs with any noticeable talent were allowed and encouraged to learn on the job, and the new medium's playing field was wide open in a way it never would be again. Despite his claims that he had flown out to Los Angeles, asked television station KTLA for a job, and was told to come back in a few years, Roddenberry's return to the West Coast was more likely made to be near his family.[6]

In 1949, Roddenberry began a five-year stint with the Los Angeles Police Department, which in the coming years provided copious material for both dramatic depiction and elaboration. Though he was the son of a cop and the brother of a cop, he attributed his entry into the Police Academy to the advice of a professional writer: "You don't know much about life and death," the (unnamed) novelist friend allegedly said, by way of pointing out that he therefore had nothing to write about. "You've seen the world. But what do you know about what people do out on the streets?"[7] Actually, Roddenberry's wartime experiences, his travels around the world as a Pan Am pilot, and his having survived a devastating crash had probably force-fed him more of life's various flavors than the majority of other working television writers. He may not have known *what* to write about, or how to do it, but by age twenty-seven, he'd certainly seen enough.

At various times Roddenberry spoke of soon-to-be LAPD chief

William Parker as an old family friend who'd been distressed to learn of Roddenberry's plans to join. "I quit my job with Pan Am and came out here from New York to see my dear and old friend, who was then Inspector William Parker in the Wilshire Division," he said. "He wasn't very enthusiastic about my plans. In fact, he did his best to talk me out of it."[8]

"I have only a hazy memory whether Bill [Parker] screamed obscenities at me or merely questioned my sanity," Roddenberry told an LAPD audience in 1984. "Become a policeman? Ruin my life the same way he had wrecked his."[9]

Roddenberry also claimed that Parker invited him to become his "chief of research" after reading "something that I had written." When Roddenberry replied that he wanted to stay a beat cop, "We argued and we agreed that I would work six months for him, and alternating six months, he would have to put me anywhere on the force I wanted to be."[10]

From mid-1953 until early 1955, before following Roddenberry's path to television writing, Don Ingalls worked with Roddenberry in the LAPD's public information unit. Ingalls says that although it's possible Roddenberry had a fifty-fifty time arrangement with Parker, he saw no indications of it, nor does he remember Roddenberry talking about such a pact. Of Roddenberry's police career before their time together in public information, Ingalls recalls only that Roddenberry had at one time been assigned to patrol division. "I don't know how he could really do that much," he says. "He wasn't in the department that long."

Neither does Danny Galindo, a renowned LAPD homicide detective who'd taken an after-hours writing class with Roddenberry at Universal-International Studios in 1950, remember Roddenberry splitting his time between the chief's office and his patrol duties.

Whether Roddenberry knew Parker as well as he indicated is in dispute. Ingalls, who believes that the two had a "friendly working relationship," says that Roddenberry consciously projected himself as the chief's peer: "Gene always had the knack of being equal to whomever he was socially involved with. It was a good knack to have. He had it and he used it, and he was treated as an equal. He didn't enter the chief's office like officer and chief of police. They were equals. Gene wasn't servile."

Ingalls and Roddenberry became chess partners, business partners, and good friends. They'd shared common experiences as bomber pilots (Ingalls in North Africa and Europe), former careers as commercial airline pilots (Ingalls at TWA), and a passionate desire, Ingalls says, "to make a lot more money than we were making at the department." Through a contact with an Amana Company sales rep, Roddenberry and Ingalls moonlighted as freezer salesmen. "We got a booth out at the L.A. County Fair with our freezers. Our gimmick was, we'd freeze up a bunch of strawberries and give people samples if they came by. We sold a lot of freezers. As a matter of fact, Roddenberry sold one to Chief Parker."

What united the two men most of all was wanting to be writers. Ingalls was founding editor of the LAPD house organ, *Beat*, while Roddenberry, Ingalls says, "wrote more formal things than I did. He lectured out at colleges on police matters." One of Roddenberry's papers was titled "Achieving Professionalism," in which he argued for striving to make police work as respected as law and accounting.[11] He also gave a talk, in late 1953, on the history of law enforcement to students at Los Angeles State College, mixing philosophic reflections on law enforcement with a general overview of its configurations over the years, beginning with Hammurabi. (In a revealing moment that may have been a reference to his rocky marriage, he said, "When two or more people come together they soon find that their individual interests clash. The emotions, thoughts, and activities of people are as different as their fingerprints. The variety of possible human activity is infinite. Despite the work of the world's religions, self-interest is still the paramount consideration of the individual.")[12]

At night and on weekends, both Ingalls and Roddenberry practiced their avocation. Roddenberry also found time to write at least one piece of fantasy prose for *Beat*. It bore a fitting title and subject for an aspiring writer who was working ambitiously toward the day when he could quit the LAPD: "The Secret Life of Officer Mitty," a take-off on James Thurber's well-known character who has a penchant for fantasy. Roddenberry's Mitty, an officer in the unglamorous patrol bureau, imagines himself variously as a member of the "Gangster Squad," a homicide detective, and a special aide to the police chief.

Roddenberry was the first to sell stories, under the pseudonym Robert Wesley (a combination of his brother's first name and his own middle name), to *Dragnet*, in 1953. Likewise, Roddenberry later preceded Ingalls's departure from the force by several months. After Roddenberry had sold two scripts to *Have Gun, Will Travel,* he gave producer Sam Rolfe a spec script written by his friend. Impressed by the work, Rolfe called Ingalls in and promptly hired him to be the series story editor. A few years later, Ingalls became producer as well. He spent the next thirty years as a television writer-producer; his last show was *T.J. Hooker,* starring William Shatner as an LAPD officer.

Over the years, prior to claiming in 1988 that he'd helped to create *Have Gun, Will Travel,* Roddenberry often mentioned that he'd been the show's "head writer." In fact, as both Rolfe and Ingalls confirm, no such position existed. "He was one of our favorite writers," Ingalls says. "And he wrote more episodes than most writers did, but there was no head writer. It wasn't set up that way. If anyone was the head writer, it was the story editor." (There were 156 episodes, of which Roddenberrry is credited with having written or co-written 27. He was never on staff.)

As he'd said, Roddenberry was indeed Chief Parker's "chief of research"—though not until late January 1955, several months before making sergeant and resigning. He took the job vacated by Albert Germann, who left Parker's office in January 1955 to become a professor of criminology, first at Michigan State University, then at California State College at Long Beach. Germann, Ingalls, and Roddenberry all wrote speeches for Parker.

Appointed chief in 1950, Parker had masterminded the resurgence of the Los Angeles Police Department, bringing it from the object of ridicule to a model worthy of respect. Considered by many critics an overzealous devotee of law and order—one who saw the world strictly in terms of good and evil, right and wrong, and black and white—Parker was nearly as well known as FBI chief J. Edgar Hoover (the two despised each other). He soon saw many of his methods and reforms emulated across the country, often to the distress of civil libertarians. In 1957, a collection of his speeches on various themes was published under the title *Parker on Police*, and became required reading for law enforcement officers; Roddenberry, of course, was one of its uncredited ghostwriters, as were Ingalls and Germann, among others.

To hear Roddenberry tell it, he and Parker differed sharply on policing philosophies, with Roddenberry playing the enlightened futurist to Parker's autocrat. While speaking the words that he had written for him, Roddenberry said, Parker would often wonder why groups he perceived as left-wing were giving him standing ovations.[13] To believe that is to believe that Parker, a member of the California State Bar and a former Harvard University student, the developer of the Police and Prisons Plans for World War II's Allied invasion of Europe, and the creator of civilian police departments for postwar Munich and Frankfurt—by all accounts a brilliant man—could not discern the difference between Joseph Stalin and Thomas Jefferson.

"Every word that came out of his mouth, he always knew what he was saying," says Albert Germann. "He was pretty shrewd. We who wrote for him knew what we could get away with and what we couldn't."

Germann explains that Parker allowed his writers to address civil liberties in his speeches in order to avoid inferences that he was overly autocratic or fascistic. "He once made a statement that was quoted time and again," Germann says. "He said, 'Most American policemen are conservative, ultraconservative, and very right wing.' Even the *L.A. Times* quoted him on that. Somebody had written that and given it to him. He'd taken it, read it, checked it over, and said, 'Yeah, that's right; that's true.' He was an honest guy. He may not have liked it, but if he believed something was true, he'd say it."

William Overend, a *Los Angeles Times* reporter who interviewed Roddenberry for a story on former policemen turned writers, says that Roddenberry illustrated the philosophical differences between himself and Parker by pointing to two passages in *Parker on Police*. The first, Roddenberry claimed, was written without him: "We will continue in our attempts to eradicate from the community those parasites who prey upon us and whose nefarious activities drain huge sums of money from local channels of trade."

The second, Roddenberry said, was written by him: "To one man it is a crime to steal a penny, but good business to steal a fortune.... Kings rule, martyrs suffer and merchants prosper according to their own convictions.... Hunger, poverty, maladjustment and other physical problems do not incite crime—they incite beliefs that may produce crime."[14]

Roddenberry intended to pat himself on the back for humanizing Parker, but the two passages he cited do not necessarily contradict each other. One can empathetically identify the root causes of some crimes while pledging to eradicate criminal activity. Roddenberry, certainly, believed that. These are his words, taken from a speech Parker gave in May 1955 to the National Conference of Christians and Jews on the campus of Michigan State University, where Germann was then teaching:

> Lacking a solution to human imperfection, we must learn to live with it. The only way I know of safely living with it is to control it.
>
> When one man assaults another or one group violently flaunts the rights of another group, the immediate and pressing issue is the conflict, not the beliefs which incited it. We have not yet learned to control what men believe, but we can control what men do. I do not deny for a moment that the final solution is the perfection of human conscience. But in the interim, and it may be a long interim, we must have order.[15]

The passages that Roddenberry quoted to reporter Overend had been taken out of context in an effort to paint himself as a legitimate Don Quixote. Rather than philosophizing that all diverse points of view are equally valid—as the "one man" quote by itself seems to imply—the speech intended just the opposite; Roddenberry was actually insisting on common standards that punish all wrongdoers, no matter their individual philosophies or cultures. One paragraph later, he wrote, "Law exists, not because we do agree on what is right and wrong, but because we do not agree." Similarly, the passage about hunger and poverty inciting "beliefs that may produce crime" was followed immediately by an unambiguous thought: "It is apparent that our way of life cannot survive if we so relax and broaden our laws that almost any individual's standard will conform with them. Such a course would be little more than anarchy. Therefore, the only alternative is to alter individual standards."[16]

In seeking to remake himself as the Great Bird, Roddenberry distanced himself from his past words and thoughts. At that first *Star Trek* convention in New York, he regaled his audience with accounts of the windmills he'd battled on their behalf, and of the forces of corporate greed and stupidity he'd opposed. With the greatness of the series reflecting from his features, he was presumed to be integrity personified. He played to it in New York, and at each of the succeeding conventions that he attended, carefully constructing a mythos and in the process breathing life into the dead series. Rumors about the return of *Star Trek* abounded. A *TV Guide* reporter at the convention asked Roddenberry about the possibility of a new *Star Trek*. "I didn't think it was possible six months ago," Roddenberry said. "But after seeing the enthusiasm here I'm beginning to change my mind. It is possible to do it from my standpoint. We had such a family group on the show that it's totally different for us. We still meet and drink together, and we're all still friends, so for this show it is possible."[17]

"*Star Trek*," said the *Los Angeles Times* in June 1972, was "the show that won't die."[18]

"Gene always said that our conventions convinced Paramount that *Star Trek* was a viable property," Joan Winston says.

Before *Star Trek* began to redefine the rules of syndication in 1970, Roddenberry could have purchased all of Paramount's interest in *Star Trek* for something in the neighborhood of $150,000. But living on modest lecture and personal appearance fees, he had neither the cash reserves nor the reasonable expectation that the

149

property would ever recoup its original investment. Instead, after accepting a small payment from Paramount, he was left with a third of any future profits, and little control over the property's direction. While he would later come to rue that decision, given the circumstances, it was the only reasonable one he could have made. Until the remarkable afterlife success of the seventy-nine episodes, which began slowly and accelerated via media word-of-mouth with the popularity of the conventions, the term "future profits" had been considered an oxymoron. There'd been no rational evidence to justify an equity expenditure, particularly when his professional services were in less demand than they'd been since he left the LAPD. Visionary or not, Roddenberry could not foresee the unforeseeable. Fortunately, Paramount would not reincarnate *Star Trek*, in any form, without his participation.

That was fine with Lou Scheimer. Early in 1973, Scheimer approached Paramount about turning *Star Trek* into a Saturday morning animated show. As president of the animation studio Filmation, Scheimer in years past had produced such shows as *Superman*, *Batman*, and *Teen Titans* for network television. The idea of resuscitating the *Trek* characters occurred to him only because he was a fan.

While negotiating the deal, Scheimer learned that animation giant Hanna-Barbera had become his deep-pocket competitor for the exclusive license. He despaired of bringing the project to Filmation, but when the ink had dried on the contracts, one of the signatures was his; he'd obviously made a deal more advantageous to Paramount than the one proposed by Hanna-Barbera.

He promptly sold the thirty-minute show to NBC daytime executive Joe Taritero, an old friend, with Roddenberry's single stipulation: that he be granted complete creative control. Scheimer was thrilled; he had wanted the series to be exactly what he remembered: one visionary's conception of a time three hundred years into the future. At Roddenberry's urging, Scheimer hired Dorothy Fontana as associate producer–story editor; Roddenberry himself acted as executive consultant, reading the scripts written by such credentialed *Star Trek* writers as David Gerrold, Sam Peeples, Margaret Armen, Steven Kandel, Paul Schneider, and Fontana.

To Roddenberry, the signing of the animated series contract, for a season of seventeen shows, seemed to be further confirmation of his career renaissance. *Genesis II*, a pilot that had been produced at Warner Bros., would soon be aired on CBS. *Questor*, a ninety-minute pilot for NBC, co-written with Gene Coon (Fontana says that Coon wrote the script and that Roddenberry rewrote it, taking the lead credit because he knew that Coon was too ill—dying in fact—with lung cancer to protest), was then in production at Universal. "Spectre," a pilot script co-written with Sam Peeples (Roddenberry's contributions apparently were to add sexual elements to Peeples's original script), was at Twentieth Century-Fox. Another Peeples co-venture, "The Tribunes," was also at Warner Bros. If all went well, by the coming fall he would have five series on the air—a far cry from the uncertainty and relative poverty of the previous four years, when his star had dimmed considerably over Hollywood.

"For a couple of years," Roddenberry said, "our only income was lecture fees I got from colleges where kids still loved *Star Trek*, even though it was not a commercial success." (Roddenberry tended to cry financial wolf. At no time was his home or vacation condo in La Costa on the sales block.)

Given the intentionally optimistic portrayal of the future in *Star Trek*—that the world survived the cold war without the superpowers leading us to mutually assured destruction—the curiosity of *Genesis II* was its underlying pessimism: Nuclear war ravages the earth in 1983.

The story begins 150 years after the moment of devastation, when scientist Dylan Hunt awakens from an experimental state of suspended animation (which he's been in since 1979). After a sexual jumpstart, he finds an underground network of high-speed trains, slave societies, nomadic savages, a race of superhuman mutants called Tyranians out to rule what remains of the world; and of course some typical Roddenberry touches: men kept as pets for women's pleasure and amusement.

Despite poor reviews of the March 23 airing, CBS ordered six scripts for which Roddenberry immediately began sketching ideas.

He commissioned Dorothy Fontana, who'd recently been his secretary for several months, working out of his home, to write the second episode, titled "London Express." When CBS decided not to proceed, Warner Brothers approached ABC, which agreed to look at a revamped and renamed pilot.

"We had to make two pilots for *Star Trek* before we had our format set," Roddenberry explained. "A pilot is an experiment to find out the way a series could go. It's not a finished product in itself."[19]

Thirteen months to the day after *Genesis II* had aired, *Planet Earth*, which substituted actors John Saxon and Diana Muldaur for *Genesis II*'s Alex Cord and double belly-buttoned Mariette Hartley, was ridiculed by reviewers. Kevin Thomas, in the *Los Angeles Times*, said that the movie "has got to be just about the funniest ninety minutes television has offered all season. What makes it so delicious is that for the most part its humor is apparently strictly unintentional."[20]

"I found it sadly funny," Leonard Nimoy says. "Gene had convinced them that, with Roddenberry, you go for the second pilot. *Genesis II* wasn't any good. But *Planet Earth* was equally bad. Depressed, defeatist, demoralized, they were the opposite of *Star Trek*."

In 1972, Roddenberry had conceived of *Questor*, the adventures of a super-advanced android in the modern world, with Nimoy in mind as the title character. Dictating to Fontana, he had described Questor for the series format: "His plasti-skin and hair have the same characteristics as their human counterparts, and he would be impossible to distinguish from the normal human male whether he were in a Turkish bath or, for that matter, in bed with a woman. He is totally functional."[21]

Questor's human companion, engineer Jerry Robinson (played in the pilot by Mike Farrell), suggests that the author projected his own personality: "Like most of us, Jerry has fantasies which picture himself as a ladies' man.... Like any young male, he will obviously pursue needs, wants and desires but always with a likable awkwardness. (It will annoy him constantly that his android friend, who has no physical need for the other sex, exudes a cool, self-contained quality which is invariably attractive to women.)"[22] In a sense, this was a regurgitation of the Kirk-Spock relationship.

Of course, the series required a beautiful young woman, Candi McPherson, chosen to be Robinson's secretary/assistant precisely because she is none too bright and therefore can't catch on to the strange comings and goings of an android whose existence must remain secret. She shares with yeoman Janice Rand before her the kind of beauty that apparently upset Roddenberry: "Perhaps her only disadvantage is the personal discomfort caused Jerry Robinson by her long-legged, sensual-looking body, which moves under a pert face in a highly discomforting way." Unlike Rand, however, Candi "considers herself a 'good' girl, saving her virginity for that day in her fantasies when she trades it for happiness ever after."[23]

Questor's premise lacked a quality that distinguishes self-contained movies with a beginning, middle, and end from weekly television series. What the missing ingredient was, Roddenberry couldn't pinpoint until seeking the assistance, as he had with *Star Trek*, of Sam Peeples. "All writers get into a slight bind sometimes," Peeples says. "You have a great idea but the underlying motivation becomes dimmed."

At the time, Peeples kept offices at Twentieth Century-Fox, where in conjunction with Roddenberry he was developing "Tribunes," a pilot about a futuristic police force based on the ancient Roman troops who held autonomous control over crime control and punishment. The script was never produced.

While consulting on *Questor*, Peeples spent a few days in Roddenberry's office at Universal Studios. (A group of *Star Trek* fans was ushered in one afternoon while the two men sat discussing the project. Roddenberry introduced Peeples as "the man whose pilot sold the show.") He suggested that the character of Questor be driven by the need to search for his creator. To the metaphysically and metaphorically minded Roddenberry, this represented brilliance. Significantly, though, Roddenberry then approached Gene Coon to write the script. (Peeples's friendly doctoring went uncredited, not at all to his chagrin; he'd performed the same service for any number of writer friends over the years.)

Except for his directorial debut on an episode of *Night Gallery* ("Death on a Barge"), Leonard Nimoy had spent an unhappy year at Universal and was anxious to leave at the moment of contract expiration. Then Roddenberry pitched him the idea of *Questor*. After reading the script, Nimoy agreed to stay for the pilot and, if sold, the series. In preparation for filming, he posed for photographs used by the makeup and art departments; the show was constructed around his character.

Weeks later, assuming that preproduction was proceeding normally, Nimoy mentioned the pilot to a friend on the lot, who said he knew its director, Richard Colla. Nimoy noted he hadn't been aware that a director was yet attached. Three minutes later, following the friend's phone call, Colla arrived in Nimoy's office.

"This is a bit embarrassing," Colla said.

"What is?" Nimoy asked.

"Well, we've hired Robert Foxworth to play Questor. I feel very bad about this."

"Don't," Nimoy said. "I'm glad to get out of here."

Before leaving, Nimoy called Roddenberry and demanded an explanation. Roddenberry stammered before managing, "They sure caught me by surprise."

"Who did?" Nimoy asked.

Roddenberry then launched into a convoluted explanation: He'd been performing the normal duties of an executive producer in preproduction—supervising the makeup and art department, consulting with the set designers, and looking at film of actors sent over by studio executives and casting directors. One of the photos was of Robert Foxworth. "They asked, 'What do you think?' I said I thought he was capable. And the next thing I know they went and made him an offer behind my back."

"I see," Nimoy said.

The waiting-for-the-guillotine pause that followed was broken by Roddenberry: "I'll certainly get back to you if he falls out."

Assuring him that he wouldn't take second position on the show, Nimoy added, "There may be some press on this, because the word was out that you were brought in here to develop this thing for me to star in. What're we going to say?"

"Well, I'll say you weren't available."

"That's not exactly the truth, Gene. I'll have to tell them what you just told me, that they sold you Robert Foxworth."

"Well," Roddenberry said, "I guess you'll have to tell your story and I'll tell mine."

Any number of Roddenberry's former colleagues agree that he preferred crawling through verbal minefields to facing confrontations. "It made him uncomfortable," Robert Justman says. "He'd rather have said yes to somebody than tell them what they didn't want to hear. "

For that reason, Roddenberry often hid behind his attorney, Leonard Maizlish, whose job was to execute the orders and absorb the punishment. "Gene excelled at telling people what they wanted to hear," David Gerrold says. "That was his genius."

But, says Nimoy, "There was nobody home when it came time to take the heat."

NBC ordered half a dozen scripts for *Questor* (the pilot was retitled *The Questor Tapes*) in anticipation of going to series. Roddenberry installed Larry Alexander and Michael Rhodes at the show's helm before moving on to *Genesis II*. Then NBC changed its programming mind; *Questor* was too much like another Universal product then in development for ABC, *The Six-Million-Dollar Man*, which was produced by Harve Bennett.

In the retelling to *Star Trek* fans, Roddenberry positioned himself as having been again crucified by the network. To listen to him explain it, he was incapable of error, either in judgment or talent. *Questor*, he said, "was the story of an android robot who was outwardly indistinguishable from a human male, except perhaps that the...programming of his computer mind made him incapable of hate, jealousy, violence, and other television star qualities."[24]

The concept of *Questor* searching for his creator, he claimed, "immediately got me in trouble with some of the television executives. One of them said, and I quote exactly, 'Whoever heard of a character in drama being interested in the reason for his existence?' In his case, I probably could have said Pinocchio."25

Inasmuch as the reviled executives had refused to green-light the *Questor* series for scripting until he incorporated Sam Peeples's advice that Questor search for his creator, Roddenberry's nose deserved to grow longer than the one on Gepetto's wooden puppet.

"It's very difficult to admit mistakes when you have a fan following of several million," says Jon Povill, his longtime friend and colleague. "They look up to you as if you're God, and you're afraid to show that God is fallible. And that, of course, is one of the major themes in Gene's work."

More difficult even than admitting mistakes is resisting the temptation, when handed the opportunity, actually to be God—particularly for those who don't believe in God. There's no one else above you; no point of reference to anything larger than yourself—neither nature nor "The Great Spirit" nor Jesus Christ nor Mohammed nor a burning bush nor Gautama Buddha; nothing external that might compel humility.

Not all humanists are necessarily devout atheists. But Roddenberry was, and in his atheism he exhibited the same certainty that religious fundamentalists do. By definition, such absolute certitude precludes the ability to examine or accept the validity of opposing viewpoints. Thus, pure reason and pure faith are mirror images. If, to evangelicals, he was an unrepentant sinner, then to him they were foolish and superstitious. Neither position leaves any room for accommodation. "I worry," he said of Jimmy Carter to his secretary Susan Sackett, "about a president who claims he has a personal relationship with God." "He felt Carter was a superstitious person, and he didn't believe in superstition," Sackett explains. "He believed we should rise above 'petty superstitions,' as he called them."

In a world of pure faith, it's possible to project yourself as the God you worship. But in a world of pure reason, there's no reason not to project your own image across the horizon—to see your own face everywhere you look, as hundreds of thousands of people expect you to be the visionary you seem to be. For a man so easily seduced by pleasure, nothing could be more seductive than to be treated as an emissary from the future. To resist such temptation, one would probably have to be a saint.

That day in June 1973 when the principal *Star Trek* actors reassembled in a San Fernando Valley studio to record voices for three of the animated episodes became a media event. Gene Roddenberry, William Shatner, Leonard Nimoy, DeForest Kelley, James Doohan, Majel Barrett, and NBC executives made short speeches, answered questions from the assembled press, and smiled for the cameras before going inside to work. All except Nimoy were glad to be there.

"The third season of *Star Trek* had been unpleasant," he explains. "It wasn't fun anymore; I didn't enjoy it. So when this came up I thought, 'Why should we go from a pretty good series to animation?' Then word came down that I was the only one who hadn't signed, and I thought, 'What am I trying to prove? Why should I be the only holdout?'"

When he received assurances that after the first session he could record future dialogue at any studio in the country and mail in the tape to Filmation, Nimoy was convinced that his frequent regional theater performances would not suffer. He agreed to provide the voice of Spock.

When they began work, Nimoy assumed that George Takei and Nichelle Nichols were out of town and would redub their parts upon return. He inquired at the first break as to their whereabouts. The response was vague and muffled. At the next break, he again pressed the point, his curiosity now less Spock-like and more urgent. Finally, he was informed that they hadn't been invited to the party.

Roddenberry, in appealing to Nimoy's status as the sole holdout, had not mentioned that neither Takei nor Nichols had been asked to suply the voices of Sulu and Uhura, despite the fact that their likenesses, to which Paramount asserted ownership, would be reproduced. According to Screen Actors Guild rules, animation performers may provide up to three voices for the same price as a single voice. Doohan, a dialectal expert, was to be both Scotty and Sulu (as well as the occasional alien), while Barrett would be Uhura and other voices.

Nimoy was outraged. "I was told that I was the only one who wasn't coming back," he told Roddenberry. "That's why I agreed to do this." Taking the position that he wouldn't be a party to deception, he swore not to return until Takei and Nichols were hired to do their own voices, or at least asked to do so.

"I couldn't figure out how they could put these people on screen and not pay them anything," he says. "I said, 'Why is this up to me to do this?'"

A few days later Roddenberry called. "Leonard," he asked, "are you taking the position that they have to be in every episode?"

"Gene, I don't want to negotiate their contracts for them," Nimoy replied. "But I will tell you that anytime they're being presented or represented in these films, they will be hired to do their voices or I won't be there."

Roddenberry stumbled over his words for several seconds, apparently thinking out loud. "Yeah, all right," he finally said, "we'll work that out."

The decision to exclude Nichols and Takei had obviously been made to save money, while the decision to hire Majel Barnett over Nichelle Nichols, a more seasoned vocal performer, was made to make money. As for his role as the show's executive producer-consultant, Barrett's husband only had to read the scripts to collect his $2500 fee per episode.

"Gene had the leverage to do what I did," Nimoy says. "He just didn't do it."

Of Roddenberry's five possible series, only the animated *Star Trek*—twenty-two episodes over a year and a half—materialized. (*Spectre*, a gothic story constructed around the relationship between a psychiatrist and an investigator of paranormal activity, was finally shot in England in late 1976 under Roddenberry's aegis. It aired in May of the following year.) His income depended on convention appearance fees and Lincoln Enterprises merchandising of anything *Star Trek*. He even sold storyboards from the animated series and Xerox copies of other writers' scripts (the latter was a Writers Guild violation for which he would later have to make restitution). He also made available for sale his own scripts, from *Questor* to *Planet Earth*.

When his son Eugene "Rod" Roddenberry, Jr., was born in the spring of 1974, Roddenberry invited two hundred people to his home for the official naming. Presiding over the celebration were a Catholic priest, a Protestant minister, and a Hasidic rabbi. "Lou," he said to Lou Scheimer, producer of the animated series, "that kid is going to get to heaven. I've covered every base." By then Gene Roddenberry knew that his professional and financial future would depend on *Star Trek*.

Fresh out of UCLA film school in 1972, Jon Povill read in *TV Guide* that Gene Roddenberry would be producing a new science fiction pilot titled *Genesis II* at Warner Brothers for CBS. Armed with his only sample of writing, a science fiction comedy script for which he'd finagled some payment from then fledgling writer-producer Ron Shusett, Povill made an appointment with Roddenberry's assistant Ralph Navada.

Povill found Roddenberry genial and gentle. With a warm smile, the producer took the script and pledged to read it promptly. Every three weeks or so, Povill called to find out whether Roddenberry considered his work promising. Each time he received a different excuse or apology for why it hadn't yet been read, and each time Povill promised to call back on a designated day in the future; in this way he provided artificial but friendly deadlines.

It took more than a year until Roddenberry read the script and was apparently impressed. By then *Genesis II* had become *Planet Earth*, but *Questor* still looked like a go. At Roddenberry's suggestion, Povill pitched some stories to *Questor* story editor Larry Alexander, who referred them to producer Michael Rhodes, who declined them. Povill was preparing a second batch of submissions when *Questor* was yanked.

Planet Earth soon met the same fate, leaving Roddenberry a man with neither series nor studio. He did, however, have an idea for a novel, and to help him with research he hired Povill at lean wages. For the neophyte employee, this seemed like a huge break. Povill would drive his old car into the area above Sunset at the end of the Sunset Strip in Beverly Hills, to Roddenberry's home on Leander Place, and park next to Roddenberry's green Mercedes that said "Gene R" on the license plate. Roddenberry may have been struggling financially, but he was living well.

Povill's job was to help Roddenberry, with facts and figments, imagine a novel that described the theoretical responses of NASA and other agencies to a massive space ship suddenly hovering in Earth orbit. "I don't know why he chose me to work with him," Povill says. "I seemed to know what he was talking about and seemed to be able to carry on that kind of conversation."

Povill's job as researcher didn't last long; Roddenberry soon quit the novel. "My suspicion," Povill says, "is that he was daunted by the size and scope of the project." But Povill was not immediately dispatched to the flatlands. Having discovered that the young writer was a decent carpenter and handyman, Roddenberry asked Povill to stay on in that capacity for the same remuneration and tend the many parts of his house falling into disrepair. Disappointed by the book's abandonment, Povill agreed and began to fix fences, walls, and plumbing. Most importantly, he baby-proofed the house for the infant Rod.

"It is fair to say that at that point in my life, I was fairly much in awe of Gene," Povill says. "As I got to know him more personally and got to suffer a bit because of his personal problems, the awe did evaporate."

As an employee-cum-guest-cum-friend, Povill may have spent more time in the Roddenberry home than in his own during the early to mid-1970s. Much of that time was passed in the backyard pool, with Roddenberry and Barrett and anyone else who happened to be there. There was alcohol and marijuana to share, and bathing suits were not usually worn. Povill and Roddenberry playfully battled each other, sitting atop kickboards, trying to maintain a precarious balance against the opponent's advances—first guy into the drink loses—laughing like kids. Then in his mid-fifties, Roddenberry impressed Povill with his competitive spirit and stamina.

A frequent dinner guest, Povill was witness to several ugly scenes between Mr. and Mrs. Roddenberry. "I spent some of my life's most uncomfortable evenings in their company as they abused each other verbally," Povill recalls. "They were sadistic. The issues, whatever they were, were never actually addressed. They would fight like mad and insult each other about stupid little things, nonsensical things, that had nothing to do with anything. It could start with a snide comment about the way the dinner was prepared, or how the silverware was set up. Then the rejoinder would come back and it would be this swapping of insults and swapping of hurts. These were arguments to get out the rage, but not to deal with the issues."

The fuel for the arguments, Povill guessed, was alcohol. "There would be prodigious drinking," he says. "Both of them. She could put it away just as well as he could." Povill, in the middle, was expected not to mediate but to take one side against the other. "It was painful, really painful. I never knew whether the invitation would be extended to stay for dinner, and Majel and Gene never knew if it was going to be a nice, pleasant dinner, which it often was.

"They were two people who were very angry at each other. Both of them suffered from the Groucho Marx syndrome of not wanting to belong to clubs that would have them as members. Gene certainly had that as far as Majel was concerned. I think he showed her considerable disrespect. He had tremendous self-loathing. My impression was that he didn't really have deep abiding confidence in what he was doing but had to project deep and abiding confidence."

Many times over the years, Roddenberry claimed that LAPD chief William Parker was grooming him to be chief of police. One of those to whom he made that claim was Bob Lewin, an early producer of *Star Trek: The Next Generation*. "Parker brought him in to be the historian of the police," Lewin recalls Roddenberry telling him. "He traveled with Parker because he was writing the history of the department. Gene would say to Parker, 'I'm at my wits' end, doing all this writing; I'd like to be active, to be out. Can you put me back in narcotics for a while?' Parker would say, 'Sure.' So he worked drugs for three months, then back to Parker, then vice for three months, or robbery, or homicide, or whatever. He did that for a long time. Finally Parker said to him, 'Do you know why I'm letting you do this?' Gene said no. Parker said, 'It's because I think you have all the potential to be a police chief some day, and that's why you're here.' Gene told me that, absolutely, he was being groomed to be police chief."

"Mitty pulled at his blue police jacket, trying to stretch the collar into something resembling a windbreak" is how Roddenberry had begun his "Secret Life of Officer Mitty," published in the May 1954 issue of *Beat*. Patrolman Mitty first fantasizes about searching out dangerous gangsters, then he pictures himself in the office of the police chief:

"Mitty," the Chief said, "I've had my eye on you. Now I need your help."

The Chief offered him a cigarette and Sergeant O'Flaherty hurried over with a light. Mitty sat down and the Chief continued:

"I'm in a devil of a mess. The theorists have us wasting manpower. I need a top-flight field man to straighten them out. You're that man!"

Mitty nodded. Already his mind was working at a furious rate, like a giant electronic calculator. Without conscious effort it was totaling appropriations and expenditures, man-hours, division areas, crime rates.

The Chief's voice filtered through. "Mind if I appoint you my special Staff Commander?"

Mitty thought about it for a brief second. "No, Chief. I'm not looking for glory. I'll get the answers. You put them into practice...."

CHAPTER EIGHT

The

Nine

IN MAY 1975, Gene Roddenberry accepted an offer from Paramount to develop *Star Trek* into a feature film, and moved back into his old office on the Paramount lot. His proposed story told of a flying saucer, hovering above Earth, that was programmed to send down people who looked like prophets, including Jesus Christ. Who or what had programmed the craft was not addressed. "Basically," Jon Povill says, "God was a malfunctioning spaceship." By July, Paramount had rejected the treatment. Roddenberry blamed the religious backgrounds of Paramount executives, including chairman Barry Diller, a practicing Catholic, for the rejection of his story. While Paramount allowed him to keep his office on the lot and encouraged him to search for film themes, he no longer received studio development funds.

That same month, Roddenberry was approached by John Whitmore, an Englishman whose name is legitimately preceded by the honorific "Sir." On behalf of "Lab 9," a company of individuals devoted to the study and actualization of paranormal events, Whitmore asked Roddenberry to write a screenplay that explored the group's belief that earth would soon be visited by extraterrestrials, collectively called "The Nine." He said that eventually Roddenberry would be introduced to The Nine through their channeler, Whitmore's associate Phyllis Schlemmer. First, though, Whitmore wanted to prepare his writer for that extraordinary experience by having him observe legitimate psychic experimentation at universities and research institutes across the country. Exposed to events beyond normalcy for which his belief system had no reasonable explanation, Roddenberry would likely shed a layer or two of skeptical armor, thus allowing The Nine's message to reach its target. Likewise, the intended movie was supposed to make Earthlings more receptive to The Nine's (eventual) arrival.

Roddenberry was reluctant, but he desperately needed money. One day before Whitmore approached him he'd complained to his secretary-assistant Susan Sackett, "If I don't get twenty-five thousand dollars, I'm going to lose the house."

On August 1, he signed a contract that was to pay him $25,000 for a first-draft screenplay based on his experiences with The Nine and his other paranormal experiences, and another $25,000 for a rewrite. Whitmore, a man of deep pockets, also agreed to pick up all of Roddenberry's travel expenses, which also eventually totaled around $25,000.

Roddenberry's first draft of "The Nine" was dated December 19, 1975:

Writer-producer Jim MacNorth, creator of the long-ago canceled but still immensely popular television series "Time Zone," is at a science fiction convention in New York, attacking the television networks in a speech that's been heard probably umpteen times by the fans, who applaud him vigorously. Miserable and cynical, he endures their adoration only because he has to—while he'll be forever famous, he's far from rich.

In his dressing room at the convention, he is approached by an English gentleman named Harwood who represents a group called Second Genesis. Harwood wants to hire MacNorth to write a screenplay about paranormal phenomena—psychic healing, out-of-body experiences, telepathy, communications with beings on other levels.

"I'm afraid that's just not my bag," MacNorth replies.

Harwood's companion, Mara, an East Indian woman dressed in a sari, gazes at MacNorth's groin and asks if he's ill.

"Mara's a healer," Harwood explains. "She can see disturbances in a body's aura."

MacNorth dismisses his guests and flies home to Los Angeles, where he's picked up at the airport by his wife, Kathy, "an attrac-

166

tive, long-limbed woman about ten years younger" than he. First, Kathy delivers the bad news: The studio has rejected his movie script for "Time Zone." Then she tells him the worse news: In the event someone else writes a good script, he won't be allowed to produce the film.

At home in bed, just as Mara has predicted, he can't get it up. In the process of explaining why not, he assures Kathy he didn't screw around with anyone else—"Not this entire trip."

Driving onto the studio lot, MacNorth stops to consult with the guard at the gate, a friend who keeps his ear to the studio rails. "[You] can't keep shoving down people's throats how you were right and how wrong and stupid they were," the guard tells him.

In MacNorth's office, his attorney Tom Keeble says the studio is contractually obligated to let him produce the film: "I am not letting them get away with this. We're also going to sue for your television profits. I can't see any way they can gross something like twenty millon on your show and still be in the red."

MacNorth is despondent over his deteriorating financial condition when Keeble shows him an offer from Harwood: $75,000 to write that screenplay for the Second Genesis people. "I am not a prostitute," MacNorth insists. To demonstrate what he means by prostitute, he calls a young aspiring actress and his secretary into his office, and offers them money for sex. The secretary immediately begins undressing, followed by the actress. Though MacNorth tells them to cease, both continue to strip. With each in the background wearing only bra and panties, MacNorth peruses the Second Genesis contract. Kathy walks in, hardly surprised by what she sees.

The contract calls for MacNorth to travel the country for three months, all expenses paid, and observe psychic experimentation. "And you commit to write only what you see and believe," Keeble tells him. "Nothing else."

On the first of his trips, MacNorth attends sessions at the "prestigious Massachusetts Research Institute," where he observes experiments on theoretical physics and telepathy—and discovers his own telepathic powers: Confirming that his wife, three thousand miles away, is indeed wearing a brown suit and an orange blouse, he also discovers that she plans to divorce him. Her attorney? Tom Keeble, in whose office she is at that moment—presumably contracting more than legal business.

MacNorth attends experiments intended to verify electrostatic auras and faith healing. A fortune-teller informs him: "You've been very foolish, sir. Yes, you've won great fights, but at what cost? A great heavy shell about yourself…so heavy…like armor…you've imprisoned yourself in it…you can no longer reach out nor can others reach in. Like Hector of Troy, you stride clashing sword and shield, you hear not, you feel not." She begins to cry. "Poor man, you must learn there is bravery also in peace. And danger…I still see danger for you."

Stopping at his house for a change of clothes, MacNorth finds a handsome young man waiting for Kathy to come home. The twentysomething-year-old shows a key Kathy has given him as proof that he belongs there.

Keeble tracks MacNorth to an airport bar, attempting to drink away his troubles. The "Time Zone" film project is suddenly popular again, Keeble says, as is science fiction in general. He calls it "the hot new cycle" and promises MacNorth vast riches if he will capitalize on the opportunity. But MacNorth refuses to abandon his contract with Harwood and Second Genesis, even though he knows that this opportunity may pass him by.

Having changed his plans to fly to San Francisco, MacNorth arrives unannounced at the Pennsylvania country estate/commune of Second Genesis. There he finds a group of people tuned in to something beyond the physical plane. He demands to know why they hired him; why they were willing to risk their money; what they were looking for. Harwood answers by telling him to suppose that he'd been hired by Louis Pasteur: "Many considered him crazy…his strange notions about invisible things around us, inside us, some helping us, others making us sick. He called them…bacteria."

MacNorth replies that he would have written the script had he seen the bacteria through the microscope with his own eyes.

Introduced to each commune resident, MacNorth also meets

an allegedly psychic cat that digs its claws into MacNorth's groin, where the trouble is.

MacNorth is led to "the cage," a ten-foot-square chamber built of copper and filled with sophisticated electronic recording equipment. This is where a channeler communicates with The Nine, which Harwood describes as "several other kinds of life forms…[who] are in touch with us about matters concerning the future of our own race."

His skepticism still intact, MacNorth visits more research institutes and observes different psychic experiments. He then returns to the Second Genesis estate, this time staying long enough to become familiar with the routine. He becomes "more at peace with my inner self than I ever believed possible."

One night, without even touching MacNorth, Mara fixes the "aural field disturbance at the base of [his] spine." With "total disbelief on his face," he mutters, "My God!" upon noticing his sudden and unexpected erection.

At last, in a communication through the channeler, MacNorth talks to The Nine. They tell him that the purpose of the film he is supposed to write and produce is to prepare humanity "for an arrival of our representatives on your planet Earth. We will call this 'The Landings.' They will occur within one of your years from the completion of the film and its viewing…"

Another member of the community, Dr. Sarat, tells MacNorth that The Nine "represents civilizations existing in other dimensions. You might think of them as other 'envelopes' of space and time which co-exist with ours."

Through the channeler, The Nine tell MacNorth that they visited Earth long ago, in humanity's infancy: "We mingled with your first ancestors and gave them of our seed from which your many races of human were formed. You were that of an 'experiment' which failed. Yes."

MacNorth prepares to leave for Harwood's manor in London, where The Nine will reveal more to him about his purpose. Still skeptical as ever, he receives a call from Keeble telling him that Kathy has died in a plane crash en route to a surprise reconciliation with him in London. Harwood, knowing how badly MacNorth missed her, had convinced Kathy to meet him there. The Nine, however, continue to insist that MacNorth and his wife will reconcile. Anguished by Kathy's death but determined to carry on anyway, MacNorth sees The Nine's obstinate prediction as proof of the project's absurdity—but a deal is still a deal.

When MacNorth arrives at Harwood's London manor, there stands Kathy, waiting; Keeble had walked her to the gate and then departed. Seeing that her plane was to have been delayed, she arranged to fly another airline.

Mr. and Mrs. MacNorth profess to be madly in love.

MacNorth writes his screenplay. Though it fails to confirm the existence of any psychic phenomena, Harwood is satisfied. He tells MacNorth that The Nine have informed him of Kathy's pregnancy. As champagne corks pop in celebration, MacNorth says that his life was indeed changed by these "lovely crazies at a Pennsylvania commune. What they made me believe is far larger, far lovelier. I believe I know now that all life is One, that we're all part of a wondrous, eternal miracle which we have yet to fully comprehend."

Lab 9's real-life headquarters that served as Roddenberry's model for the screenplay were in Ossining, New York, on a fifteen-acre compound complete with two large houses, a barn, several garages, a pond, and a small waterfall. One of the homes was occupied by Whitmore and the channeler Schlemmer; the other by several budding psychics and their mentor, Andrija Puharich, a former physician who through his writings (*The Sacred Mushroom*, *Beyond Telepathy*) became a renowned chronicler of paranormal phenomena. It was Puharich who'd brought the world's attention to the spoon-bending activities of Israeli "psychic" Uri Geller.

Roddenberry's research and the writing of the first draft of "The Nine" took up most of the late summer and fall. He visited the Ossining compound several times during his research, and he and Barrett stayed at Whitmore's manor in England, where they met several of Whitmore's friends, including British Broadcasting Company notables.

During one of Roddenberry's longer visits to Ossining, Puharich claimed that he was deciphering cryptic messages, in Hebrew, through a wristwatch that kept stopping and starting; the position of the arms each time it stopped, he said, indicated a Hebrew letter. Roddenberry asked for a demonstration. Puharich replied that he'd already deciphered most of a short message and could therefore anticipate the final letter, which meant that he knew when the watch was due to stop next. Ten minutes before then, they placed the watch on the kitchen table and passed the time talking. With less than a minute to go, everyone drew silent, all eyes on the watch. Exactly on cue, it stopped. "There was a ten-second silence," Schlemmer says, "then Gene let out a long loud 'Shiiiiiiit!'"

Schlemmer recalls another occasion when several of the young psychics staying in Puharich's house were invited to a get-together with Roddenberry, who wanted to ask them questions. He was, to be sure, highly skeptical. In the midst of the discussion one young woman went into the kitchen and dished out some ice cream for herself. Realizing how impolite it would be to eat it in front of the others, she brought out bowls and spoons and the half gallon tub for them, then returned to the kitchen for her own bowl. About to put a spoonful into her mouth while walking back into the room, she let out a yell as the spoon began bending; the ice cream slid onto the floor. In a moment, several other spoons began bending.

"Gene was very puzzled by this," Schlemmer says. "I remember him looking at all of the spoons and cutlery and trying to figure out how this happened. Not everyone's bent. It seemed it was a chain reaction which often happens with metal bending."

Tony Morgan, a friend of Whitmore's and a member of the governing board of the BBC, had met Roddenberry during a visit to the compound one weekend in September. According to Whitmore, Morgan's diary entry for the date said of Roddenberry: "Nice man, perplexed by John, Phyllis and Andrija—but then, who wouldn't be?"

When Roddenberry finally met The Nine through Schlemmer, his questions indicated that he was at least agnostic on the possibility of their existence; either that or he was respectful of his hosts' and employers' uncommon beliefs and practices. In the communications, which were taped for posterity, his tone of voice is unfailingly polite and engaged. If he was in fact feigning interest just to pick up some quick money, he demonstrated enviable skills as an actor.

He asked: "Is there any sign or method by which this writer, if he is told by other people that this could represent negative forces—the communications and all—that he could confirm to himself that it is positive forces? Of course, if he deals with religious people, some of them are going to be frightened and insist that it could only be negative, and he will need a way of confirming to himself that these represent positive forces; that he's not being duped or not the butt of some cosmic clown or that sort of thing that is often discussed in these areas."

Schlemmer, in a strained halting voice, replied for The Nine: "By that of their knowledge, by that of their benefit, to that of the planet Earth, you will have of the understanding. We had explained that there would be of those that could create of difficulty, that of the power cannot sustain, within that of your ear, within that of your heart, within that of your mind, if it feels not right, then that of the essence of which they convey to you, then we give to you our assurance, it is not right."

"I see," Roddenberry replied.

Later, he sat in on another "communication" with Schlemmer, Puharich, and Whitmore. "I have been well aware in my heart of the love and affection and goodness that surrounds these people here," he said. "But of course I'm asking my questions in relationship to an audience who will reflect many viewpoints and have not had this experience."

The Nine, through Schlemmer, asked if he would be interested to hear about some of his past lives: "At the time in that of what you would call of the Bible," she said, "we would relate of two of your times if you would have desire."

"Yes, I would."

"You were of one that was called of a one that was named of

Jonathan, that was in relationship to that of Moses," Schlemmer began. "Our Sir John, and that of our doctor, may explain of that in relationship to you. It is in truth that you are of the son of one that was called of Gershom. You were of—how may we say?—we must have understanding of that of relationships within this of the planet Earth. You are of a son of a son of Moses. And that of the time of the Nazarene, you were of one that was called—there is of confusion, with this of the name. They call of him John, but in truth his name was of Jonah, and he was in relationship to that of the one of Peter as that of the Father. Yes."

Whitmore tried to clarify The Nine's convoluted syntax: "That he was the father of Peter?"

"I will have other consultation for verification, our Sir John," Schlemmer said. "This is what they had asked of me to tell to that of you." After a brief silence, she continued, "That is so. He was of recognized as that of the father of Peter."

After some highly convoluted references to "Altea" and "Atlantis," Schlemmer as The Nine implied that Roddenberry may have been the Roman god Jupiter as well: "You have of the knowledge of Jupiter, of love. Would you like of us to call of you Jupiter, or would you prefer of that of Jonathan, or of Jonah, and there are many from the time forward that we have not related. Or would you like to be known as that of the gentleman of Altea?"

If Roddenberry was flattered to think that he'd been the grandson of Moses or the father of the apostle Peter or even Jupiter himself, his tone of voice indicated equanimity. "I think I prefer Jonathan," he said.

"We may call of you, of your name, of this day, if you would have of that desire. Yes. Do you have of a question?"

"Yes," Roddenberry said. "In these previous lives did I learn things that will help me with this very difficult task?"

"If you will review of that of Jupiter and that of Jonathan and of that that was Jonah, you will find within there many of the elements that are within that of yourself. And they will bring of the knowledge that is within that deep within of your soul, to that of the front, to bring to you—how may we say to you?—those qualities that are needed to complete of this task. You have within of you of all of the abilities. This was of your choosing. You have brought of much knowledge to this planet Earth, and without that of your knowledge, you in truth have been in service. They say I have made of a wrong statement, that you have been in service and in truth you were knowledgeable of that. It is just that within those of your existence and of acquaintance you truly had not brought forth of the knowledge that within of you, you in truth know that you are in of service to this of the planet Earth, and that you have of the knowledge that you— And when we say of this to you, we wish for you to know that it is not to give to you of that of flattery, for we find that we give not flattery to those that cannot— I am sorry. They say that I am speaking in that of confusion. When we speak to you, and we tell of you of who you are, it is not to give to you of flattery, for we do not do that. As our Sir John and as our doctor is aware, if there is one who would ask of questions that cannot assimilate and cannot in truth understand, we do not answer until they are in that moment when they can. We are aware and we know that you know that you in truth are of a special one. And we say this to you with all of the love, and all of the knowledge that you too have of great love for this of the planet Earth, and of understanding. You know within that of your heart, that you have been of a benefit, and that you have been inspired. Yes."

"May I describe a problem I believe I have and to ask for advice?" Roddenberry asked. "My problem as I have begun to see it today, is I find myself drawn into this circle of love. I find myself, while I know so little about it, most attracted by it, most admiring of the thing that it has caused. And yet I know that in order to do the job I have been given, that I must not be pulled in too far until my story is written, because I must still retain some perspective."

"You must not be biased," Schlemmer said. "You must give it the viewpoint of that of one who is detached. We understand."

Roddenberry's first draft "did not meet the hopes and expectations that we had," Whitmore says. "We liked and approved the autobiographical nature of the story he produced as a vehicle for telling the story, but we felt he never captured the essence or the import of The Nine material itself."

That the screenplay is based firmly in autobiography is beyond doubt: the strained relations with Majel, allusions to unlimited infidelities, his desperate financial situation—all of them were accurate. Whether or not he was, or had been, impotent cannot be known. But the love-hate relationship with the fans was most assuredly true, as Whitmore found out when he accompanied Roddenberry to a *Star Trek* convention in New York. "My strongest memory of this," Whitmore says, "is noting the almost godlike awe in which he was held by the Trekkies as the fount of all knowledge—when, in fact, he was rather naive. He obviously knew that their admiration was misplaced and that he could never meet their exaggerated expectations."

Whitmore had the contractual right to demand a rewrite, for which Roddenberry was to be paid $25,000. Roddenberry was tired of The Nine but not of the paycheck. He took the money and turned the rewrite over to Jon Povill—for $4,000. Povill recognized Roddenberry's intensely autobiographical draft as embarrassingly authentic. His own much superior draft, though still not the message Whitmore had hoped to articulate in a feature film, posed an intriguing dramatic conundrum: Assuming The Nine to exist, why was James MacNorth unable to accept them?

"I took all the accumulating evidence of The Nine and made it more and more threatening to the Roddenberry character," Povill explains. "Ultimately, the story became: 'What if Rod Serling wakes up one day and finds himself in *The Twilight Zone* for real?' This is, 'What if Gene Roddenberry wakes up one day and finds himself in touch with extraterrestrials, and he can't deal with it?' In that way, I was able to walk a line as to whether or not the extraterrestrials were real or not."

As he continued to work on the script, Povill maintained his agnosticism on the possibility that The Nine may indeed exist. He soon felt a sense of responsibility that temporarily paralyzed him. He recognized that if the purpose of the script was to prepare Earthlings for the arrival of these entities from beyond, then he may have been unwittingly setting up the world for an invasion of evil intent; he couldn't be sure that The Nine were necessarily benevolent. "It was a very powerful, palpable fear that I had to deal with," Povill says. "I transferred the strength of that fear to Gene—to the Gene character. I gave him the ego fear that his only success in life had not been his." Povill posited that The Nine had chosen James MacNorth as their channel for the television hit 'Time Zone'; that they, not MacNorth, had created the series.

Except for vague utterances of approbation, Roddenberry avoided talking to him about the rewrite, Povill remembers. "Nothing was mentioned about any of the personality traits I'd given his character," Povill says. "He didn't say anything, which is odd because in my draft the Roddenberrry character, when confronted by what becomes overwhelming evidence that this other reality is real, has a nervous breakdown and hallucinates that he hijacks 'Time Zone''s version of the *Enterprise*. And he interacts with The Nine as Captain Kirk would interact with the Klingons."

Not until he showed the script a year later—1977—to Harold Livingston, producer of what was to become the television series *Star Trek II*, did Povill realize that his work had struck a nerve. "Gene was tremendously insecure about *Star Trek* being his only success," Povill recalls. "Harold said, 'How could you give this to him? How could you show it to him? This is Gene. This is Gene. Finally I understand Gene.'"

Whether Roddenberry believed in anything beyond the physical universe, extraterrestrials included, is in dispute. His opinion on the subject seemed to differ with the days of the week, or the state of his career.

Susan Sackett says that Roddenberry's enduring fascination with states of consciousness can be traced to an out-of-body experience he claimed to have had as a young boy: "He suffered from childhood allergies and illnesses, and his eyes didn't work very well. He tired easily and had asthma. He told me that one afternoon he just felt so bad that he wished he wasn't in his body. Suddenly, he found himself across the room staring back at his body. He vividly remembered that."

Noting that his references to reincarnation sometimes contradicted themselves, Sackett says that she once came right out and asked him whether he believed in it. "And he said something about, 'I believe that we continue, but you don't come back with all of your thoughts intact. You're not the same being. You become one with the All.' So he believed in something that was bigger than himself, in that respect."

Even an atheist may come to be favorably disposed to reincarnation when told that in past lives he was both the grandson of Moses and the father of Peter (and the supreme Roman god). But before his death, Gene Roddenberry, whose fame and fortune were earned by populating outer space with a diversity of life forms, rejected the idea of extraterrestrials as hooey. Early on in *Star Trek: The Next Generation,* he discovered that Tracy Tormé, one of the show's most talented writers and a young man to whom he'd developed an almost grandfatherly devotion, was planning to adapt a book on UFOs into a film. "He called me into his office," Tormé recalls, "and told me that he was just amazed and highly disappointed in me for believing in any of that crap. And I said, 'Well, Gene, you know a lot of the UFO stuff is crap, but a small percentage of it really isn't. The more you research it, the more you find there is something real at the very heart of it.' He was very disdainful of that and said that UFO nuts had been hounding him for years and that it was all crap, absolute crap, and that there hasn't been one case that stands up to any evidence. He was very militant about it. I know that a lot of people in the UFO world would be surprised to hear that Gene Roddenberry was so anti-UFO. I was surprised, too. But I think later on where that came from was his friend Isaac Asimov and also Ray Bradbury, who are tremendously anti-UFO. I remember how worked up about it he was. It was almost like, 'Tracy, it's beneath you to be involved with a heinous subject'—almost like it was child molestation."

Roddenberry's experiences with The Nine may have indeed stirred in him some philosophical uncertainties about paranormal occurrences or extraterrestrials. But, as the anecdotal evidence suggests, he had little trouble dismissing those doubts after cashing the final check from Lab 9 in late 1976: Roddenberry offered channeler Phyllis Schlemmer a job as a writer. "He started out with an offer of fifteen hundred dollars a week," she says. "I said no, and he kept raising it until he reached five thousand a week. When I said no then, he realized I was serious. I think he thought all I was doing was using my imagination." Whether or not he was hoping that her acceptance would confirm his skepticism, he abandoned the matter. (His proposal to Schlemmer was undoubtedly inauthentic, inasmuch as he wasn't in a position to extend such an offer.)

A year later, Roddenberry entertained the visiting John Whitmore for a day, both at home and on the set of *Star Trek: The Motion Picture*. "It was very peculiar," Whitmore remembers. "He never asked about anyone at Ossining."

After Roddenberry failed to sell his screenplay for the proposed *Star Trek* feature film, he invited Jon Povill to try his hand—on spec, of course. Povill's treatment received the standard Roddenberry declination: "This would make a great episode if we were still doing the series." But in a few months, Roddenberry called to ask if Povill would collaborate on another idea he'd had. "I got off the phone with him," Povill says, "and shrieked with joy." Six months before, while physically moving Roddenberry's belongings into his once and future offices on the studio lot, Povill had predicted to Susan Sackett that Gene Coon's old office would someday be his. That someday had arrived. "I was ecstatic. I was going into Paramount to write a *Star Trek* feature for Gene Roddenberry."

The ecstasy faded rapidly as the two men began working on a time travel idea that Roddenberry claimed as original but which Povill recognized as containing a number of elements from his own version. "Now, suddenly," Povill says, "ours wasn't a pure relationship. We were collaborators, and problems started to crop up because he wasn't actually writing this thing; I was. We were having our same sorts of discussions, but now I was trying to take his concepts and make them coalesce into a cohesive story. And I had trouble doing that because they didn't coalesce. There were some gross inconsistencies."

With Roddenberry's eyes welling up whenever Povill pointed out story problems, the task of clarifying these inconsistencies became political as well as intellectual and creative. "I found myself tiptoeing around his feelings," Povill says. "That's what you do if you can see that you're giving someone pain—genuine emotional pain—by criticizing what he's said."

The pain that misted Roddenberry's eyes sprang from insecurity. He'd become Jim MacNorth, creator of "Time Zone," purveyor of alien lives he didn't believe in, tilting at imaginary windmills, taking paychecks from fans, daily facing the shrinking limits of his own talent.

"I would say he was going through a pretty bad depression in those days," Susan Sackett recalls. "He seemed to suffer from depression on and off all of his life."

"Gene was desperate to find an interesting story to tell," says Leonard Nimoy, "because he was given the opportunity of a mandate. He was handed a large canvas and told, 'Here, produce one of your great masterpieces.' Imagine the terror of looking at this empty white frame and wondering what to put on it."

Roddenberry and Povill's story failed to generate studio enthusiasm and was discarded along with the ideas of countless other writers. Roddenberry knew about some of these other writers' efforts, but most were pitched without his knowledge. For two years, Paramount had turned down more ideas than anyone could log or count. Writers with even tenuous connections to *Star Trek* or science fiction came in to pitch. The response, always, was "not big enough. We need bigger." A case in point was John D. F. Black's "End of the Universe," about a black hole that has begun to attract and consume all matter in the universe; the *Enterprise* is sent to forewarn planets. "The end of the universe wasn't big enough," Black recalls.

Unlike *Star Wars*, which came to the audience in June 1977 as a blank slate, *Star Trek* had a past to be measured against. And while that past carried a built-in audience for whatever product appeared on the screen, it also created expectations that blank slates do not have to meet. Everyone at Paramount knew what a

179

Star Trek feature ought not to be—a magnified television episode—but no one could articulate what it should be. "They were preoccupied," Nimoy says, "with this idea that it must have size and stature."

The matter was made moot when the Paramount Pictures braintrust—chairman Barry Diller and president Michael Eisner—decided to create a fourth television network of independent stations using a new *Star Trek* series as a launch pad. After premiering with a two-hour pilot, *Star Trek II* was to air from eight o'clock to nine o'clock every Saturday night and be followed by a series of made-for-television movies; additional nights of programming would be added as success warranted. "There just seemed to be an undercurrent of attention for *Star Trek*," Eisner says. "We wanted to get a nice strong base on which to build the night." All the original actors signed on, with the exception of Nimoy, who'd filed suit against Paramount for unpaid merchandising royalties.

It is difficult to imagine a studio pinning such ambitious hopes on the revival of any other series so many years after its original cancellation. But *Star Trek* had become the tale wagging the dog, achieving a critical mass larger than the sum of its individual stories, characters, and themes. As a symbol of a more perfect world to come, it transcended its original entertainment medium and grew into a social movement, a philosophy, even a religion. "It was a cult," Eisner says, "and it seemed to me at the time that the cult was large enough to start a fourth network."

On college campuses and at *Star Trek* conventions, Roddenberry was seen as the knight errant by young audiences bereft of heroes after Vietnam and Watergate. "Gene enjoyed playing the guy who was perpetually running for office, but claimed he was not a politician," Nimoy notes.

Roddenberry assumed the executive producer's role for the new series. He uttered no protests about its proposed time slot, though it is reasonable to assume that Saturday night was as inconvenient for the target audience's attendance as he'd claimed Friday nights had been ten years before. "Gene was not a major player in the motion picture business, or even in television at that time," Eisner says. "When we decided to go forward, he was enthusiastic."

Robert Goodwin was named line producer and Harold Livingston creative producer. Jon Povill was hired as "assistant producer"—in effect, Roddenberry's gofer, the same job he'd held for a few years. But because he was vastly more familiar with *Star Trek* than was Livingston, he sat in on all story conferences and soon became the liaison between Livingston and Roddenberry; the two had developed a terrible dislike of each other. "I noticed he either drank a lot or was on dope," Livingston says of Roddenberry. (Several people, including Povill, say that Roddenberry was snorting a fair amount of cocaine at the time, in addition to his usual prodigious drinking.)

Paramount had ordered thirteen episodes plus the two-hour premiere movie, all of them to be made without Nimoy. Roddenberry was apparently undaunted by the actor's lawsuit against the studio, and even less daunted by having to explain to the fans why Spock would not be back aboard the *Enterprise*. He offered Nimoy the role of Spock, but in only two episodes out of every eleven. Nimoy's agent, Sandy Bresler, responded that it was questionable whether the actor even wanted to return—"So why don't you offer him his choice of how many episodes he wants to do?" Refusing to reconsider, Roddenberry reiterated the initial offer, which ended the discussion.

"I was insulted," Nimoy says. "He was taking the position that he would use me as he saw fit—plug me into his plans. I said, 'I will not accept a part-time job on *Star Trek*.' I thought it was a reduction from what I'd had previously."

The *Star Trek II* producers intended to accumulate all thirteen finished scripts before attempting the writing of the pilot. Story assignments began to be handed out. When Jaron Summers pitched "The Child," Povill liked the core idea but not the story line, and suggested an alternative. Summers agreed and wrote a fast first draft. As a test, Livingston asked Povill to do the rewrite. Povill passed, performing quickly enough and proficiently enough, in Livingston's opinion, to move up a couple of notches on the employment ladder.

"I told Gene that I wanted Jon to be my story editor," Livingston says. "He said, 'He's not ready.' I said, 'Bullshit, you just want to keep him for yourself and hold him back. If you don't hire him, I'm going to quit.' So he hired him, but he never forgave me for that."

Roddenberry had not mistrusted Povill's talent; he'd simply not wanted to lose his all-purpose handyman, gofer, collaborator-sounding board. "I was his personal source," Povill says. "Harold had been advocating for some time that if I was sitting in on all those story meetings and performing the functions of a story editor, that I should be the story editor. Gene resisted that. He said, 'You shouldn't move him along so fast.' I think he was afraid that once I got out there and once my talent was recognized, that I wouldn't be there to help him. And there was some truth to that."

Unable to find a writer for the two-hour pilot, Livingston assigned himself the first draft of "In Thy Image," Alan Dean Foster's story of a space probe that has transmogrified in the three hundred years since its launch and is now searching for its creator. Roddenberry's rewrite, unanimously considered inept by the production staff, touched off a war between the two men that continued on and off for the next year, through draft after draft after draft of what was eventually to become *Star Trek: The Motion Picture.* "My perception," says Livingston, "is that he wanted what *he* thought was the best product; it didn't matter what anybody else thought."

Star Trek lore holds that Paramount nixed the television series and turned "In Thy Image" into a feature film after noting the blocks-long lines of fans waiting to see *Stars Wars* (and then, six months later, *Close Encounters of the Third Kind*). What's more correct is that George Lucas's gargantuan success saved *Star Trek* from the outright oblivion it would have suffered when Paramount's parent company, Gulf & Western, decided to abort the expensive and risky fourth network because of instability in the economy (Gerald Ford's presidential campaign in 1976 featured buttons that read "WIN"—whip inflation now). No network meant no series.

A moderately priced feature, on the other hand, stood a chance of becoming a profits bonanza. It seemed likely that a high percentage of those standing in line for *Star Wars* tickets had been, or would be, *Star Trek* fans, too. "I doubt whether there would have been the impetus to change *Star Trek* from a television series to a movie without *Star Wars*," Michael Eisner concedes. (The efficacy of a fourth network was established a decade later, when Barry Diller inaugurated Fox Television, while the wisdom of anchoring an upstart network with *Star Trek* was ratified when the syndicated *Next Generation* became the founding program on what is essentially an ad hoc network of affiliated stations.)

By the same measure, the first *Star Trek* movie may not have been produced were it not for the forestalled series. *Star Trek II* had acted as a bridge, a comfort zone between the studio's intention to find a suitable project and its determination to begin production. All of the momentum, energy, and enthusiasm that had accrued to "In Thy Image" can be traced to its acceptance as a television pilot. If the story had been proposed from scratch as a feature, it's possible that it, too, would have ended up in the landfill of rejected ideas. But for the small screen, Paramount felt no compulsion to present astounding grandeur. That allowed a script to develop, and now that script was matched with an urgency, initiated by *Star Wars*, to get a finished product into the marketplace; there was no time to wait for something more perfect.

When it became clear that the original modest budget of $8 million for the as yet untitled *Star Trek* motion picture would not be adequate—special effects alone might eat much of that—director Robert Collins was jettisoned in favor of Academy Award winner Robert Wise. Entirely unfamiliar with *Star Trek*, Wise hadn't been aware of Spock's importance until his daughter and son-in-law insisted the film wouldn't be *Star Trek* without him. Wise's contract required Paramount to make a robust effort to cast Leonard Nimoy, who'd made clear that he would not even read a script so long as he and the studio remained legal antagonists. Nimoy had rebuffed several broadside and backdoor attempts to sign him, because none acknowledged the litigation.

The responsibility to return Nimoy to the family became Jeffrey Katzenberg's. Katzenberg had worked in marketing and distribution at Paramount Pictures in New York until Michael Eisner asked him to come west and run the proposed syndicated network. After the network's annulment, he'd remained in California as the executive shepherd in charge of the *Star Trek* film.

Katzenberg flew to New York, where Nimoy was appearing on Broadway in *Equus*. He watched the play and afterward the two men, who'd never met, had dinner together. They talked for hours that night, as they did the following day, and the day after that, discussing all the dirty laundry having to do with unpaid merchandising royalties and unauthorized use of the *Star Trek* blooper reel for (Roddenberry's) profit. For the first time since originally making his demands, Nimoy believed that he had Paramount's attention, not just the obligatory regard of its business affairs department. He was perched in the catbird seat, holding something the studio wanted.

Resolution of the matter soon followed, coinciding with the end of Nimoy's run in the play. The actor returned to Los Angeles and on a Friday afternoon his attorney came to his home and presented him with a sizable check and papers to sign in satisfaction of the agreement. One hour later, a Paramount messenger dropped off a copy of "In Thy Image," by Gene Roddenberry. (Livingston's name was not on it.) The next morning Roddenberry, Jeffrey Katzenberg, and Robert Wise arrived to discuss his participation: Would he or wouldn't he reprise Mr. Spock for the big screen?

The immediate problem was that the script Nimoy had just read did not include Spock. He asked if this was the story they planned to tell.

"I was fishing," Nimoy says, "for something that sounded like, 'We're considering this,' or 'We have some ideas in mind we'd like to discuss with you.' There was none of that. They took the pretty firm position that this was the script." Nimoy inferred that the filmmakers' sole concern was whether they had the green light to inject Spock into an existing framework. His character, therefore, would not be integral to the story; but then, as he read it, neither were any of the other characters, including Kirk. In this tale of a space probe essentially hijacking the *Enterprise* and threatening the Earth, "We all became passengers, in a sense. We don't know whether we're supposed to honor, or obey, or confront, or cooperate with, or support. Ours wasn't goal-oriented behavior. What made the series so good was that we would locate the problem, come up with a solution, and implement it. The movie had none of that; and at the end, we discover that it was kind of an empty quest."

Katzenberg and Wise, in their focus on Nimoy, had not discussed with Roddenberry what Spock's role might be. They'd just assumed that the creator would create something marvelous. When Nimoy asked, "What do you intend to do with the Spock character?," Katzenberg and Wise turned simultaneously to Roddenberry.

"We posit the following idea," Roddenberry said: "Spock has gone back to his home planet of Vulcan in an effort to rid himself of the last vestiges of any human emotion in order to attain a purer state of Vulcan logic. And in so doing, he has a nervous breakdown."

Nimoy wanted to laugh but didn't. For months he'd rebuffed Paramount and Roddenberry, and now, on a Saturday morning, one day after agreeing simply to consider participating if the project seemed worthwhile, this was the best the film's spiritual father had to offer. "It was a pretty sad state of affairs," he says. "I stammered through something that sounded like, 'I'm not really sure that that's the most heroic thing we can do with the character.'"

With the issue still to be resolved, Roddenberry and Katzenberg excused themselves so that Nimoy, as he'd requested before their arrival, could spend some time alone with Wise. "I'm at a loss here," Nimoy told Wise. "I'd like to be in your movie, to make a contribution. But I'd like to be in it in order to *make* a contribution, not just to give Paramount the right to announce that they've gathered the entire cast. I don't know what to do."

"Come aboard," Wise said.

At that point, Wise had yet to discover a fundamental truth that foreshadowed some of the problems soon to burden the production. Uninitiated in the *Star Trek* universe, he naturally relied on Roddenberry to be his tour guide through the final frontier, believing that the creator and the series had been one and the same. "I don't think he realized," Nimoy says, "that he wasn't necessarily going to get the best of *Star Trek* simply because he had Gene Roddenberry."

CHAPTER NINE

Soon

to Be

a Major

Motion Picture

HOWARD STEVENS was dining with a friend at the Cock 'n Bull on Sunset when he overheard a familiar, if thick-tongued, voice. Scanning the dark room, he located Gene Roddenberry, obviously drunk, bending the bartender's ear. Approaching, he asked, "Gene, what're you doing here?"

Roddenberry was surprised to see a friendly face. "Majel and I had a fight," he said. "She threw me out of the house."

"Why don't you join us?" Stevens suggested.

"Delighted," Roddenberry said, sliding off the bar stool.

The two had met a couple of years before, in 1976, when Stevens was hired to introduce Roddenberry to a student group at Morris County College in New Jersey. An aspiring comic who regularly played New York's Improv and Catch a Rising Star, Stevens had performed on the same campus a week before; and because his act included a long, satirical take on *Star Trek*, he was asked back as emcee of Roddenberry's appearance.

Roddenberry had mistaken Stevens, who'd picked him up at La Guardia Airport and taken him to dinner before the engagement without identifying himself, for a member of the Morris County faculty. When Stevens began his introduction with selections from his *Star Trek* routine, Roddenberry had enjoyed the comedy as much as the students. "I thought you were going to screw up the evening when you started," he'd told Stevens while being driven back to New York City's Chelsea Hotel, the renowned hub of literary creativity where Arthur C. Clarke was alleged to have written the script to *2001: A Space Odyssey*. The next night Roddenberry had taken in Stevens's show at the Improv.

Some weeks later, Stevens had called Roddenberry to say that he would be in Los Angeles for several days, filming a television special with comedian Freddie Prinze. Roddenberry had instructed Stevens to phone when he got in and, true to his word, had extended generous hospitality, taking him to dinner, granting the use of an extra car, and offering a spare bedroom. Excited by his career prospects, Stevens had in fact stayed permanently in California, though not for long in Roddenberry's home. But even after he'd found his own apartment, Stevens, Roddenberry, and Majel Barrett had continued their friendship.

Stevens had been in the *Star Trek II* offices one day with Jon Povill and Susan Sackett when Roddenberry called from his condominium in La Costa. Knowing that Stevens did excellent impressions, Roddenberry had said, "You gotta do me a favor. Call back in a few minutes and do your Jimmy Stewart. Ask for Majel and bust her chops."

When the phone rang in the condo, Roddenberry had pretended he couldn't get to it. "Hello?" Barrett had said.

"Is this M-m-majel Barrett," had come the voice.

"Why, yes," she'd said enthusiastically, recognizing without being told that the speaker on the other end of the line was her all-time favorite actor.

"This is Jimmy Stewart."

"Yes, Mr. Stewart. How are you?"

"Well, I'm down here in La Costa, and I just heard that you Roddenberrys were here too. I hope I'm not imposing."

"Oh, no, Mr. Stewart, not at all. It's such a pleasure to hear from you."

"Well, good, because I just want to say: Nurse Chapel, I've always had the hots for you."

At that, Stevens had identified himself. And for the next two years—until the wrap party for *Star Trek: The Motion Picture*—Barrett was palpably cool to Stevens, who never revealed that her husband had put him up to it.

"Gene, Majel's pissed at me," Stevens confided in Roddenberry each time he felt the chill.

"For what?" Roddenberry would ask.

"Because of the Jimmy Stewart thing."

"Nah."

In part because of his relations with Barrett, Stevens believed, he'd not seen Roddenberry for several months before overhearing him at the Cock 'n Bull. Joining Stevens and his friend at their table, Roddenberry made casual small talk, dishing out and catching up on old news. "You know what I did today?" he said nonchalantly. "I signed a deal to do a *Star Trek* movie."

"Gene, that's great, that's fabulous," Stevens said.

"And do you know how much they're paying me?" Roddenberry asked. Two years before, he had revealed to Stevens that his personal appearance fee had soared over the years, as though tied to the *Star Trek* popularity index. Speeches that originally earned him just airfare and expenses, then several hundred dollars, were, by 1976, bringing in anywhere from $3500 to $10,000 each. "It's like winning the lottery every day," he'd noted. (Roddenberry apparently confided in Stevens a great deal. He told him that he'd chosen Gene Coon as *Star Trek* producer based on his reaction to seeing Nichelle Nichols dressed only in a knit sweater. He said that when he was still married to Eileen, he would spend afternoons at Barrett's apartment, making love to her in the shower, then have to hide his pruney fingers from his wife. In the 1980s, he complained to Stevens that he'd just sent a check to Eileen for half of the initial royalties on the *Star Trek* home video package and that she'd accused him of hiding other profits. "I could have doctored the books if I'd wanted to," he said. "But I didn't. I sent the money immediately. Now she's got her lawyers calling up and saying, 'There's more. We know there's more. Where is it?' I don't have to give her anything, and now she gives me this shit.")

"No, Gene, how much are they paying you for the *Star Trek* movie?" Stevens asked like the dutiful second-banana.

In a voice that Stevens remembers was full of amazement, not conceit, Roddenberry said, "Five hundred thousand dollars."

At the end of the evening, Roddenberry paid the check. He was obviously too drunk to drive. With his friend following behind, Stevens chauffeured Roddenberry home in Roddenberry's car and tried to help him sneak into the house without Barrett hearing. Stymied by the tightly latched windows and immovable side doors, Stevens finally activated the automatic garage door, which at two in the morning no doubt awakened Barrett, if not the entire neighborhood.

"Thanks a lot," Roddenberry said sarcastically.

To convey adequately the misery that was the production of Star *Trek: The Motion Picture,* Jeffrey Katzenberg has constructed an allegory. In it, he plays a feisty street fighter from back East who's invited out to the wild, wild West. Wearing a ten-gallon hat and hand-tooled boots, a six-shooter poised in his hip holster, he arrives at the gates to the place called Paramount. His new employers, two gents named Barry Diller and Michael Eisner, are standing out front, on that rootin' tootin' street named Melrose, to welcome him. As they explain with great enthusiasm exactly why he was born to the job for which they've hired him, and why this thing called the movie business is going to be the greatest experience of his life, he can hear the faint rumbling of something huge in the distance. He wonders why these guys Diller and Eisner don't seem to be distracted. Trying to ignore the rumbling, he continues listening to their stories. But he can't completely ignore it, because it's getting louder and louder, obviously closer and closer. Why aren't Diller and Eisner bothered? Is he the only one who can hear it?

"Finally," he says, "the noise is deafening. And I turn around and there, coming down Melrose, is this runaway stagecoach drawn by eight of the largest Clydesdales that you've ever seen. They're so crazed, there's foam coming out of their mouths. And just as this runaway stagecoach comes right in front of the Paramount gate, Barry and Michael say, 'Here,' and they hand me the reins. Boom! This thing takes off. That's how I recall *Star Trek*—a runaway stagecoach. I'd never been on a stagecoach before. I didn't even know what a stagecoach did. And there I was, being dragged down the street, torn to shreds. Not a chance in the world was I getting this thing under control."

Most of the film's myriad problems are well known in *Trek* lore: $5 million—and several months—lost when special effects wizard Robert Abel failed to deliver a single usable frame; the ongoing dispute between Roddenberry and Harold Livingston over the script; and a producer, in Gene Roddenberry, who by unanimous consent was a woefully inept manager. Compounding all of these problems was Paramount's implacable determination to debut the film in 1979, which meant that everyone worked to the point of exhaustion.

"On a scale of one to ten," Katzenberg says, "the anxiety level on that film fluctuated somewhere between eleven and thirteen."

To Michael Eisner, "It was a nightmare."

That nightmare may have been best symbolized by the acrimonious relations between Roddenberry and Livingston. Livingston had been off the Paramount lot for more than four months, since the dissolution of *Star Trek II*, when he heard through the grapevine that the script from which the film was to be made no longer bore his name. Unless Roddenberry had begun anew from scratch—an impossibility, Livingston knew—he deserved at least some credit. He called the studio to complain, and demanded clarification. His status as the script's co-writer, he was assured, would be expressed unambiguously at the March 28, 1978, press conference.

The mood at the press conference announcing the impending production *Star Trek: The Motion Picture* and the reunion of the entire original cast was festive and ebullient, almost as if an armistice had been signed. And in fact, Paramount's five-star generals—Gulf & Western chairman Charles Bluhdorn, Paramount chairman Barry Diller, and Eisner—turned out to christen the launch, which at the time was budgeted at $15 million and scheduled for the following June.

As much as he craved being the film's author, Roddenberry realized that he could not create from nothing; he needed someone else's first draft. Dennis Clark, fresh off *Comes a Horseman*, was hired to integrate Spock into the script—sans nervous breakdown. Clark didn't last long, however. He and Roddenberry mixed like ammonia and chlorine, Roddenberry having gotten the relationship off on treacherous footing with a misconceived practical joke reminiscent of those he'd played during *Star Trek*. He had temporarily replaced Clark's longtime assistant with Grace Lee Whitney (the once and future yeoman Janice Rand) in the role of the repugnant, sassy secretary. Clark ill-appreciated the attempt at humor, which more than anything told him that he and Roddenberry were destined to clash over core values.

At ten o'clock on a Sunday night in April following Clark's departure, Livingston's home phone rang. Livingston answered.

"Hello, how are you? How are you doing?" Roddenberry asked. "Haven't seen you in a long time."

Livingston recognized the distinctive voice, caught somewhere between tenor and alto. "What kind of trouble are you in now?" he asked.

"Well," Roddenberry said. "We've hired Bob Wise to direct. This is the big one, and we'd like to talk to you."

"What do you want to talk to me about?"

"We'd like you to rewrite the script."

"You mean my script that you rewrote that someone else rewrote?"

"Yeah," Roddenberry said. "But we want you to go back to the original. And you've got to write in Spock."

The conversation concluded with their making a breakfast date at which Wise would also be present. A few minutes later, a messenger arrived with a copy of the script. Livingston read it before going to bed. His perception was that it had been rewritten perhaps a dozen times, each draft worse than the previous one. It was unintelligible and unshootable.

"Mr. Wise," Livingston said at the meeting, "what I think you should do is take cyanide." Then he turned to Roddenberry: "Gene, you're finished."

Livingston's first condition of employment was that Roddenberry not be allowed to write, rewrite, or otherwise put words to paper. Livingston was granted complete autonomy over the script.

A few weeks later, Roddenberry violated the agreement for the first of what would be many times. Finishing his inaugural draft, Livingston handed in a copy that was to be sent to Eisner and Katzenberg, who were in Europe on business. Some days later Eisner called to say that he thought the work was terrible. Livingston, taken completely by surprise, checked with Eisner's secretary to be sure that the correct script had been sent. Comparing drafts, Livingston discovered that what the executives had received was Roddenberry's quick, surreptitious rewrite.

He walked out for the first of what would be many times, all of them catalyzed by what he considered Roddenberry's editorial meddling. Paramount brought him back with renewed assurances—and a great deal of money. But if Roddenberry had in fact been warned off the script, he continued to put his stamp on it anyway.

Jesco von Puttkamer, the NASA scientist who acted as the film's technical adviser, visited Los Angeles often during and subsequent to the filming; he and Roddenberry became reasonably close friends. "Gene was drinking quite a lot and smoking a lot of pot, which I advised him to quit," von Puttkamer recalls. "When he made up his mind, he was so hard-nosed. He'd rather go down with the ship than change his mind about things. He always came out a winner. He always had his way, even if it sometimes took months and years."

"More than anything else," Katzenberg says, "Gene was devoted to protecting the essence of *Star Trek*. Whether he went too far or not, he believed that his was *Star Trek*'s sole voice."

Livingston agrees that Roddenberry knew everything about *Star Trek*—but nothing about structuring a motion picture script. "Gene was a great idea man and a good story man," he says. "He

195

just couldn't execute. That's not unusual. What took him sixteen speeches to accomplish, I could do in a few lines."

The two writers battled each other daily, the first draft of a scene leading to a rewrite, leading to another rewrite, and another, and another. Rewritten scenes were not only dated but timed, and bore the rewriter's initials. During production, Leonard Nimoy arrived at Livingston's home every night at nine, after filming, to help polish the following day's scenes. Livingston credits him with keeping the tinderbox situation from exploding. "Nimoy was very useful," he says. "He enhanced the script considerably."

Throughout the long writing process, Roddenberry became annoyed if someone he considered a member of his camp preferred Livingston's work to his. "He expected me to support him any time there was any disagreement over what some aspect of the story should be," says Jon Povill, the film's associate producer. "He felt I was being tremendously disloyal, but I was loyal to the project. I think he knew that somewhere inside of him, but in his eyes it was still disloyalty."

The irony of Roddenberry's expectation of loyalty lay in the history of his own treatment of Povill, first when his young protégé had been in line for story editor of *Star Trek II* and he'd resisted the promotion, then when Povill was named associate producer after a stint as the film's production coordinator. As associate producer, Povill's duties involved standing in for producer Roddenberry or director Wise at various meetings and acting as the point of access for hiring and firing; they also included writing. His initial salary, $600 per week, was $700 less than his story editor's salary had been, and only $100 more than his production coordinator's salary.

"I was working very much shoulder to shoulder with Wise, Roddenberry, and Livingston, all of whom were making pretty hefty bucks," Povill says. "I felt that I should be making at least a thousand dollars a week." Incensed by the underpayment, he stormed into the office of production manager Phil Rawlins and was informed that Roddenberry had set the figure. Povill insisted that he be raised to his benchmark, and Rawlins returned to Roddenberry, who pursued the matter with the studio.

A week later, Povill received his first check under the new salary structure—$800.

"What the hell is this?" he said to Roddenberry, not bothering to contain his anger. "Nobody negotiated with me. Nobody talked to me. With all that I'm doing, I should be getting at least a grand a week."

"It wasn't my responsibility," Roddenberry said. "It was Bob Wise."

Povill went to Wise. "You want a thousand, you've got a thousand," Wise said. "It's fine with me."

At that, Povill marched into Katzenberg's office and reiterated his harangue, concluding with: "I've talked to Roddenberry, I've talked to Wise, and they said it's OK with them if I get a thousand." Impressed by Povill's fury, Katzenberg referred him to vice president of production Lin Parsons.

"Who gave you this eight-hundred-dollar figure?" Povill asked Parsons.

"Roddenberry," Parsons said.

On a film that ultimately cost $45 million, Povill says, "Gene wanted to look like he was saving money."

(Roddenberry was never known for his generosity. When Susan Sackett began as his secretary in 1974, she was paid a weekly salary of one hundred fifty dollars. Aware that her new boss had hired and fired her predecessor in a space of five days, she was frightened that she might meet the same fate. But three weeks later Roddenberry called her from somewhere on the road, where he was delivering a lecture. "I'm so pleased with the job you're doing," he said. "You're going to get a raise." Five dollars a week.)

In the course of cosmological and philosophical discussions, both related and unrelated to work, Roddenberry and Povill often landed on the subject of revenge. "Gene thought of himself as a person who really relished the opportunity to take revenge when wronged," Povill says. "He liked the concept. He liked the idea of payback. It gave him satisfaction. He didn't like the idea of someone getting the better of him"—as Hal Livingston would on the *Motion Picture* script.

When it came time to divvy up the glory in 1979, producer Roddenberry credited the screenplay to himself and Livingston. Livingston protested. "I wrote this," he said.

"No, a lot of this is mine," Roddenberry said. "Look at the initials."

"I'm not going to argue," Livingston countered. "We'll let it go to arbitration." And it did, briefly, before Roddenberry withdrew.

Livingston, however, did believe that Roddenberry deserved to share story credit with Alan Dean Foster, and strong-armed Foster into agreeing. Roddenberry refused, in Livingston's estimation, "because if he couldn't have screenplay, he didn't want anything."

"I made the decision not to take writer's credit since I was receiving credit as the producer and as the creator, and it just reached a point where too much credit becomes almost laughable," Roddenberry claimed.[1] Livingston, he said, "felt he deserved the credit, and my policy is to never get into a credit dispute.... That was my policy all through *Star Trek*. If a writer felt he wanted it and wanted it badly enough to have a Guild action on it, I'd withdraw."[2]

He extracted his revenge on Livingston after the film had completed production, when Livingston discovered that Roddenberry had signed with Simon & Schuster (a division of Gulf & Western) to adapt the screenplay in novel form.

"What're you doing, you son of a bitch?" Livingston said angrily. As the screenwriter and the author of several novels, he believed the opportunity to re-create the script in prose should have been his. Even more aggravating, the book's advance had fetched $400,000.

"There's nothing you can do about it," Roddenberry said.

The deal giving Roddenberry the right of novelization, signed long before Livingston came on the scene, hadn't been intended as revenge. But if the sentiment he expressed to Povill accurately reflected his beliefs, his getting the opportunity to rub Livingston's face in what he wanted, just as Livingston had rubbed his face in what he'd wanted, must have been profoundly pleasurable.

"He had his moment," Livingston says.

On March 30, 1979, the National Space Club in Washington, D.C., honored Gene Roddenberry at the annual Robert Goddard Memorial Dinner, named for the American physicist who'd been a pioneer in the science of rocketry. Excusing himself temporarily from his writing of the novelization while postproduction on the film proceeded without him, Roddenberry took Barrett to the nation's capital, where for three days they were ushered about by Jesco von Puttkamer, technical adviser on *The Motion Picture*. (In a letter thanking him for "the literally dozens of friendship courtesies which you extended," Roddenberry told von Puttkamer to prepare for the imminent arrival of a mailed gift: "Have no idea what it is, but, knowing Majel, I would suggest you do not open it in the presence of impressionable children and/or bureaucrats.")[3]

With their presence at the Goddard dinner, the assembled scientists, technicians, writers, even space-interested politicians, were crediting Roddenberry for having furthered the cause of space travel—for, in some sense, laying the grass-roots groundwork that enabled funding of the space shuttle program. As the Americans raced the Soviets to the moon in the 1960s, von Puttkamer explains, "money was no object. If we wanted another test, we got it." But in the early 1970s, President Richard Nixon sensed diminishing returns from the moon landings, both in terms of science and public interest, and he terminated the Apollo program. Offering a different agenda, he beefed up the National Cancer Institute—with dollars that might have gone to NASA—and predicted a cure for cancer by the end of the decade. Rather than landing an astronaut on Mars somewhere around the year 1990, according to the existing plan, NASA had to choose between the shuttle program and erecting a space station. Constrained by budget, the shuttle research team could not afford experiments that might fail—defeating, of course, the purpose of experimentation.

"We had to eliminate funds here and there and still somehow get it flying," von Puttkamer says. "We couldn't say, 'It can't be done.' Instead of cutting away fat, we cut away meat. That ultimately led to the Challenger disaster [in 1986]."

The mood at NASA in the early 1970s was depressed, almost defeatist. "People like me were feeling very down," von Puttkamer says. "We wondered what was happening to this damn nation, turning its back on progress. Is America giving up? Is this whole two-hundred-year experiment a failure? That's how it seemed, especially for an immigrant [German] like me, who'd come to this country for these qualities, which all of a sudden didn't seem to apply anymore. It was during these passive times that most people at NASA started noticing this *Star Trek*, which was in reruns. Those characters were whooshing through space, expressing a totally positive attitude toward the future. It was upbeat. No cynicism. Naive, maybe, but the message was that, 'Hey, guys, the future's going to be good.' I finally felt that maybe hope wasn't lost after all, that a nation that can put something like this on television still has a sense of value somewhere."

Roddenberry, who was fifty-seven, mounted the dais at the Goddard dinner and, when the enthusiastic applause subsided, began his remarks. "I have been uncertain how to properly express appreciation for the honor being done me here this evening," he said. "Fortunately, as sometimes happens to science fiction writers, my problem has been solved by an extraterrestrial document which has fallen into my possession. I have here an English approximation of that document. Some of you, of course, will believe that this is merely a story that I've invented these few moments at this microphone. Not true. I pledge to you that these are authentically the notes of a life form whose basic origins were other than this planet. At the time of writing, that life form had lived fifty-seven years among us—so perfectly camouflaged as a human that this alien at times even believed itself to be human. At those times it sometimes foolishly believed also—as some humans do—that a few years of accidental existence on this dust speck are somehow the alpha and omega of life and consciousness in our universe."

It was a curious conceit he invoked, that of pretending to be an alien from outer space. But Roddenberry often positioned himself as the outsider, alone on an intergalactic parade stand, watching the world from a perspective not shared by any other human. "I was considered 'that slightly demented person' whose proof of his dementia," he said, "was that he had created *Star Trek.*"[4] At a distance from the fray, he appeared to remain aloof, detached, unperturbed by today's events because he could foresee the time when enlightenment was the outgrowth of reason. (In the early 1980s, Roddenberry began a novel which he called "Report to Earth," about an alien named Gaan who observes Earthlings and their customs. "The secret is identifying with the alien so completely that prejudice about myself and Earth begins melting away," he said. "Somehow the shedding of personal prejudice seems to open up a person's mental processes. You think in new dimensions and at new speeds. The more I polish Gaan and practice putting myself in his place, the more discoveries I make."[5] According to Susan Sackett, Roddenberry never completed the novel because he could not work without a deadline: "Gene was not a driven person. He was an eleventh-hour writer. He did his best work under the gun."

Roddenberry may have been correct in his optimistic evaluation of the future; time will tell. But his otherworldly prescription for getting us there was, ironically, wrongheaded. A case in point is his assessment of the Japanese attack on Pearl Harbor, which he once described as the act of a country "trying to elbow her place in the sun." As the alien in our midst—the creator of *Star Trek*—he said, "You begin to look upon these things from a broader perspective. Here is a planet on which this war happened. You tend to forget, 'Okay, I was an American fighting for America.' You look at all the people. You understand also the nice things about Japan. You take a philosophical look to all of these things. It was a couple of systems that were clashing then, too. Japan felt that she had a right to be dominant in her sphere of the Pacific. It's easy to get angry about it, and there were times I did. But looking back on it from a perspective of science fiction, you tend to look upon whole countries, whole peoples."[6] There are, of course, as he noted, many wonderful and beautiful aspects to Japan. Its attack on Pearl Harbor, however, did not happen to be one of them; nor was its imperialist invasion and occupations of China and Manchuria. Japan of the 1930s had joined the Berlin-Rome Axis only because it shared with Hitler's Germany both the dream of a country without borders and common enemies in the Allied powers, who opposed their expansionist plans. If Roddenberry anticipated that reason alone would lead to a better world three centuries hence, his revisionist view of history was illogical. In the *Star Trek* future, people are seen to revel in their diversity—language, culture, customs, religions, looks—but standards of ethicality are common to all beings.

From his perch in outer space, Roddenberry began to believe that good and evil were simply matters of opinion, and that motive was more important than behavior; a good cause therefore mitigated the worst excesses. Referring to the Mideast kidnappers who in 1988 held several Western hostages in Lebanon, he said, "I am amazed to see [them] treated as bad guys always. Many of these people have legitimate complaints. The world is not as simple as we lay it out—good guys here and bad guys there. I am very concerned and want to find a way to get into the fact that most of the warfare and killing going on in the world is going on in the name of...organized religion. I think we have to attend to that."[7] Besides the fact that that oft-repeated statement about killing and dying in the name of religion is a canard and has been for at least two centuries, the irony of his comment was that the kidnappers he defended as having "legitimate complaints" had indeed acted in the name of religion.

There was further irony in Roddenberry's reflections on right and wrong in *Have Gun, Will Travel.* "I'm not pleased," he said, "with scripts where I fell off the wagon and created a crafty fast gun who was evil, without questioning very much why he was evil, and had Paladin slay him."[8] While the dramatist is expected to motivate his villains for the sake of storytelling, in the real world evil behavior, regardless of its motivations, deserves appropriate punishment. That's the only way societies, particularly of the type

Roddenberry's optimism envisioned, can endure. When he wasn't
an alien, Roddenberry recognized that; he referred to it as "civiliz-
ing and taming the solar system."[9]

Displaying a sardonic sense of history, Jeffrey Katzenberg points
out that principal photography on *Star Trek: The Motion Picture*
began on August 9, 1978, and that the film opened December 7,
1979—Nagasaki Day and Pearl Harbor Day, respectively. "Never
in the history of motion pictures," he says, "has there been a film
that came closer to not making it to the theaters on its release
date." Thousands of prelabeled film cans on the dock at the lab
awaited the prints, which were then shipped immediately to theaters. If they'd not made the delivery date, Paramount would have
had to repay $30 million in guarantees already received from the
exhibitors. "Barry Diller had said, 'I don't care if you deliver blank
film. Put a title on it; it doesn't matter. You will deliver. We're not
giving the money back.'"

In Jon Povill's opinion, the film that went out in those waiting
cans was essentially a rough cut: "No one saw it in its entirety
before release."

That *Star Trek: The Motion Picture* was an immediate hit did
not assuage Paramount. Somebody had to take the rap for the fias-
co—Roddenberry. Whether or not it was entirely his fault was aca-
demic: While he had been involved with preproduction set design
and costuming—"Not that he overshadowed Robert Wise," Povill
says—he was rarely present during production, particularly in the
latter stages. The complicated postproduction processes, including
the design and insertion of opticals and special effects, had been
supervised in their entirety by Wise. "Gene was thoroughly
decent," Wise says. "But he wasn't around too much. He was not
a presence. I did all the postproduction myself."

"Gene simply didn't have the skills to be a film producer in
terms of the size and scale of these things," Katzenberg says.

At some point it had begun to seem that money was no longer
funding production and postproduction, but was disappearing

without a trace. "This was probably the only movie I've ever been involved with," Michael Eisner says, "that got out of control on a budget basis." Katzenberg tells of Diller casually inquiring how much over budget the film was one particular day. Half a million, Katzenberg responded blithely. Diller's face began to redden with rage, which burst Katzenberg's cork; he began laughing hysterically. "What're you laughing about?" Diller managed through clenched teeth. "Well, Barry," Katzenberg said, "I'm laughing because there's no controlling it. It is truly the beast that's eating the entire corporation. It is going to bring us to our knees, and I have no control over it. And the fact that you think I have control over it, or that I might have had control over it, or hoped I had control over it, forget it." After starting out at less than $2 million, the final budget was closer to $45 million—about $35 million more than *Star Wars* had cost—making it the most expensive film in the history to that time of Paramount Pictures. Had *Star Trek: The Motion Picture* failed at the box office, Paramount's operating capital—some of which was used the following year to fund Steven Spielberg's *Raiders of the Lost Ark*—would have been severely depleted; and quite possibly, the creative brain trust of Diller and Eisner would have been shown the door. (Eisner admits he almost fired Katzenberg during production.)

Only extraordinary pent-up demand for anything *Star Trek* enabled the studio to dodge that bullet. Fans were not deterred by uniformly scathing reviews and poor word-of-mouth. They waited in blocks-long lines to see the film because it was the first *Star Trek* in ten years. Next time—and there would indeed be a next time, given the size of the waiting audience, which overwhelmed the studio's loftiest estimates—they would not be so forgiving. The goods would have to be on the screen. Getting them there, however, would be someone else's job.

Producer Harve Bennett had been on the Paramount lot only one week when he was called to a meeting in Barry Diller's office. Hired by the studio's television division because of his extraordinary series batting average—*The Six-Million-Dollar Man*, *The Bionic Woman*, *Mod Squad*, and *Rich Man, Poor Man* —he had no reason to believe that the meeting was to be anything other than a debriefing. Walking into the luxurious suite, he immediately recognized Diller, who'd long ago been his assistant at ABC; Eisner, with whom he'd worked at the same network; and Paramount television chief Gary Nardino, who'd hired him. He did not recognize the elderly gentleman occupying the principal chair. "This is Charles Bluhdorn," Diller said. Bennett was flabbergasted. He knew of the self-made chairman of Gulf & Western and, like many, considered him a legend.

"Sit down," Bluhdorn said. "What did you think of *Star Trek, the movie?*"

Bennett understood immediately that he was being interviewed to produce the sequel. Producing feature films had long been his career goal, but forks in the road and, ironically, success had kept him from pursuing it. His mind began racing, remembering that while watching *Star Trek: The Motion Picture* his two children had gotten up from their seats half a dozen times for trips to the lavatory and candy counter. Should he tell the truth, or fudge a little, not knowing who in the room might be offended by candor? "Well," he said, "I thought it was boring."

"You see, by you bald is sexy," Bluhdorn said to Eisner, referring to the actress Persis Khambatta, whose head had been shaved to portray the Deltan Ilia in the film. He turned back to Bennett. "Can you make a better movie?"

"Oh, yes," Bennett said. "Yes. I can certainly make a better movie."

"Can you make it for less than forty-five fucking million dollars?"

"Mr. Bluhdorn—"

"Call me Charlie."

"Charlie, where I come from I could make five or six movies for that."

"Fine, do it."

It was a measure of how synonymous Gene Roddenberry had become with *Star Trek* that *The Motion Picture* had been "a Gene Roddenberry Production." At the time, that titular honor was usu-

ally granted only to successful or bankable producers; Roddenberry had been associated with a single success—and that on television. Even more telling, his credit had appeared ahead of "a Robert
Wise film," Wise being a four-time Academy Award winner (the
director and producer of both *West Side Story* and *The Sound of
Music*). This was strictly a matter of marketing. "It's not *Star Trek*
unless I say it's *Star Trek*," Roddenberry often said, his declaration
establishing hegemony then and forever over the domain. "Paramount was scared to death that Gene would go out and tell all the
Star Trek fans that they're making a terrible movie, that they've
taken *Star Trek* away from him; that if they had any love for *Star
Trek*, they wouldn't go see the film," Povill says. "That was Paramount's great fear." And it was the reason that on the as yet unwritten sequel to *The Motion Picture*, Roddenberry would assume the
new title of "executive consultant." For a fee comparable to his
producer's salary on the first film—and a percentage of the net
profits—he would be expected to offer opinions along the way and
then grant his imprimatur, thus keeping the fans engaged; this was
the origin of the creator emeritus title. But essentially, his new job
was not all that different from (the way he handled) his old job.

"When I received the assignment," Bennett recalls, "I asked,
'What is Roddenberry's part in this?' The answer from Eisner and
Diller was, 'We are paying him to be a consultant.' Then I asked if
that meant I had to report to him. The answer: 'Absolutely not. Just
consult with him; give him that to do.' That is all I was told."

Bennett had never seen *Star Trek* on television. After screening
all seventy-nine *Star Trek* episodes in preparation, he came up with
the idea of mining the criminal Khan character played by Ricardo
Montalban in "Space Seed." Executive producer Bennett constructed a plot around Khan's unexpected rescue from exile and
subsequent all-consuming revenge: He has to kill Kirk, no matter
what the price to himself. When Bennett committed enough of
the story to paper, he suggested to Roddenberry that they meet
to talk.

"No, no," Roddenberry said, "I'll put my comments in writing."

For the next ten years in which Bennett produced four *Star

Trek films, the only substantive communications between Roddenberry and Bennett took place in memos. Roddenberry's memos to Bennett were frequently damning and occasionally vicious; having been removed from the bridge of his starship, he considered the new commander to have taken power through mutiny. "Gene cast me immediately as an interloper," Bennett says. "There wasn't a single issue in the four feature pictures of which I was the producer and frequently the writer that was not resisted in memo by Gene." Any change or innovation that deviated from the template in Roddenberry's head was challenged, even vilified. In the second film, he complained about the death of Spock; in the third film he criticized the destruction of the *Enterprise*; the fourth, he declared, was "not good science."

"It was clear to me," Roddenberry said, "that bit by bit they were trying to take out the important things in *Star Trek*. Whenever you have a hit of any kind, there are always people who want to change it and make it their hit. They felt that by changing *Star Trek* sufficiently into their own image of what science fiction should be, then they would be the 'Gene Roddenberry' of the future. I didn't ever think it was impossible that they would become that person, except lack of talent for science fiction. If someone had come along and made *Star Trek* better, I would have been caught in a trap. But I would have liked the fact that *Star Trek* got better. But it never did. It got worse."[10]

Roddenberry's memos to Bennett reflected that contempt. Meanwhile, word got back to Bennett through the grapevine that Roddenberry was leaking his ridicule to the fanzines. Yet whenever Bennett saw Roddenberry in person—generally in the parking lot, occasionally on the street or at a rare studio event—Roddenberry was cordial and warm. "Never face-to-face did he say any of the things that he would write in memos," Bennett recalls. "Gene could be a very pleasant person passing you in the parking lot." Bennett thought it was schizophrenic. He didn't see the method behind Roddenberry's behavior.

For Roddenberry, who suffered an almost phobic aversion to confrontations, and whose image was that of an evolved pacifist, the memos provided deep cover. Their shelter allowed him to play the old cop game of good Gene–bad Gene. The bad Gene of the memos did his dirty work, the good Gene of the flesh and blood was to be loved and adored. "It was in the memo that Gene made money," Bennett says, "and it was in person that he made friends, or ingratiated himself, or became the idol."

The bifurcation of good Gene and bad Gene had existed long before Harve Bennett came on the scene. One of the most obvious facts of Roddenberry's life was that nearly everyone who worked with him regularly in a creative capacity on any incarnation of *Star Trek* eventually disliked or distrusted him. Meanwhile, Roddenberry's friends such as Christopher Knopf, Sam Rolfe, and E. Jack Neuman, all unassociated with *Star Trek*, express admiration for him as a warm and intelligent companion.

"Gene never developed a sense of his importance," Knopf asserts. "He may have known he was very important, but he never conveyed, 'I am the oracle.' I never felt that he was egotistical; never for a second. He was always interested in what you were doing. He was a dear, sweet man."

To Neuman, Roddenberry was supremely self-effacing, not the self-aggrandizer that he became in relation to *Star Trek*. "I never heard Gene boast about anything he did or achieved," he says.

Rolfe, likewise, reflects on his friend's memory with fondness, even after discovering that Roddenberry claimed to have been head writer and co-creator of *Have Gun, Will Travel*. "That was Gene," he laughs.

The three writers, however, were noncombatants in the *Star Trek* wars. They were civilians, and in their company he was off duty.

Early in *Star Trek II*'s story development, Bennett sent an outline to Eisner and circulated copies to the seven other people required by protocol; Roddenberry stood at the top of the copy list. The story's key event was the death of Spock, which Bennett intended to effect in a surprise at the end of act one, the way star Janet Leigh was killed forty minutes into *Psycho*. "I wanted to do it so suddenly that it took your breath away," Bennett says.

In a memo, Roddenberry objected vehemently. By agreement, Bennett was required to consider Roddenberry's thoughts in good faith and reply to them, but not necessarily to incorporate them. "He had a lot of constructive thoughts," Bennett remembers. "I would estimate that about twenty percent of the points that he made were included in some form in the next step, the next outline, or the next script draft. A lot of the stuff I took very seriously; I took it with the respect of a student to a teacher. He was the creator of *Star Trek*. He knew the characters. So I would take his comments when he said that Spock or Kirk would never say such and such." Responding to Roddenberry's protest, Bennett explained why he believed Spock's death would increase the film's entertainment value, and yet not be a violation of the fan's trust.

Three weeks after the outline's distribution, Paramount received a barrage of letters, all saying in one way or another, "Don't kill Spock." (Were it not for that profoundly dramatic moment of the character's death, Leonard Nimoy would not have returned to *Star Trek*. He had already announced his disinterest in continuing when, one night over coffee, Bennett asked him, "How would you like to have a great death scene?" Nimoy looked up and said, "Fascinating.") In another memo, Roddenberry referenced the outcry to bolster his continuing objection. Bennett replied that the death of Spock was an important dramatic moment, and that the fans ought not to be in a position to determine the film's creative course.

Roddenberry perceived the fans as his allies; Bennett knew it, Paramount executives knew it, and Roddenberry knew that they knew it. Through computer networks, conventions, and fanzines, he was tied to the vast and ever-growing fan universe, and was not hesitant to wield his influence to his advantage. He'd made clear that he thought Spock's death was a betrayal and would prove harmful to the franchise. Studio executives feared Roddenberry would withdraw his imprimatur and trigger an official or unofficial boycott. In several meetings, the fans' potential reaction was noted, and for a time it appeared that they would have the last word. Bennett fought for the film he wanted to make and was ultimately backed by the studio. He had, after all, been given a mandate by

Charles Bluhdorn. But now that Spock's death would no longer be the *Psycho*-like surprise that Bennett had anticipated, the big moment was moved to the climax. The question was, How did so many fans find out about the proposed plot point? With eight people receiving the memo, each of them connected to several others, there was a staggering number of possible leakers.

Before the film opened in 1982, Bennett attended his first *Star Trek* convention. Wandering the convention floor, he happened upon a Lincoln Enterprises booth and saw a copy of his original outline—"My typewriter, my misspellings," he says—being sold for $50. Still, this was not conclusive evidence that Roddenberry had been the one filling the grapevine with rumors and inciting the legions to riot.

Both critically and commercially, *Star Trek II: The Wrath of Khan* (directed by Nicholas Meyer from a screenplay by Jack B. Sowards of a story by Harve Bennett and Sowards) was a success. Its failure would have almost certainly ended the films instead of creating a feature series, the popularity of which engendered television's *The Next Generation*. Yet until 1987, when in an otherwise critical memo about *Star Trek V* he included an offhanded line of gratitude "for the things you have done...to realize the highly valuable *Star Trek* property we have," Roddenberry never offered Bennett praise or thanks for in essence resurrecting *Star Trek*.[11]

While scripting *Star Trek III*, Bennett dutifully copied Roddenberry on all drafts, which included from the beginning the dramatic destruction of the *Enterprise*. Even though Kirk effected the starship's suicide to foil the Klingons in a highly dramatic moment comparable to the death of Spock, Roddenberry complained—and soon fans began protesting. This time, the connection between complaints and protests would be established.

To prevent the type of leaks that had plagued the previous film, Bennett had instituted security measures—at the studio, in the special effects houses, and with all editorial matter. To protect the scripts and outlines, executive producer Ralph Winter devised a system that secretly differentiated distributed copies so that each bore a single distinguishing feature. If on page 5 the word "five" appeared somewhere in context, then that was considered copy number five. A copy of a script surfacing with five on page 5 could be traced to the person listed as having received script five. That is exactly what happened when a fan appeared in Bennett's office one day holding an early draft of the script. "I thought you might want to see this," the fan told Bennett. "It's on the street. It probably explains why you're getting all that mail."

Bennett searched for the clue and matched the number to his master distribution list. It had been Roddenberry's copy. Now Bennett understood that there would never be a chance to surprise any audience, even in previews—and nothing could be done about it. By leaking the script Roddenberry had violated no statutes, not even a contract clause. This was the way it was going to be: Roddenberry would try to invoke democracy in the creative process by stuffing fans into the ballot box. But all their votes didn't equal Paramount's support for Bennett. At the denouement of *Star Trek III*—before the climax of the reborn Spock coming to his senses—Kirk initiates the starship's self-destruct sequence. "I thought it was a foolish piece of waste," Roddenberry noted after the film's release. "I don't know what they gained by losing the *Enterprise*, other than a moment in a film. The *Enterprise* was really one of our continuing characters."[12]

In Roddenberry's earliest memos to Bennett he reiterated the idea that in the twenty-third century human nature will have evolved and conflicts between peoples eliminated, that *Star Trek* is about the inner turmoil of coping with the infinite, that *Star Trek* represents the ideal. Bennett thought those were lovely thoughts but, after extrapolating the messages of seventy-nine episodes, not entirely valid. He pointed out to Roddenberry that the series environment had been inarguably paramilitary: the *Enterprise* is a ship at sea bearing weapons and shields; even when they aren't used their presence indicates potential hostilities. Despite long periods of peace, the Indians—that is, the Klingons and any other unfriendly tribes discovered in deep space—act up from time to time and have to be subdued, through fistfights and phaser fights, as well as more destructive and ingenious means. Further, in three hundred years or three thousand years, the *Enterprise* crew would still be human beings who react to the same drives people do today—or else they'll all have become like Spock. (Roddenberry himself had inadvertently ratified this view in an interview several years before. *Star Wars*, he said, "was not about humanity. *Star Wars*...is really a fantasy about princesses and kingdoms and knights and things in another galaxy. *Star Trek*, on the other hand, is about humanity, about us, about our children's children.")[13] Roddenberry returned the memo with one suggesting that Bennett had missed the point, which was that in the twenty-third century human nature will have achieved higher strata of consciousness. To that Bennett wrote, "Dear Gene, With all respect I believe that technologically the world will change considerably in the next three hundred years. But I believe that since human nature has not changed in the last four thousand years, it is unlikely to change in the near term."

Optimism was the tent pole of Roddenberry's philosophy. "Gene was truly an optimistic man," Christopher Knopf says. "I never heard a negative from him, not about anything. He always had a twinkle in his eye." But the show itself, as Bennett argued, often ignored the mandate for drama's sake.

Mindful of the gulf between him and Bennett on this issue, Roddenberry repeated the edict in virtually every memo. "He thought I was trying to do a revisionist *Star Trek*," Bennett says, "whereas I perceived it as trying to replicate what had worked in the show, and thereby pay homage to the founder."

One of the first Roddenberry memos Bennett had read was a push for the second film to be a time travel story—as, Roddenberry insisted, *Star Trek: The Motion Picture* should have been. Alluding to the popularity of "City on the Edge of Forever," he'd outlined a convoluted plot about Kirk and Spock returning to 1963 in order to prevent the assassination of John F. Kennedy. Bennett had responded at the time that the drama of the premise is inescapably undermined by the audience knowing from the get-go that the heroes can't and won't succeed. Roddenberry interpreted the rebuff as a repudiation of all time travel stories.

A good time travel story surfaced nearly half a dozen years later, when Bennett and Nimoy devised *Star Trek IV: The Voyage Home*, in which the *Enterprise* saves twenty-third century earth from destruction by rescuing two humpback whales from present-day San Francisco and transporting them to the future. After reading the proposed outline, Roddenberry noted that he'd been advocating time travel stories since day one, and trotted out the assassination treatment with the directive that it was the tale that deserved to be told.

Directed by Leonard Nimoy, *Star Trek IV: The Voyage Home* concluded the trilogy that had begun with the second film—number three picking up where number two ended, number four starting with the last scene of number three. It was the most popular of the six feature films, at least in terms of box-office receipts, and, not surprisingly, it's the one for which Roddenberry claimed the most credit. "I was still smarting from *Star Trek III*, which I did not consider a great job, nor is it rated with the fans as a great job," Roddenberry recalled. "All my memos on this said, 'Okay. This is an opportunity to do the *Star Trek* we know, to do the *Star Trek* characters we know—to make them strong. Let's bring back the television format.' And *Star Trek IV* was, I believe, the result of that effort. I even forced them into time travel, which the studio front office had, in their wisdom, objected to time and again. I met with Harve and Leonard from the first, because I was determined to bring back the *Star Trek* that I knew and that I thought worked. Unlike the previous ones, I was very involved in this film."[14] Bennett and Nimoy both say that Roddenberry was, if anything, less involved on *IV* than on the previous two films, and note that the "television format" had already been reestablished with *The Wrath of Khan*.

With the benefit of hindsight, Roddenberry claimed to have great prescience as a fortune-teller. "I think they didn't like time travel, which is odd, considering that years later their most successful movie was a time travel story which took place in *Star Trek IV*," he said three years after the film's release."[15]

If Roddenberry had had his way with the plot, *Star Trek IV* would likely have failed, both critically and commercially—and not just because the outcome would have been predictable. It is true, of course, that anyone watching *The Voyage Home* knows instinctively that Kirk, Spock, and the *Enterprise* will bring back the whales in time to save the earth, just as he knows that James Bond will somehow find a way out of peril, no matter how dire circumstances seem. The difference is that in the film Nimoy and Bennett made, Kirk and his crew were bound to succeed; in Roddenberry's version, which injected a grim note of historical realism, they'd have been bound to fail. And that, more than Spock's death or the destruction of the *Enterprise* in order to save the crew, would have violated the fans' faith in *Star Trek*'s optimism. Both Spock and the *Enterprise* were, after all, reborn. But even Bones McCoy couldn't have helped JFK.

Early in 1991, after he had turned over the producer's hat to his former associate Ralph Winter, Harve Bennett met with Gene Roddenberry for the final time. Bennett wanted Roddenberry to clarify the falsehoods and misconceptions he believed were contained in the galley proofs to a *Star Trek* coffee table book written by Roddenberry and Susan Sackett. (In the book, which remains unpublished because of legal entanglements, Roddenberry's quotes were to have stood out from everyone else's, in bold, just as in *The Making of Star Trek* his words had been printed in all caps.) Roddenberry, sitting behind his desk, said, "Yes, fine," to each of Bennett's points, and motioned to Sackett, who was taking notes, to effect the appropriate changes. At the conclusion of the meeting, Bennett rose to leave. Then he stopped. "Gene," he asked, "can I say something to you?"

"Sure," Roddenberry said.

"I've been a sharecropper in your plantation for almost ten years," Bennett said. "I've had a great time, but I'm leaving now. In ten years I have never, ever, said anything in public that would in any way distress you or reflect badly upon our relationship."

"That's true," Roddenberry agreed.

"I have listened to everything you had to say. I have honored you and respected you. I know how much money in profits I've put in my pocket and yours these ten years."

"Yes."

"Well, I have one request."

"What is it?"

"Just once, in a public place, would you just say that I've done a good job?"

"Of course," Roddenberry said. "But everyone already knows that."

"Everyone is not you. I really would love to see somewhere that Gene Roddenberry said Harve Bennett did a good job. As I leave, I would really like to feel that I was a member of the *Star Trek* family—and that only comes if you say so."

"Absolutely, of course," Roddenberry said.

To Bennett's knowledge, Roddenberry never uttered the magic words. The natural place for such a proclamation would have been the television special celebrating the twenty-fifth anniversary of *Star Trek*, in September 1991. But Bennett's name was not the only one missing amid all the glory handed out on that show.

CHAPTER TEN

The

Clothes

Have

No Emperor

O N AUGUST 7, 1986, one month shy of *Star Trek*'s twentieth anniversary—and weeks before his sixty-fifth birthday—Gene Roddenberry appeared on stage in a sold-out Los Angeles auditorium for a seminar sponsored by New York's Museum of Broadcasting. The subjects: *Star Trek* and Roddenberry, who a year before had been the first writer to receive a sidewalk star on the Hollywood Walk of Fame. There were the usual questions about Spock and his creator and the show's history, and the usual remarks about logic and network executives and what the future holds. Then someone in the audience asked about the possibility of reviving *Star Trek*.

"Our main actors would not do another television series," Roddenberry replied. "Television is twelve hours a day. Television is miserably hard work. I wouldn't produce a television series again myself. I had two daughters at that time—teenagers. And for four years I was never home. And these basic years of their lives I was never there. Fortunately, we're good friends now. But I have a twelve-year-old. The networks do not have enough money to get me to abandon my twelve-year-old in these key years of his life."

What did interest him, Roddenberry said, was not the resurrection of the old series but a sequel series "dealing with the new issues of the nineties."

His questioner rephrased Roddenberry's words into something a little pithier. "Sort of like, '*Star Trek*, The Next Generation,'" he said.

The title appeared to stick. Roddenberry nodded his head, glanced to the side, and rubbed his face quickly. If ever there was a new *Star Trek*, he went on, it wouldn't be a weekly series; producing one is the equivalent of turning out "half a motion picture" a week. "You should never ask a person to do that."

In early September, Paramount sponsored an extravagant twentieth-anniversary bash. Dozens of "A" list celebrities joined virtually anyone who'd ever had anything to do with *Star Trek*. The food, with an international theme, was delicious: Uhura's African, Scotty's Scotch, Sulu's Japanese, Chekov's Russian, and so on. It occurred to a number of the invited guests, including Robert Justman and David Gerrold, that something more than Paramount's largess and gratitude stood behind the lavishly opulent celebration of its number one cash cow.

They were right. Only a month later, on October 10, Paramount announced that, beginning in the fall of 1987, a new weekly *Star Trek* with all different cast members would appear in first-run syndication. (The studio was having difficulty selling product to the major networks, but its programs like *Entertainment Tonight* and *Solid Gold* were performing spectacularly in first-run syndication. Unlike dramatic shows sold to networks, which studios or production companies generally finance at a deficit to the network's license fee in the hope of scoring on the come, first-run syndicated hits can bring vast riches from the first—the way *Star Trek: The Next Generation* would.)

Named to create and produce the new series: Gene Roddenberry, who had just completed a treatment program for alcoholism at the Schick Shadel facility in Santa Barbara. Although Roddenberry's friends say his son gave him more joy than anything else in life, apparently there was enough at stake to entice him from Rod's side and overcome his dread of producing "half a motion picture" a week. He accepted $1 million as a bonus simply for signing the contract, which entitled him to a consequential salary as well. (He soon plunked down more than $100,000 on a Rolls-Royce but complained to staff members when Majel Barrett spent $35,000 on a Mercedes.)

Money, however, was only one of the several reasons for his decision—and perhaps the least of them. By 1986, his return as producer would not have been a strict bread-winning necessity. Classic *Trek* had been paying handsome profits (A.C. Nielsen rated *Star Trek* the number one syndicated show on television), and his fees and profits on the three motion pictures (number four, *The Voyage Home*, would be released that fall) were into or approaching seven figures, making the hundreds of thousands being generated annually by Lincoln Enterprises mere gravy. More likely, pride had become Roddenberry's prime motivation.

Until he affixed his signature to the contract, he had played the reluctant groom. "When Paramount came to me and said, 'Would you like to do a new *Star Trek*?' I said no," Roddenberry recalled. "I wanted no part of it."[1] But the record is unclear whether he initially declined Paramount's offer to "catch lightning in a bottle" for the second time or whether at the outset he was not invited to try.[2] The latter seems more likely, given the studio's initial commitment to film twenty-two episodes at a cost of $1.2 million each, which in sum was the budget of a major feature film, and Roddenberry's reputation as an undependable producer. With the experience of *Star Trek: The Motion Picture* still vivid in Paramount's corporate memory, he did not engender overwhelming confidence as the guarantor of an enormous investment. Studio executives respected his influence with the audience more than they did his creative skills. If that hadn't been true, they would have entrusted him with the creative side of the ledger on the feature films and hired a competent line producer to actualize his vision; or at least they would have compelled the films' producers to heed his suggestions.

Several months before heralding the show's return, the studio had hired writer-producer Gregory Strangis to oversee the *Star Trek* reincarnation. Working without fanfare or official announcement, he began devising characters—one of whom was a Klingon member of the Federation—and concepts for the series that was to take place about a century after the original show; Kirk and crew, he presumed, had long been dead. Not displeased with Strangis's preliminary efforts, Paramount may have tried to dissuade Roddenberry from returning to the new series. "They said, 'Maybe you shouldn't [try to catch lightning twice], because it's impossible,'" Roddenberry recounted, after the show was a hit. "My ears perked up over the word. Nothing's impossible. The hardest thing was to believe you could do it."[3]

Sensing Paramount's unexpressed preference that he not be aboard would have pushed Roddenberry to try to prove himself. "Gene had a certain amount of rightful outrage over people trying to exclude him from his mother-lode contribution to *Star Trek*," Adam Malin says. As the president of Creation Entertainment, Malin often hired Roddenberry to provide the keynote addresses at *Star Trek* conventions. "Gene felt he had to do it all over again, to show that it was him. Right on stage he said that if he did it a second time nobody would ever again say that it hadn't been him. He used far stronger words than those. He was plenty pissed off that history had so rapidly forgotten his contribution, and he was determined to do it again. He couldn't prove that he was the big kahuna of the *Star Trek* movies, because he was emasculated from having the producer's role. So he felt that by executive producing *Star Trek* again he would put the definitive Roddenberry imprint on *Star Trek*."

Roddenberry did not, in fact, enjoy the contractual right either to control *Star Trek*'s destiny or to demand the job of executive producer. Paramount could have insisted that he butt out; but the presumption was that Roddenberry controlled millions of viewers the new show needed to attract. Studio executives believed—and Roddenberry knew they believed—that a discouraging word would travel at warp speed through fandom and doom the series before its birth. Concerned already about producing the show without the original cast, Paramount didn't need anything else kindling its fears. That invisible fine print conferred all the rights Roddenberry cared to exercise; his leverage was in direct proportion to the amount of the proposed investment. "Paramount still owns the basic copyright on *Star Trek*," he explained in 1989 to an audience at a convention produced by Malin's company. "The reason that I have some say on *Star Trek* is that Paramount is a little afraid that all of you would commit revolution."[4]

When Roddenberry chose to enter, Strangis was shown the back door exit. A representative from the studio's business affairs department informed him that he was relieved of his duties because Roddenberry would be taking over. "It wasn't done as well or as kindly as it could have been," Strangis remembers.

"I think it's just as well for you that they didn't do the show they had in mind," Roddenberry told the same fan audience, recounting how he'd been enticed to return. "I saw [Strangis's] outline—the one they had in reserve in case I still said no. It was the U.S.S. *Enterprise* run by a group of space cadets. And in the outline, the principal word [sic] of dialogue I heard was, 'Gee, whiz.'"[5]

To elevate his importance at the expense of the work done by Strangis, Roddenberry appropriated for his use some of the circumstances that had just prompted Harve Bennett's departure from Paramount. Bennett had wanted the sixth *Star Trek* film to flash back in time, to when Kirk and Spock attended Starfleet Academy. But Roddenberry reviled the idea of "The First Adventure" and publicly compared it to the slapstick *Police Academy* films. Only he, he later claimed as his primary objection, had ever been able to create a successful *Star Trek* character. "That's not creating a character," Bennett says. "It's casting." With Roddenberry gathering fan support behind him, Paramount disregarded Bennett's four-film track record and asked him to find another subject for *Star Trek VI*. He left instead.

The outline Strangis had written centered on the Klingons and the Federation joining together, overcoming their mutual distrust, to battle a common enemy. "I was looking for conflicts and intrigues and fun," he says. "And gee whiz, I've never used 'gee whiz' in my life."

Now all Roddenberry had to do was create. "I lie on my back, staring at the ceiling," he said, describing the creative process.[6] (A year and a half later, he claimed to have an "Orwellian" fear: "that friends and associates will think I bed down at night and space out in my pajamas.")[7] Apparently, however, the ceiling held no answers. Four days after the series announcement he took David Gerrold to lunch. Gerrold congratulated him and asked what he was planning creatively.

"No, no, no, no, no," Roddenberry said. "Before I discuss my plans, I want to hear your vision of *Star Trek*. What would you do if you were creating it?"

For years Gerrold had been contemplating how he would improve *Star Trek* if ever it came back; his 1973 book *The World of Star Trek* had included several of his suggestions. "We start with an older, more thoughtful captain," he said. "He's the star, and he doesn't beam down. The mission team is headed by the first officer, who does beam down; this avoids that Kirk-Spock rivalry, where Spock became so important that Kirk was no longer fully in command of the ship. So we have two male leads, one who's a very thoughtful man, and one who's the action lead.

"Yeah, all right, we can do that," Roddenberry said.

Such brainstorming sessions followed for almost a week. Gerrold wasn't surprised that Roddenberry devoured his ideas so hungrily. Almost fifteen years earlier Roddenberry had admitted to him, "Every time I sit down at the typewriter, I feel like this is the time that they're going to find out I'm faking it." For that, and for the cordial relationship they'd shared since Gerrold had written "The Trouble with Tribbles" in 1967, he felt compassionately protective toward Roddenberry. On October 20, Roddenberry hired Gerrold on staff, apologetically paying him only $1,000 per week, far less than Writers Guild minimum for a staff writer. The first offer had been for $750. Gerrold had refused, taking the higher figure only when Roddenberry promised that after ten weeks, "I'll take care of you," which meant that Gerrold would be executive story consultant at a significantly higher salary. As a bone, his employment contract was backdated ten days, to the first lunch with Roddenberry. This may have been a far from magnanimous gesture, one possibly suggested by attorney Leonard Maizlish, the constant presence in the *Next Generation* offices who would soon be seen as Iago to Roddenberry's Othello: ownership of Gerrold's ideas before he was an employee might fall into a legal gray area.

What Gerrold didn't know at the time was that Roddenberry expected him to ghostwrite the series bible—that is, in some sense, to create the show.

Roddenberry had also asked two other former *Star Trek* staffers to the dance, Robert Justman and Edward Milkis. "He did it in usual Gene Roddenberry fashion," Justman remembers. "He called me up and said, 'Hey, Bob, I'm going to be running some science fiction films here at the studio, and maybe you'd like to come by and watch them with us and have some lunch.' I had already suspected, when I saw the Paramount people at the twentieth-anniversary party, that there was going to be a new show. So I knew what he meant. I think he wanted to feel me out first, to see if I was interested."

Justman and Roddenberry had maintained an agreeable relationship, seeing each other perhaps once a year. But in truth, except for their common working experiences (Justman had also produced *Planet Earth* for Roddenberry) and Justman's uncommon loyalty, there was little to hold Justman and Roddenberry together as friends. Justman and his wife, Jackie, often felt uncomfortable around the Roddenberrys, once picking up broad hints about partner switching. While Roddenberry was the quintessential scene-stealer, Justman remains modest and self-effacing, finding it painful to take rightful credit for his accomplishments and contributions. Not until his hiring on the new series as supervising producer did he gently confront Roddenberry on Roddenberry's implicit promise to bring him on board the production crew of the first *Star Trek* film; once the project had been given the go-ahead, Roddenberry never took and never returned any of Justman's calls. ("Gene never called me unless he wanted to find out if I was interested in working with him on a project," Justman explains. "It always worked the same way—always, on every project I worked with him. He'd call and say, 'I'd like to get together and have lunch next week.' He never once called me without purpose. So about the time I read that the film had been green-lighted, he called and asked me to lunch the following week. I said, 'Sure, Gene, I'd love to.'" But the following week Roddenberry didn't call. Nor would he accept Justman's repeated calls. Justman even had his agent try, to no avail.) "You broke my heart," Justman told him.

At that first screening the four men watched *Aliens*. Roddenberry was particularly drawn to the gutsy female Marine character, Vasquez, who near the end blows up herself and her partner, taking several aliens with them. Roddenberry included in his eight-page preliminary series bible a character based on Vasquez, Macha Hernandez. Also included in the bible, which was shorter on ideas than on inconsistencies, were some typically Roddenberrian touches, such as the character of Lieutenant Commander Troi, "a four-breasted, oversexed hermaphrodite," and a Yodaish midget named Wesley Crusher. Roddenberry knew that his conception of the series was far from complete, and with Paramount pressuring him to devise the first draft of a bible so that everyone could see where at least $25 million was going, he turned to his team.

Though Justman was brought aboard primarily for his production skills, he, like Gerrold, hit the ground in a sprint, turning out reams of memos with ideas for the as yet untitled new *Star Trek*. He suggested that the twenty-fourth-century *Enterprise* have children aboard; that the ship employ "an android, programmed by Starfleet Command with all of the familiar abilities and characteristics of Spock fused with the leadership and humanistic qualities of Captain Kirk"; and that there be something aboard the *Enterprise* called a "holodeck," where crew members go for recreation to experience virtual reality. He conceived of and wrote several back stories to explain the characters. Despite Roddenberry's insistence that there be no Klingons, Justman proposed bringing aboard a Klingon who was loyal to the Federation. "Including a Klingon," Roddenberry later bragged, "was a tip of the hat to my belief that humanity's progress is constant."[8] (Justman later conceived of the visuals for the main title sequence.)

Gerrold wrote dozens of memos on all aspects of the show, both philosophical and practical. He suggested "some kind of additional makeup effects for the android crew member—a golden shade for his skin, for example," a new stardate computation formula, a new warp speed computation; that the structure of the show avoid classic *Trek*'s Kirk-Spock-McCoy dominating troika; that the apparent movement of the stars in relation to the *Enterprise* be more scientifically accurate; that the starship's captain be a woman, and that there be a chaplainlike character whose job is to tend to the crewmen's interior life.

Even before Roddenberry had first met with Gerrold, he and Majel Barrett had taken Dorother Fontana to dinner at a Century City restaurant. He'd solicited Fontana's opinions on the new series and, satisfied with her responses, indicated that she would soon become an integral member of the team. Until there was a permanent place for her, he'd said, he would be interested in her reactions to all in-house memos, copies of which would be sent to her home. Fontana had agreed to the arrangement, hoping that it wouldn't be unpaid for long, and she, too, soon began commenting on the material. Among her memos was the suggestion to change Captain Picard's first name from Julien, which had been bestowed by Roddenberry; one of her recommendations was Jean-Luc. Not surprisingly, Fontana took particular exception to Roddenberry's four-breasted woman. "I really hate Lieutenant Commander Troi," she wrote. "I honestly believe you will offend most women, and maybe a lot of men with this character. Besides, how are you going to arrange those four provocatively shaped breasts? Four in a row? They had better be small. Two banks of two? Do you know how much trouble women have with the normal number—keeping them out of the way of things, I mean. Four straight up and down? Don't be silly!"[9]

Fontana's, Gerrold's, and Justman's idea output contrasted sharply with Roddenberry's; after years away from series work, Justman says, Roddenberry experienced difficulty in getting up to speed. Contributing few memos of his own, he culled ideas from those sent to him and, in editorial meetings, directed Gerrold to include them in the bible that would bear the Roddenberry byline. "I don't know any other way to do a series this complex," he later said. "You have to have one point of view; you can't put it together by committee."[10]

Roddenberry well may have believed that the act of culling

entitled him to be copyright holder on any *Star Trek* idea. A case in point is his memo to Gerrold dated October 29. "Let's build into a series regular the handicap of blindness," he wrote. "This crew member wears a prosthetic device which gives only fair normal eyesight but results in powerful telescopic and microscopic vision." His wording sounds as if the idea had sprung from his own brain, but in fact, two days before Gerrold had sent him a memo headlined "Handicapped Crew Member." Among the possible handicaps Gerrold had cited was "blindness—compensated by some kind of electronic eye which gives our crew member augmented vision. Perhaps he/she can see well into the infrared or the ultraviolet, as well as telescopic and microscopic focusing."

Roddenberry's memo also proposed having children aboard the Enterprise. "Let's settle for now on a starship feature designed to give our crewmen (crewpersons?) the most normal possible lives and the kind of emotional stability that makes for the soundest possible kind of professional decisions and conduct. That feature is a starship capable of providing our characters with the essential of both community and family life, the latter complete with children if desired. No, we do not have children under foot in starship operational areas, but we do have large areas of the vessel given over to home life, recreation, entertainment, schooling and etc."

Again, Roddenberry omitted any reference to Robert Justman's memo of twelve days earlier, which had entertained the same suggestion. "To expect people to leave everyone and everything they hold most dear for such a long journey is, I think, unconscionable," Justman had written. "Why should our *Enterprise* crew be denied the opportunity to live a full and rewarding life? Therefore, I propose that we have men, women, and children on board throughout the whole new series. There would be births, deaths, marriages, divorces, etc.... What we would have then is, indeed, '*Wagon Train* to the Stars.'"

For eight weeks Gerrold composed and assembled the bible. He would write several pages, present them to Roddenberry, and receive them back with comments scribbled in pencil. Roddenberry would say, "Tell me about the characters." Gerrold would respond, "No, Gene, it's your show. You tell *me* about the characters." "No," Roddenberry would respond, "you tell me what you want." When bible pages were discussed in meetings with Justman and Milkis, Roddenberry presented them as his own work. One time Gerrold offered input and was chastised by Roddenberry. "A captain shouldn't speak," he said, "when he's in a roomful of colonels." He called Gerrold frequently with instructions to write sections on the difference between science fiction and fantasy, on the kinds of stories that could never be considered; and to include a glossary of scientific terms. Making the necessary changes and inclusions on his own computer, Gerrold kept the only disk copy of the bible, from the first to the last draft.

The byline, however, was Gene Roddenberry's; Gerrold typed it himself, acting on instructions. He soon discovered that Majel Barrett planned to sell photocopies to fans, through Lincoln Enterprises, at $10 each. In essence, Gerrold believed, Roddenberry was paying him to produce a popular souvenir item (tens of thousands had been sold from the original series).

With the bible completed and no "creative" producer à la Gene Coon yet on staff, Roddenberry assigned Gerrold to begin screening writers and stories. Gerrold wasn't being paid as a story editor, and he performed his duties hesitantly, anticipating his upcoming contract renewal. But at the end of December, he wasn't offered either story editorship or the promised job of executive story consultant. "Take it or leave it," Roddenberry said of the offer to be a staff writer for twenty weeks at a Writers Guild minimum of $1,547 per week. Disappointed and insulted, Gerrold countered with a higher figure, to which Roddenberry reiterated in the name of their friendship his pledge to "take care of you later on."

Then Roddenberry pulled out his big gun, the one he'd already used several times on Gerrold over the ten weeks. He claimed that Paramount had been unfamiliar with his work and hadn't wanted him on staff, that he'd fought valiantly to get him this far, and that it was up to Gerrold to earn the studio's full faith; doing so, he estimated, would take at least a year. Gerrold did not contest Roddenberry's allegation, though it seemed unlikely to him that Paramount should not know that he was the author of "The Trouble with Tribbles," one of the most popular episodes of the original series, and, from the studio's perspective, one of the best-selling videocassettes. He did, however, note that at the age of forty-three, he was the same age as Roddenberry when he created *Star Trek,* but instead of being a neophyte as Roddenberry had been, Gerrold had twenty science fiction novels and twenty years of television experience.

Star Trek: The Next Generation received its title in late November, but the series format had not yet been finalized when Robert Lewin met with Roddenberry in January for consideration as creative producer. The two had known each other at Desilu, Lewin having written for *Mission: Impossible,* and talked about old friends in common. Then Roddenberry explained that he wanted the show to be set in the twenty-fourth century and asked if Lewin, the producer of such show's as *The Man From Atlantis* and *The Paper Chase,* had ever written or produced science fiction. Lewin said that he hadn't but was interested in the subject, and suggested that he be allowed to noodle for a while. A week later he returned to describe his Henri Rousseau–like vision of life in the twenty-fourth century: All wild animals, he told Roddenberry, will be domesticated. "They don't prey on each other. They're fed by civilized people. They have a diet and are allowed to roam free. In Central Park the elephants and lions and deer just wander around. There are no real race distinctions. And all buying is done on credit. It's four hundred years from now. We've got to have learned a lot. Everything is controlled, but there's a lot of freedom."

The specifics of Lewin's postulation may not have been enacted directly into the series, but Roddenberry obviously believed that he'd found a philosophically kindred spirit. "When can you start?" he asked.

When Lewin began the first week in February, he worked closely with Gerrold and Fontana. Gerrold had accepted Roddenberry's promise that he could contribute scripts, while Fontana was technically not even on staff. In late November she had been asked to meet with Roddenberry, Justman, and Edward Milkis, the supervising producer. At the meeting she'd pitched four story ideas, all of them met with enthusiasm. Apologizing that she wasn't yet on staff, Roddenberry then told her to start thinking about a story for the pilot episode to take place on a staging planet. Fontana had consented, but before leaving she made clear her wish to be named an associate producer–staff writer at the first opportunity. Continuing to read, comment on, and write memos, she'd begun work on the pilot story, for which she received the green light to script near the end of January. All during that time she and Gerrold had met, at Roddenberry's request, with other writers to hear story pitches and develop them into assignments.

Roddenberry instructed Lewin to use Fontana as his story editor. She didn't know that, nor did Lewin realize that Fontana was not a staffer until after almost a month he happened to mention that his contract wasn't yet finalized. "I don't have one at all," Fontana replied. Lewin went directly to Roddenberry and tendered an ultimatum that he name her story editor.

"Because she'd once been his secretary," Lewin says, "he always treated her like one. He expected gratitude and devotion and unlimited respect and admiration." (At a *Star Trek* convention in 1989, Roddenberry was asked about Fontana. "She started out as my personal secretary," he said. "It was the second season. I called her into my office. I said, 'Dorothy, you are now story editor. You're going from $178 dollars a week to one thousand.' She cried. She was apparently frightened of the show."[11] In fact, Fontana had resigned as Roddenberry's secretary in the fall of the first season to pursue her free-lance writing career, and was made the show's story editor soon after completing the script for "This Side of Paradise." As a secretary, her base salary had been $300 a week, though she usually earned significantly more because of overtime.)

Only then did Roddenberry begin to negotiate for Fontana's services as a staff writer. His first offer was below Writers Guild minimum, as it had been with Gerrold. Fontana refused. The next offer, though higher, was also under Guild minimums for staff writers "with additional capacities." She refused again. Then Leonard Maizlish became involved. A lawyer with a reputation as a legal piranha, Maizlish had begun showing up daily in an unexplained capacity. His salary, if any, was not coming out of Paramount's pocket. Playing the part of Roddenberry's factotum, he appeared to serve no other clients; Roddenberry and Roddenberry's interest in the show were his only concerns. And by all accounts, his presence was appreciated only by Roddenberry. To everyone else he represented bad news. If you saw Maizlish coming, you knew he had something to say you didn't want to hear. Good news, Roddenberry would have given himself. Both men would lay any blame on the studio executives; it was *their* fault for this or that. Of course, the excuse contradicted Roddenberry's frequent crow that Paramount had wanted him back so badly that he'd received complete and total autonomy.

Maizlish sat down in Fontana's office. He asked why she'd refused to accept either "excellent" offer. Fontana replied that both offers fell below her guild's minimum pay for the duties she'd be performing—nor did either of them demonstrate the sort of retroactive generosity she'd been led to expect ("We'll make it up to you...") after working for two months. The third offer for $3,000 a week, presented by Paramount as the final offer, after she threatened to file a complaint with the Writers Guild if she received another insulting offer, was accepted. She received the title of associate producer but was prevented from performing any production tasks, essentially making her the show's executive story editor—a job worth far more than she was earning. She, like Gerrold, never received an assigned parking space, the only staff members not to.

Gerrold sensed that Maizlish brought out the worst in Roddenberry. He noticed it in his own treatment as soon as Maizlish came on the scene. Roddenberry called Gerrold disloyal and a "loose cannon" for disagreeing with him. Behind Gerrold's back, Roddenberry frequently spoke disparagingly of Gerrold, complaining to other staff members that he was "disruptive"; the staff members had seen no evidence of that. "Let me explain it to you in terms of a dog pack," Roddenberry told them. "The biggest dog is in charge of all the others, and I'm the biggest dog here." He claimed that the studio wanted to fire Gerrold, but that he'd interceded; and that Gerrold didn't understand science fiction. Though Gerrold had been in virtually every story conference—more, even, than Roddenberry—Roddenberry refused to grant him a script assignment for two stories other staff members had liked. On the verge of tears because of one particularly abusive tirade questioning his skills as a "team player," Gerrold pushed back. He said that he resented being a so-called partner for three months who'd been excluded from the fun part—writing scripts—after doing the grunt work, and accused the Great Bird of the Galaxy of doing something distinctly un-Bird-like: breaking his promise. Perhaps stunned by the anger, Roddenberry initiated a deal memo that afternoon for Gerrold's "Blood and Fire," an AIDS allegory about which the writer felt passionately.

After only a week of work, Gerrold was ordered off the script and onto the second draft of the bible, one to be more fully developed than the fifty-page original version he'd put together. "I'll work with you closely on this one," Roddenberry said. "It's very important, much more important than your script right now." Reluctantly, Gerrold expanded the bible with Roddenberry's input. But while looking through a Writers Guild manual he discovered that the writers of series bibles are entitled to additional remuneration. He raised the subject with Maizlish, who retorted that writing the bible was the job he'd been hired to do and suggested that if he reiterated his complaint in the future, he'd be fired.

There was Roddenberry and Fontana and Milkis and Justman. Only John D. F. Black, *Star Trek*'s first editor, was missing from the original crew. Justman called him to come in and pitch. Black went, though he didn't have any stories in mind. He had only one science fiction idea and had been saving it for the proper moment to write it as a feature film. Just tell us what it is, the writing staff pleaded. He did. The story would take place on a planet that looks similar to Earth with one obvious exception: There's no crime—not in the cities, not in the countryside. The *Enterprise* crew eventually discovers that every so often the planet's leaders meet and, by random selection, identify one area or city in which every transgression —from jaywalking to removing mattress tags—becomes a capital crime; the offender is summarily shot. And because the populace never knows which city is being targeted at any given time, everyone is always on best behavior.

Justman fell in love with the idea and knew Roddenberry would do the same. Black retold it to Roddenberry, who said he just had to have it—had to! A week or so later, Black delivered the story treatment, and in a few more days returned to hear Roddenberry's notes. He sat in Roddenberry's office with pen and paper, writing down Roddenberry's objections and observations, then went home and back to work. After turning in version two he found himself again in Roddenberry's office, listening this time to comments that not only seemed to have nothing to do with the story but were delivered with accelerating vehemence. "Oh, by the way," Roddenberry said suddenly, in the midst of what had become a tirade, "we desperately need a bottle show, so I'm doing 'Naked Time.'" (A "bottle" show saves production money, because all the scenes take place on already existing sets with few, if any, additional actors. "The Naked Time" was Black's first *Star Trek* script.)

"What do you mean you're 'doing' 'Naked Time'?" Black asked.

"I'm ripping it off," Roddenberry clarified. "You don't mind, do you?"

"What the hell can I do about it?"

"Nothing."

When Black left (he learned the next day that his "Justice" script had been given to another writer, Worley Thorne) Roddenberry asked Fontana into his office and mentioned that he'd begun a script idea called "The Naked Now," inspired by Black's twenty-year-old story. He handed her a 750-word synopsis and the first ten script pages. Being up to his elbows, he said, he didn't have the necessary free time to finish the job, would she be interested?

Fontana had begun work on the pilot script, "Encounter at Farpoint," in early December, turning in the first draft outline a month later and the revised outline two weeks after that. Then she started the first draft script, all the while continuing with her still unpaid services as story editor without portfolio. What had complicated the scriptwriting were ongoing discussions with Roddenberry over whether the material was to fill two hours, one and a half hours, or a single hour; the length changed on a weekly basis because, he said, no one had yet determined whether the pilot episode would include a "history of *Star Trek* section" along with a behind-the-scenes look into the *Star Trek* world, or whether the story itself would suffice. (John Pike, head of Paramount domestic television, had pushed for an hour. Roddenberry and he had an ongoing dispute over the show's length.) At last Roddenberry and Maizlish had instructed her to write a ninety-minute script that would be tacked on to the thirty-minute "prequel" Roddenberry planned to write. By mid-March she had turned in her second 90-page draft of "Encounter at Farpoint" and agreed to contract terms a few days later. Yes, she told Roddenberry, she was indeed interested in developing Roddenberry's adaptation of Black's story into "The Naked Now."

Finding Roddenberry's material lacking in substance, she informed him that she would develop her own story from the premise. Though he agreed with her plans, Roddenberry initiated a deal memo that named him and Fontana as the script's co-writers, with Fontana to receive sixty to ninety percent of the script monies; he contended that he'd already written "the first part." She protested to producer Bob Lewin that this arrangement had not been her understanding, and that if she was not to receive the full story and script assignments then she would decline the assignment. Lewin promised to inquire.

Three days later, right before a staff meeting and luncheon,

Maizlish called Fontana into an unoccupied office. There was a problem, he said: Paramount wanted Roddenberry to write "The Naked Now," but that with his approaching deadline on the "Farpoint" prequel and all the other tasks necessary to the start of production, there wasn't enough time to do everything. Fontana replied that she would gladly withdraw from "The Naked Now" assignment and devise her own original material for the show.

"No, you don't understand," Maizlish said. "Gene's problem is that he needs the script written because Paramount wants a Roddenberry script."

"Well," Fontana said, beginning to suspect his ulterior motive, "if Paramount wants a Roddenberry script, then they certainly don't want a Fontana script." She reiterated the solution: that Roddenberry should write "The Naked Now," and that she would come up with new stories. When Maizlish began again to state his solution, she interrupted him. Under no circumstances, she said, would she write a first draft outline, a second draft outline, and two complete scripts for half the money, half the credit, and half the residuals.

The next day Roddenberry called Fontana into his office. He repeated what Maizlish had told her, and she repeated her position. "If Paramount is so hot to get a Roddenberry script," she said, "then you should certainly write it, Gene."

"Now I know what kind of friend you are," Roddenberry bellowed, his tone choked with hurt and astonishment. This was Shakespearean tragedy on a real stage. Act one: King Lear is surprised that his daughter doesn't love him the way he believes she should. Fontana wasn't a "team player," he said. "I went to the mat for you to get you the associate producer credit. Paramount didn't want you, and [associate producer] Eddie Milkis threatened to walk if I gave it to you. But I did it, and this is how you repay me."

The explanation was new to Fontana, but it didn't change her position. She said she was sorry that he didn't approve, and expressed surprise that she should have to remind him that the Writers Guild, of which he was always claiming charter membership, considered such arrangements unethical and illegal.

Roddenberry persisted. At last Fontana suggested that she write the script for full price. Inasmuch as Roddenberry was the show's executive producer, he could rewrite her work to his liking. The two versions would then be submitted to the Writers Guild arbitration board. Take it or leave it. He took. (The WGA arbitration committe gave teleplay credit to Fontana, with story credit to Black and Fontana.)

Fontana asked Milkis whether he had issued an ultimatum over her receiving the title associate producer. He had not been happy about it, he admitted, but had not threatened to resign. Then she approached Rick Berman, the show's co-supervising producer, who had come from the studio's executive ranks and was there as Paramount's guarantor. No, Berman said, "at no time" did the studio demand a Roddenberry script.

As punishment, apparently, Fontana's office was moved into a cramped space outside of which was a large generator that pounded and roared all day; entry was through a heavily traveled corridor that housed photocopiers and other office machines; a busy—and noisy—elevator was next door. "Gene's anger at Dorothy really got to the point where it was cruel," Bob Lewin says.

Roddenberry's anger may have flowed, at least in part, from brain damage. A diabetic who suffered from and was treated for extremely high blood pressure, he created dangerous physiologic reactions and long-term damage by continuing to drink heavily against medical advice. The result: probable cerebral vascular disease and some alcoholic encephalopathy (brain structure variations). According to David Plotkin, a Beverly Hills physician who specializes in internal medicine, "Any of those could make him forgetful, angry, difficult." Roddenberry's sobriety, begun at the Schick Shadel hospital in Santa Barbara the previous fall (where he complained to the medical staff of having relationship problems with Majel Barrett, whom he believed was an alcoholic),[12] lasted at most three months, Susan Sackett recalls. After Roddenberry's death, Schick Shadel's chief of staff, physician P. Joseph Frawley, reviewed Roddenberry's medical records for the final five years and discovered a *Valley of the Dolls* type of drug use and abuse that few people except his doctors had suspected.

Apart from drinking immediately upon awakening, Roddenberry also variously ingested both prescribed and illegal substances: quantities of Nyquil, Valium, cocaine, Seconal, Desyrel (an antidepressant that causes drowsiness, particularly when used with other drugs or alcohol), Ritalin (a stimulant when used by adults; generally used by children to counter the effects of hyperactivity), Trandate (for high blood pressure), Micronase (for diabetes), Dexamil (a stimulant), Prozac (an antidepressant), Norpramin (another antidepressant), and a range of diet pills.

If as an alcoholic and addict, he needed an excuse to justify abusing himself, Roddenberry had a good one in his difficulty recreating *Star Trek*. It upset his equilibrium, as well as his plans to prove himself as the Great Bird, to recognize that his contributions to the final product would be skimpy. Who better to take out his disappointment on than those who'd been there at the beginning and from whom, therefore, his inadequacies could not be hidden? "I don't know how much he drank," Gerrold says, "because I'm not sure I ever saw him sober."

In refusing to kiss Roddenberry's ring, Fontana and Gerrold tacitly acknowledged his status as a mortal, dooming themselves in the process. After Gerrold finished the second draft bible, he returned to the outline for "Blood and Fire." Over the following month, his story about a mission team that cannot be beamed back aboard the *Enterprise* because they've been infected by an insidious parasite was repeatedly criticized by Maizlish; he'd become Roddenberry's point man and proxy, often writing memos on scripts and outlines, and sitting in on most story meetings, often without Roddenberry. He once fell asleep during a casting session, snoring loudly as an actress auditioned for her part. Sometimes he attempted to rewrite scripts. He worked on Michael Michaelian's "Too Short a Season," Roddenberry admitted to Lewin, "just to help my thinking on it." Inasmuch as Maizlish was a lawyer, not a writer or producer—or even on staff in any official capacity—this was a contravention of Writers Guild rules.

Gerrold eventually worked with Herb Wright, the second writer-producer hired on the series, and finished constructing the "Blood and Fire" story. Roddenberry read it, made some brief suggestions, and ordered a script. Gerrold took less than two weeks to complete the first draft. He turned it in and departed on a four-day *Star Trek* cruise for which fans had paid to mix with *Star Trek* principals. While on board he received a telegram from Roddenberry: "Everybody loves your script. Have a great cruise." When Gerrold returned, however, Roddenberry told him that the script was "a piece of shit."

Roddenberry's abrupt change of opinion remained a mystery for only a few hours, until he handed Wright his notes on the script and, mistakenly, Maizlish's as well. Wright gave them to Gerrold and somewhat ominously suggested he read *both*. They were virtually identical, which meant that those written by Maizlish were the source material: His comments were intended for Roddenberry's eyes only. (Some months later staff writer Sandy Fries turned in the first draft of his script about Starfleet Academy, one that had been ordered quickly because of a dearth of product in the production pipeline. His office mailbox filled with favorable memos from the other writers and producers and Roddenberry verbally complimented Fries on the script's excellence, saying he had relatively few comments. The next morning Fries brought his tape recorder into Roddenberry's office to receive notes for the second draft. Roddenberry didn't get right to the script. Instead, he schmoozed with Fries, as though they were old friends—or as if Roddenberry planned to take him under his wing. After twenty minutes or so, Roddenberry said, "We're going to have to part company." Similarly, staff writer Johnny Dawkins was let go by Roddenberry without apparent reason and with no explanation after pleasant small talk.)

Maizlish's role and duties had become clear. He was Roddenberry's personal story editor and creative pinch hitter, standing in for a man who was often confused and seemed wholly irrational. To Rick Berman, however, who was then co-supervising producer (and later executive producer), Maizlish's role was no more obtrusive or unusual than many agents who accompany their clients virtually everywhere. "You'd be surprised at the number of big stars," he says, "who feel they can't go to the bathroom without their agent being there."

Maizlish was Roddenberry's tether. "I am convinced that Gene really lived in the twenty-fourth century," Bob Lewin says. "It was in his head night and day. There wasn't a question you could ask him about the twenty-fourth century that he didn't have an answer for. Many times I would hear him say, 'They would not do this in the twenty-fourth century,' or 'They wouldn't do that. In the twenty-fourth century things are different than that. You've got to understand, in the galaxy then this is the way it's done. This is the way your military is set up.' He'd go on and on and on."

When Herb Wright arrived in *The Next Generation* offices on March 30, 1987, as the second writer-producer, Roddenberry treated him like the golden boy. Wright had earned the job not for his work on *Night Gallery*, which was probably the closest he'd come to the genre, but because Roddenberry had read and loved an unproduced Western script of his. "You're the only other writer besides me," Roddenberry said, alluding to a *Have Gun, Will Travel* episode, "who ever put a camel in his Western. You're unusual." Wright, however, had worked on enough series to know that the golden treatment couldn't and wouldn't last.

At the beginning, Roddenberry often took Wright to lunch at Nickodell on Melrose, where he would order drink after drink and regale the new producer with stories of his heroics during the war, his exploits with women, and his experiences as a cop. Though he'd been groomed to be Los Angeles's chief of police, he told Wright, he hadn't wanted the job because it wouldn't allow an outlet for his "creative juices." "That was something he talked about a lot," Wright says, "his creative juices."

The stories bore the ring of truth to Wright, who'd looked forward to meeting and working with the Great Bird of nearly mythological fame. And indeed, the man, the myth, and his demeanor dovetailed neatly in those days. "I liked Gene," Wright says. "He could be very winning, very charming. He was obviously well read and intelligent." And then Roddenberry's erratic behavior began.

First were his unexpected tirades. In the middle of script and story meetings he would sometimes suddenly—and unpredictably—detour into invective, usually about women. Wright recalls a story in the works about a planet on which women are superior to men. Patrick Barry's "Angel One" was an old concept that Roddenberry had used himself several times—on *Planet Earth*, for instance, ten years before. In a meeting with Wright and Barry, Roddenberry prefaced his comments with the mandate that the planet's women be fairly represented; they are, after all, he noted, the superior gender. "But of course," he said, "you'd never want to let women actually get *into* power. All women are cunts, and you can't trust them." The trigger for such diatribes was usually his ex-wife, Eileen, who had filed a lawsuit against him, alleging that he had conspired to hide profits from *Star Trek*, of which she owned 50 percent. "He'd just go off on her," Wright says, "and he was pretty vulgar about it, too. You never knew when it was going to happen. He'd just go off onto a tangent and all of a sudden there'd be a soapbox pulled out, and he'd do a number. Then he'd take a breath and calmly go back to work. He was antiwoman, for sure." (In the middle of one of these flights, he stopped to note that of course he was in favor of equal rights for women. "I support the NRA [*sic*]," he asserted.)

Like John D. F. Black before him, Wright had no reason to suspect Roddenberry of allegiance to anything other than the best show possible. But over the months it became apparent that there were other factors operating.

One morning after he'd been on staff for several months Wright sat in Roddenberry's office, making chitchat before receiving notes on a script he'd written. The script lying in front of him, Roddenberry turned to the first page and began his recitation.

After a moment or two, Wright stopped him. "Hold on a second, Gene," he said, "you're giving me notes on a script I didn't write."

"Yes, you did," Roddenberry said, and resumed giving his notes.

Wright stopped him again: "Gene, really, I didn't write that script."

Roddenberry's voice became more insistent: "Yes, you did."

The script, as Wright knew from having read and commented on it a few days before, had been written by Bob Lewin, whose name was on the title page. It could have been a simple case of mistaken identity. Wright did not think so. After all, he was twenty years younger, considerably taller, and the owner of a great deal more hair than Lewin. The incident, Wright concluded, indicated senility—and indeed it may have been; on several other occasions Roddenberry quite obviously didn't recognize him or anyone else around him either.

Schick Shadel's physician Frawley later agreed: "In reviewing all of the documentation available," he wrote, "it is my opinion that the patient suffered from a gradually recognized dementing condition or conditions which were exacerbated or accelerated by his use of both licit and illicit drugs and alcohol, as well as his underlying medical problems of hypertension and diabetes, and his depression... These conditions resulted in impaired memory, thinking, mental function and personality changes, apathy, loss of energy and depression."[13]

Since Frawley's diagnosis corresponds to the period beginning more than two years after *The Next Generation*'s early days, Susan Sackett suggests another explanation besides senility for Roddenberry's behavior with Wright: Roddenberry so hated being wrong that he would rather conduct the meeting than admit to having made a mistake. "Plus, he was terrible on names and faces," she says.

"When you're with the executive producer, and he tells you, 'This is your script and here are the goddamned notes,' you listen," Wright says. He withdrew a tape recorder from his briefcase and turned it on. He nodded his head appropriately when Roddenberry seemed particularly emphatic. He asked no questions. At the conclusion of the half-hour meeting, he stood up, offered thanks, and walked out. Passing by Lewin's office, he dropped off the tape. "Here's Roddenberry's notes on your script," he said.

Wright's experience can be seen as a metaphor for *The Next Generation*'s early years, when Roddenberry's actions—and *inac*-tions—sent the creative staff through a revolving door. In the first three years, twenty-four writers and writer-producers came and went, which is at least triple the rate of attrition for the average hour-long dramatic show.[14] The joke among former *Next Generation* writers is that they were "one of the eight thousand members of the Writers Guild who worked on *Star Trek: The Next Generation*." Lewin, an industry veteran, brought writers in with whom he'd worked on other shows. They would pitch stories that Lewin liked; invariably, Roddenberry shot them down. Lewin would persist, asking if there wasn't *something* in the story that could be salvaged and developed. Roddenberry would suggest that the writer rework the story based on his suggestions, but when the reworked story arrived, he'd do the same. This put Lewin in an inherently compromising position: According to Writers Guild rules, a producer is allowed only two meetings with a writer on the same story before having to hand out the assignment. "I can't ask you to come in for another meeting," Lewin would tell the writers, "because if it's a third meeting, I'm obliged to hire you, but I don't think I can get you the money for a story sale yet." The writers didn't care. They wanted to be part of the *Star Trek* team. Some had been fans of the show for twenty years, and to them Roddenberry was a living legend.

"He was an idol," says free-lancer Marc Scott Zicree. "The thought of working with him was irresistible. Then they found he had feet of clay. He became a fallen hero. They saw that he wasn't in his right mind, and they had to work around him rather than with him. The general feeling I picked up from being around the offices was that he was an enormous impediment to the creative process. He didn't help it."

Not surprisingly, what usually incited the ire of anyone who put words to page was Roddenberry's insistence on rewriting the scripts as they came in, no matter how good they may have been. "I forgot how bad the writers in this town are," Roddenberry once complained at a staff meeting. Writers would carefully incorporate his notes into a script and devise stories that hung together well. "Then he'd rewrite it and it wouldn't work," Lewin says. "Then he might give it to me to rewrite and I'd try, but I couldn't. Then I'd give it to somebody else. Eventually it was dropped. We dropped a lot of stuff."

In time, the writers began to attribute his inconsistency and caprices to the biochemistry of blood alcohol. "It was quite common knowledge that he would give notes in the morning and come back after drinking at lunch having forgotten what he'd said," Zicree says. "He'd give completely different notes."

By mid-season of the first year, *Star Trek: The Next Generation* had developed a reputation as a dysfunctional work environment. "The writers had spoken to each other," Lewin says. "The word was out: Don't go near the show." For months not one agent or free-lance writer called the studio, inquiring about possible script assignments.

Lewin blames Roddenberry, as both a bad administrative executive and bad story editor, for the chaos; and Roddenberry blamed everyone around him, never admitting that self-examination might be in order.

Though they differ in detail, the complaints against Roddenberry echo those uttered during *Star Trek*. In fact, not much had really changed in twenty years. It only seemed that way, with ten times as much money per episode making the problems that much more obvious. In 1987 he was still the same randy rewriter he'd been in 1967. The first time around he had blamed network censorship and studio cheapness. But now, with Paramount committed to spending whatever it took, and without a network to enforce rigid content restrictions, he rewrote the twenty-fourth century into the same adolescent boy's fantasy. Inhabitants of the planet Betazed, including the four-breasted Lieutenant Commander Troi, were plagued by rumors that they "engage in almost constant sexual activity."[15] The Ferengi, he wrote, "have prodigious sexual appetites, and it is said their genitals are of a shape and dimension that Earth women have found as enjoyable as their sexual techniques."[16]

This was the same Roddenberry, inserting sex and sexual innuendo into almost every script that crossed his desk—for instance, "The Naked Now," on which Dorothy Fontana used her pseudonym of J. Michael Bingham after Roddenberry gratuitously made Captain Picard and Data objects of sexual desire. Of course, in Roddenberry's world, he and Picard were one and the same. "Our captain is an older man, thoughtful, compassionate, hard, but fair—and very irresistible to women," he would say, pausing for just a moment before concluding: "Executive producers have that problem, too."

The utopian future Roddenberry argued for was the place in which man took and gave pleasure at will, without restriction or restraint, unencumbered by societal convention. If he did indeed reside mentally in the twenty-fourth century, as Bob Lewin suggests, then his time machine was sexual fantasy.

Roddenberry was in his La Costa condominium one day when he telephoned writer Tracy Tormé to offer suggestions on a story. Tormé had been Roddenberry's privileged child for some time. Expressing an almost grandfatherly affection for the young writer who'd been turning out some of the show's best episodes, Roddenberry had often invited him for impromptu rides across the Paramount lot in his golf cart just so Tormé could hear his stories and advice. Tormé had submitted "Genius's Pain" to the staff and Roddenberry some weeks before, and Roddenberry was calling to share that the title had awakened in him some infrequently expressed feelings: that genius really is pain, and that the breadth of experience is divided between pleasure and pain. People use the words good and evil, he noted, but they're really talking about pleasure and pain; pleasure and pain are opposing poles of the Earth's axis. There was the pain of dealing with networks, the pain caused by an ex-wife, the pain of alimony. On and on, for fifteen minutes Roddenberry recited a litany of all the different types of pain.

Tormé, anxious to return to work, patiently grunted "uh-huh" every so often.

Then, abruptly, Roddenberry's tone lightened, signaling a change of subject. "But my idea of pleasure," he said, "is of course waves and waves of come exploding out of me."

Before his burst of laughter could be heard, Tormé slapped his hand over the mouthpiece, held the phone away, and leaned his head out his third-story office window. After laughing for a full minute, he punched the mute button and put Roddenberry's voice on the speakerphone—Roddenberry was still talking about coming.

Like sexual gratification, like the portrayal of the captain as a perfect leader, the emphasis on an optimistic future wasn't new; and it, too, was writ overly large by a man with a lot of money, an aversion to Judeo-Christian beliefs, and few inhibitions. Not only would the future be peaceful, it would be virtually utopian: Members of the Federation, he posited, have evolved to the point where they no longer conflict with each other, because conflict itself is obsolete.

Preposterous or not, the edict became a towering hurdle to the writers. Conflict being the engine of drama, what was there to dramatize? Roddenberry refused requests to allow the characters at least a bone of contention—anything on which to build a story. "The weakness of the show at the beginning," Tormé says, "was that it was too passive. Everyone liked each other too much." And as Marc Zicree discovered, the characters were also prohibited from growing more fond of each other.

This was the enlightened future, one which obviated the institution of marriage, as well as organized religion. Prompted by a script in which a male character blurts out "Will you marry me?" to a female, Roddenberry chastised his writing staff. "All of us have accumulated by now during our twentieth-century lives a staggering burden of soon-to-be outmoded values and political ideas, capitalistic and other economic assumptions, religious habits, Western industrial world prejudices, and so on," he wrote.[17] (At the Episcopal marriage of *Next Generation* star Jonathan Frakes, Roddenberry was so offended by the liturgy that he very nearly left before the I-do's. "He was going nuts," Rick Berman says.) But in his rush to perfect posterity, Roddenberry failed to delineate just what replaced these obsolete institutions. As a consequence, viewers of both *Star Trek* and *The Next Generation* know a great deal about numerous alien cultures but almost nothing about life on twenty-fourth-century Earth. That it has become a paradise free of poverty and prejudice is a given; the means are not. If nation-states have been eliminated, by which culture's rules does the Federation govern? Judging by the evidence, it would seem to be a Western culture, one that adheres to the standard Judeo-Christian ethic that Roddenberry abhorred. And how, one wonders, does his philosophy of infinite diversity through infinite combinations apply to Earth, which boasts countless disparate cultures, if the Federation speaks for everyone? Why is there never a mention of elections? Is Western-inspired democracy destined to be one of the "outmoded values and political ideas"?

Roddenberry disliked being challenged. "Allow me," he said, "the consistency of my inconsistencies."[18] (Wright included in an early script the *Enterprise* firing a warning shot after being fired on. Excising the scene, Roddenberry contended that the starship was not allowed to fire back; it was something the captain would not do, despite the act of war. And yet, in rewriting the script "Code of Honor," he included a scene in which the *Enterprise* uses all its resources to fire upon a planet—as a warning.) The most ironic of those inconsistencies was how little like utopia were the *Next Generation* offices. "During my two years there," Tormé says, "there were several people who felt this place was an insane asylum"—one whose chief of psychiatry was nuttier than the patients.

One example of that lunacy may be seen in Roddenberry's infamous "Ferengi memo," a description of the alien race that is an unwitting psychological self-portrait. Besides their "prodigious sexual appetites," the Ferengi are "connivers and manipulators." They "consider themselves too civilized to employ brute force, except when they can label it 'cleverness.' The act of winning is a most important thing in their system of values. They would agree with the twentieth-century human athletic coach who said, 'Winning isn't the important thing—winning is the only thing' [*sic*]." The Ferengi, who are twenty-fourth-century "robber barons," believe "that it is nature's way to reward the clever at the cost of the weak. They believe in the law of quid pro quo and believe it is dishonest to take or receive without fair payment, although their idea of 'fair' is that which profits them the most." The Ferengi consider themselves "the 'good guys' who live in perfect accord with nature's immutable laws of survival. They are honestly puzzled with humanity's concept of good and believe it means only that humans are demented."[19]

The Ferengi memo was a smoking gun. Its circulation sent twitters through *The Next Generation* creative staff, who now understood implicitly, David Gerrold says, that the biggest problem the show had was with its executive producer.

"I seem to be saying that *Star Trek* is an inspired vision of the human future, which it is not," Roddenberry once admitted. "I really don't believe that honestly. I've made *Star Trek* for a twentieth-century audience using twentieth-century people and morals and situations. Were I to present the twenty-third or twenty-fourth centuries as I really believe they will be, the audiences would hate me. I'd probably be arrested."[20]

It was the real-life betrayal of *Star Trek* principles that first disappointed and then angered Roddenberry's colleagues, particularly those like Gerrold and Fontana, who'd been there from the beginning and believed in Roddenberry. When Gerrold was cut off from his "Blood and Fire" script and told that Herb Wright had been assigned the rewrite, he volunteered to follow Wright's instructions and do the rewriting himself, even though, as his contract had not been renewed, he would receive no additional compensation. Already overburdened by the work load, Wright thought that was a terrific idea but needed Roddenberry's permission first. Gerrold then went downstairs and stuck his head in Roddenberry's office. "Gene," he said, "I know you guys are maxed out. Let me do the last rewrite on 'Blood and Fire' for you. Whatever you want, tell me, and I'll do it."

"That's great," Roddenberry said. "You've always been a true friend, David. You're always there for me. I'll tell you what. Just go up to Herb's office again and make sure it's OK with him. It's fine with me if it's fine with him."

As usual, Gerrold used the stairs instead of the elevator to go from the first to the fourth floor. When he got back to Wright's office to let him know that Roddenberry had approved the arrangement, Wright was on the phone. His face looked grim. "Right," he said. "Yeah, sure. I'll tell him." Hanging up, he looked at Gerrold. "I don't lie for anybody. That was Gene. He told me to tell you that it's not all right with me for you to do the rewrite."

As soon as Gerrold left to contemplate the bewildering turn of events, Wright's phone rang again. It was Leonard Maizlish, emphasizing the finality of Roddenberry's dictum—just in case Wright hadn't understood the first time.

Wright was soon to have his own problems with Roddenberry. They began the day when the studio's wishes were gently made known to Roddenberry: The chaos and confusion obviously plaguing the writing staff and affecting the quality of scripts might be alleviated by putting Wright in charge. Roddenberry, the executives suggested, should become "creative consultant." Roddenberry rejected the proposal and from then on distrusted Wright. In his eyes Wright was now the enemy—a turncoat. Wright, he felt, had tried to engineer a palace coup—how else to account for Paramount's suggestion? "Herb was accused of being disloyal," Gerrold says. "Gene and Maizlish were terrified that Gene was going to get pushed out of all authority, the way he'd been in 1980 with the films."

"Gene," says Justman, "had a lot of animosity towards Herb."

Wright didn't take Roddenberry's hostility personally. He likened the situation to Castro taking Havana and then killing all the captains because there could be only one leader. Sensing a no-win situation on Gerrold's "Blood and Fire" script, Wright had discarded the existing drafts and notes, and had begun anew on a related concept. More than halfway through, he discovered that

Roddenberry had incorporated many of Wright's situations into a script he was writing at the same time. "Hold on there, Gene," Wright said. "I wrote this. This is mine."

"Oh, well," Roddenberry said. "I'm sure your fertile imagination will think of something else."

It did, and Wright soon turned out a first draft that was generally well received by other members of the staff. The last to read it, Roddenberry scheduled a Monday morning meeting to go over notes. Wright arrived at the appointed hour. Roddenberry picked up the script from his desk and threw it against a wall. This was the worst *Star Trek* script he'd ever read, he said, beginning a nearly hour-long tirade. Wright just nodded his head at each of the complaints. He'd previously been subjected to Roddenberry's displays of fury, as had most members of the staff. But hearing that his script had showed "contempt for the show" startled him. He asked how. The stage directions, Roddenberry said, had too many adjectives. "I felt like Mozart—too many notes," Wright recalls. "All I could say was, 'OK, Gene.' Unfortunately, that was one time when he knew he was talking to me."

In late July 1987, David Gerrold filed a grievance claim with the Writers Guild of America. Pointing out that he was the primary—and unpaid—author of the show's bible, he asked that the Guild take up his quest to receive a partial "created by" credit on *Star Trek: The Next Generation*. (He knew all along that he'd have to settle for cash, not the credit.)

Roddenberry informed the writers of Gerrold's claim during a weekly staff meeting. He inquired whether anyone had had foreknowledge of Gerrold's plans. No. Then Leonard Maizlish, who was by now Roddenberry's second mouth, asked Dorothy Fontana directly whether she'd known. She said no. He asked again, and she repeated her answer. Later that morning, Herb Wright met with Roddenberry and Maizlish over a script, and in an aside Maizlish asserted that Fontana had almost certainly been aware of

Gerrold's imminent claim. Why that should have mattered, he didn't say. But Wright warned Fontana that she ought to defend herself. Meeting with Roddenberry alone, Fontana noted that Gerrold would have been stupid to announce his actions ahead of time, particularly with other staff writers.

"He *is* stupid," Roddenberry snapped. "He's never written a single word that we could use on the show, so how could he claim to write the show bible?" He then promised that Gerrold would be sorry for attacking "me and my family like this."

Nearly two weeks later, on August 10, Roddenberry ordered Fontana into his office for a meeting. Fontana suspected that the stated goal of discussing her script, "Lonely Among Us," was specious, inasmuch as she'd completed the second draft over a week before. After Roddenberry improvised a few minutes of chitchat, her suspicions were born out when Maizlish walked in. Fontana turned on a tape recorder, as did Roddenberry.

"Let's turn to another subject," Roddenberry said. "Leonard is very concerned about a possible suit that we may have with David, and we're curious what your position was. You were in the same office with David for a while and you were here during all the beginnings. And for us to be left with the fact that from the very beginning you were here and are unable to say that *Star Trek* is mine—this is a very difficult thing for us to face. My feeling of those days and my certainty is that you must have known that I created it."

"I was not in on those discussions, Gene," Fontana replied.

"You were in on the creation discussions," he insisted.

"No," she said. "I got memos."

When Maizlish tried to pry some testimony out of her, she suggested that Roddenberry's office was not the proper locale for the adjudication of a Writers Guild matter.

"This is not a Guild matter," Roddenberry said sharply.

"It certainly is," Fontana said.

"It's *my* matter, and you've been a part of this," he answered.

Maizlish tried to appeal to a sense of family, noting that everyone else on staff with any knowledge of these events was cooperating with them. He asked what source materials she'd used when writing the pilot, "Encounter at Farpoint."

"I was given material that was a writer's guide," Fontana said, "and we also had memos that touched on subjects that were not yet included in the writer's guide."

"For all you know," Roddenberry said, "David might have created that and I used it?"

"I wasn't sitting there during the discussions when this material came up," she said. "How can I say that I was when I wasn't?" What he wanted her to say wouldn't have been the truth, though she knew she had everything to gain politically and professionally by playing ball. She admitted to knowing this: that she'd referenced a tall stack of memos, some of them written by her, some by Robert Justman, some by Gerrold; a few, even, by Roddenberry.

When Roddenberry asked whether she'd read the original bible pages that he'd written by himself, Fontana recalled that she had read something in late November or early December, but since the work wasn't credited she hadn't known who'd written it, Gerrold or he.

"It is not my habit in working on first bibles to say 'by Gene Roddenberry,'" he insisted. "Otherwise everything has those credit lines. Was that not true of the first bible that I did not put 'by Gene Roddenberry' on it—the one on the old show?"

Fontana said she did not remember and would have to check her files.

Maizlish assumed a more litigious stance, as though this were a deposition. He implied that her friendship with Gerrold, as well as her office's proximity to his, might have given her some insight into what it was that Gerrold might have been working on. He even found it suspicious that she should say that Gerrold worked for exactly *eight* weeks on the second draft script, comparing it to everyone knowing "where we were when John Kennedy was shot. It's curious to me that you pick out an exact number of eight weeks."

The questions focused on Gerrold. What memos did he have? What was he doing in his office? How long did his assignments take him? Unable to substantiate his own contributions, Roddenberry knew he would have to mount a thorough defense. But to do that he needed to know what weapons the opposition held.

"And you say to us that if this matter went to arbitration or court that you would not be a witness for David?" Maizlish asked.

"No, I couldn't say that," Fontana replied. "I would be asked questions, I would hope, by whatever side as to what I knew about it."

"How could you be a witness for David, on that basis, if you know nothing?" Roddenberry wondered.

"I wouldn't be a witness *for* anybody," Fontana reiterated testily. "I assume the Guild would ask questions if they thought I had any information to give them."

Later, Roddenberry asked for Fontana's opinion of the claim's validity.

"I don't know what the claim fully is," Fontana said.

"You have no opinion on whether I created this show," he replied.

"I don't know."

"I find that remarkable."

"I'm sure you do, Gene. But there are memos extant—"

"I want to hear that from you," Roddenberry implored. "We have been associated for twenty-one years—"

"However, there are memos—"

"You must know something about me."

"There are memos extant," Fontana said, "that imply other people had input. So what's the extent? I don't know."

"I always welcome input."

"I don't know the full extent because I wasn't there."

"Well, you have no opinion on whether I'm honest in saying I created it, huh?"

When Fontana explained again that she believed this to be strictly a matter for the Guild, which would weigh the evidence before deciding an outcome, and that her opinion about any particular aspect was immaterial, Maizlish responded that a Guild matter was "something for somebody who's a stranger and who's standing on Melrose and had nothing to do with any of the people.

You've been deeply involved in this." That Maizlish, on Roddenberry's behalf, should now invoke friendship, struck Fontana as tragically funny.

"I find this astonishing—astonishing, Dorothy," Roddenberry said.

"My position, Gene," Fontana said, "is that I don't want to be involved in this fight."

"You have known me for twenty-one years—"

"Almost twenty-three," Maizlish corrected.

"I gave you opportunities," Roddenberry said.

"That's true," Fontana said.

"And you think it should be handled by the Guild."

"Yes, it should. This is a Guild matter."

"And you have no opinion on it," Maizlish said. "Is that fair?"

Roddenberry and Maizlish continued to grill Fontana on what she might have known about Gerrold's grievance. At one point, Roddenberry lamented that Gerrold could have expressed his complaints directly to him. The meeting ended with Fontana agreeing to supply photocopies of all memos in her files; Roddenberry would have had them anyway.

On the day following the meeting, Fontana received a painfully apologetic call from Majel Barrett, disinviting her to a birthday party for Roddenberry. The next day she was summarily removed from her pleasant fourth-floor office, into which she'd recently moved, and reinstalled in a first-floor hell-hole that made her original office seem almost luxurious. When she issued a memo stating that intrusive noise made it impossible to work at the studio, she was denied permission to work at home—as every other staff writer often did; all of them, however, were males. This, apparently, was the rub: Roddenberry's belief that she had betrayed him found its expression in mistrust of her gender. In one staff meeting, he yelled at her for some positive comments she'd written in a memo about a Herb Wright script, contending that she'd done so only because he was "young and handsome." In another meeting he tried to embarrass her in front of Bob Lewin. "When Dorothy had to make changes on her first *Star Trek* script," he said, referring to 1966, "she broke down and cried."

"In your dreams, Gene," Fontana replied. "I've never cried over a script in my life."

By undermining her, Roddenberry tried to punish Fontana for his own failures. He could not acknowledge that she already had credited scripts before her first *Star Trek* assignment. Since then, her free-lance career had produced a string of prestigious network assignments and publishing successes. She was the writer Roddenberry wished to be.

In February 1988, a few months after leaving *Star Trek: The Next Generation*, Fontana filed a grievance with the Writers Guild. Alleging that she had performed the function of a story editor without receiving appropriate compensation, she settled more than a year later, before the arbitration hearing, and received an unspecified amount.

Then came David Gerrold's turn before the arbitrator. Having insisted that there be no settlement before the full hearing, Roddenberry watched in silence as Gerrold's side began its parade of witnesses and introduction of evidence. Roddenberry's attorneys attempted a cross-examination, but it was based on emotion, not reason or facts. Before even half of the plaintiff's case had been presented, Roddenberry caved in. The terms of both settlements, Fontana's and Gerrold's, prevent the winners from discussing the case; there can be nothing on the record to change the historical view. "Gene Roddenberry," said *TV Guide* in its mid-season review of *The Next Generation*, "has lost none of his ingenuity or his taste in selecting stories."[21]

"Our continuing characters are the kind of people that the *Star Trek* audience would like to be themselves," reads a passage in the 1989 series bible that bears Roddenberry's signature. "They are not perfect, but their flaws do not include falsehood, petty jealousies and the banal hypocrisies common in the twentieth century."[20]

Star Trek: The Next Generation debuted in the early fall of 1987 and was an immediate ratings hit. A syndicated show sold to 210 stations, many of them network affiliates, it aired on different days and in different time slots from market to market. Virtually every station soon reported significant viewership increases over whatever had occupied the time slot the previous year. In Los Angeles and Denver, its September 30 debut—a Wednesday—outpointed all network competition, as it had on the twenty-eighth in Miami. In New York, where it aired on Monday nights, *The Next Generation* on WPIX often beat the major network competition. Overall, ratings climbed during the coming months. From Paramount's perspective, even better than the raw numbers were the demographics. The series continued to add just the right kinds of viewers advertising agencies spend zillions to reach. This assured the studio a hefty profit, since *The Next Generation* was being offered to stations on a barter basis, in exchange for minutes of airtime that Paramount itself sold to sponsors.

Having a hit series was a first for Roddenberry. He noted in press interviews and before audiences that he was *The Next Generation*'s prime mover. "I wrote or rewrote the first thirteen episodes," he said. "I didn't take credit because I didn't want to lose some excellent writers. What you try to do is turn what's inside your head into images and pictures; that's always a better guide than a format sheet."[23] (In fact, Roddenberry had assumed co-credit on three of the early stories.)

Roddenberry did not comprehend the irony of his bow-taking. *Star Trek: The Next Generation*, like *Star Trek: The Motion Picture* eight years before, was a hit despite itself. Initial reviews were mixed at best. The show, said the *New York Times*, "fail[s] to take flight."[24] While the first reviews for classic *Trek*, as it had come to be known, had also been generally poor, the difference twenty-one years later was that reviewers had seventy-nine original episodes and four feature films against which to judge the new product.

Much more important than reviews, however, was the public response. Fans were generally disappointed with the first episodes, and continued to watch only because of pent-up demand—because this was *Star Trek*, not just some ordinary new show that gets a courtesy look. No other series would have been supported long enough, by fans and the studio, to find its voice. And the devotion paid off. In the second and third years the new series became as much of a phenomenon as the original series. Not coincidentally, the later shows contained far less of Roddenberry's imprint; with him as shepherd, the quality had been uneven at best. "By two-thirds of the way through the first season," Rick Berman says, "Gene had all but stopped writing and rewriting."

With each passing year Roddenberry contributed less and less to the show. "The last three years," Berman says, "virtually the only thing he did every day was to get into his golf cart and go down to the set to chat with the actors." Meanwhile, the cumulative effects of his alcohol consumption increasingly took their toll on his health. He already seemed frail when, in September 1989, he went to Tallahassee, Florida, for a brief family reunion and became ill. Later, after an MRI, his doctors concluded that he'd had a stroke—apparently one of many; the magnetic image indicated "multiple cerebral infarcts."[25] Muscular weakness began affecting his right arm that fall and his right leg the following year. To compensate for his trouble in walking, he began to use a cane and was then confined to a wheelchair. Neurological tests showed a continuing deterioration of his mental faculties, often with severe memory impairment.

Through it all he defied his doctors' orders by continuing to drink. Christopher Knopf recalls the backyard party at Sam Rolfe's house in 1990 when Majel Barrett, noticing her husband holding a drink, pulled Knopf inside to express her anger and hurt.

In addition to the other damage it caused, Roddenberry's alcohol intake exacerbated his aphasia. He would often sit in company, staring straight ahead as though far away. Trying to respond to a question, "he'd forget what you asked," Knopf says. "It was terrible to see his mind going."

In early June 1991, Creation Entertainment organized a twenty-fifth-anniversary salute to *Star Trek*, assembling the entire original cast at the Shrine Auditorium in Los Angeles for what essentially turned out to be not a commemoration of the show but a tribute to Roddenberry. Several thousand wildly enthusiastic fans, some from as far away as Germany and England, screamed as each actor did a solo turn in the spotlight. After William Shatner, the last of the stars, came Robert Justman, who also gave a speech of gratitude for all the fan support that had kept the series alive for two and a half decades. Then he introduced Roddenberry, who was pushed in a wheelchair onto center stage by his son Rod. The majority of the audience had known that Roddenberry was sick, but until that moment they hadn't realized how sick. As one, they rose, applauding and screaming without letup for a full five minutes. Their appreciation moved Roddenberry to stand briefly. "It's amazing to have so many people wishing you well," he finally said before admitting that he was "really too moved tonight to talk."

When he was unable to turn an apologetic phrase about the "quaver" in his "writer's voice," it became clear to everyone in the auditorium that his illness was not confined to the legs. But contained in that jumbled, aphasic thought was the wish he'd always been strong enough to hide from his public: "A writer's soul," he concluded, "endures in the face of adulation."

With an expression reflecting childlike bemusement, Roddenberry's words were heartbreakingly poignant. To be considered a writer, to have the soul of a writer, and to receive adulation for being a writer—this was Gene Roddenberry's animating dream. This was what had driven him. Every act, every decision had been in the single-minded service of artistic bravado.

Now, finally, too weak and too disassociated from his ego to express pretense, Roddenberry had revealed less of his ambition and more of his vulnerability. And out had come a haiku.

Then a punchline: "Let's bring out the dancing girls now."

On a Tuesday afternoon in October of that year, Roddenberry was wheeled into a screening room at Paramount to see the final cut of *Star Trek VI: The Undiscovered Country*. Scheduled for a November release, it was to be the last motion picture made with the original cast. Producer Ralph Winter, who'd succeeded Harve Bennett after being his executive producer, was there waiting for him. Roddenberry, who looked frail well beyond his seventy years and two months, said he was cold. Someone fetched him a blanket and the film began.

When the lights came back up, Winter asked Roddenberry for his opinion. He considered the answer important. In the past, he and Bennett had noted, a Roddenberry thumbs-down on any aspect had cost Paramount some money. It being in his best interest not to like something about every film, Roddenberry had always withheld endorsement until the last moment. So Winter was surprised when Roddenberry admitted that yes, he'd enjoyed the film. "Good job," he said. "It's very good."

Two days later, on October 24, while being wheeled down the hallway to his doctor's office for a scheduled appointment, Roddenberry briefly convulsed before falling unconscious. Unresponsive to emergency rescue efforts, he died in minutes.

Winter was one of the people reporters called in the media frenzy that followed the death of the Great Bird. They wanted to know: Had Gene seen the movie before he passed away?

Yes, he had, Winter told them. He liked it a lot.

The next day Winter got a call from Leonard Maizlish. Gene didn't like the picture, the lawyer said. "He wanted fifteen minutes cut."

The Undiscovered Country was a critical and commercial hit. With Kirk leading the *Enterprise* against Klingon aggression and finally coercing a tense peace, the story was a parable of the cold war. But for executive producer Leonard Nimoy, who'd collaborated on the plot with director Nicholas Meyer and Winter, there was something unsatisfying about the film. Not until he recalled having visited Roddenberry's home several months before, to get script notes from an obviously sick man, did he recognize what was wrong.

"We're using the Klingons as flat-footed, two dimensional heavies," Roddenberry said. "The loss here is that we have the opportunities to learn more about them."

The advice had gone unheeded. "But he was right," Nimoy says. "Gene was absolutely right."

ENE RODDENBERRY is often compared to *Twilight Zone*'s Rod Serling. Both men created speculative fiction series that became popular phenomena (and prospered beyond expectation in syndication), and both achieved fame unknown by others behind the television camera. But the comparisons are facile. Besides being profoundly prolific, Serling was a writer's writer; he never rewrote another writer's script. And yet, when he died (in 1975), he took *The Twilight Zone* with him, as failed efforts to revive it have proven.

The *Star Trek* universe, however, has expanded in Roddenberry's absence, penetrating popular culture in ways that are unprecedented for a television series. When *Star Trek: The Next Generation*—"the most successful first-run drama series in the history of television syndication," according to *TV Guide*—ends its first run in the summer of 1994, it will be followed by at least two, and most likely more, feature films starring the *Next Generation* cast.[1] Carrying the weekly television baton far into the future will be its spin-off, *Deep Space Nine*, which premiered in January 1993, and yet another series. (At Paramount, *Star Trek* is known as "The Franchise.")

To log every known piece of *Star Trek* merchandise and memorabilia requires several thick volumes. *Star Trek* novels regularly occupy the best-seller lists. Klingon as a second language is being learned by new devotees every day. A religion based on *Star Trek* was founded recently in Texas. Prominent citizens of the world, like the Dalai Lama and physicist Stephen Hawking, profess devotion to *Star Trek*—not least because of its philosophy.

"I finally feel that I have become a philosopher, junior grade," Roddenberry said near the end of his life. "There's hardly a subject you could mention [that] I haven't spent time thinking out while writing *Star Trek* scripts. You spend years dreaming up strange new worlds, and they build up into something quite real."[2]

Notwithstanding his humanistic philosophy, Roddenberry left a familial legacy that begat less optimism than acrimony.

In early 1993, a Los Angeles Superior Court judge removed Majel Barrett as executor of her late husband's estate, citing improprieties in her administration. At the time, Gene Roddenberry's will was facing a contest from his younger daughter, Dawn Compton, who had alleged that her father had not been mentally competent to understand the intricacies of the will he signed in August 1990. The estate's total value was estimated to be at least $30 million, but Roddenberry bequeathed only $500,000 to each of his three children, with the vast remainder going to Barrett. Son Rod is likely to benefit far beyond either Dawn or her sister Darleen, since it is his mother, not theirs, receiving the wealth. Further, the terms of the will enable the executor to pay down the costs of the will's administration using these cash gifts, as well as the $175,000 bequest to his secretary and lover Susan Sackett, even if the costs reduce the value of the gifts to zero.

In the will, Roddenberry appointed his brother Bob, a retired police officer living in a mobile home, as Rod's guardian in the event of Majel Barrett's demise. But he didn't leave Bob a dime even though his sister and his mother each received $300,000.

Before the adjudication of the contested will, the judge decided in a separate decision that Roddenberry's Norway Corporation had fraudulently hidden millions of dollars of *Star Trek* profits from Roddenberry's former wife, Eileen. He ordered the estate to pay the fifty percent of the profits to which she was entitled, plus significant punitive damages. Court testimony and sworn depositions revealed a particularly messy and bitter conflict, indicating that hostility between the two had not abated since the 1969 divorce. In one of the case's less disagreeable assertions, Eileen Roddenberry testified that the idea for *Star Trek* came out of family camping trips: She'd encouraged her husband, she said, to amuse their daughters, snuggled into their sleeping bags, by making up stories about the stars that filled the night sky.

METHODOLOGY AND SOURCES

THE RESEARCH that was molded into a narrative for this book came from a variety of sources. At UCLA's theater arts special collections department, I studied several thousand documents—various drafts of scripts, memoranda, letters, contracts, and so on—having to do with the original *Star Trek* series. Other documentary evidence—memos, scripts, letters, and such—was obtained through the private collections of people who'd known and/or worked with Gene Roddenberry. The National Archives, the Federal Aviation Administration, the Smithsonian Institution, the National Aeronautics and Space Administration, the *Los Angeles Times*, the *New York Times*, the Writers Guild of America, the Los Angeles Police Department, and the Museum of Television and Radio were among the institutions that provided substantial support; many others, of course, contributed.

I also relied heavily on the memories and reminiscences of people who had known or worked with Gene Roddenberry. I always weighed the information according to the subject's relationship to Roddenberry, his or her reputation, and his or her credibility (which I determined by cross-checking and verifying assertions). Much of the information was given on the condition that it be used as background, and I included information from those interviews only if it could be verified elsewhere; consequently, there are no unattributed quotes.

For the most part I avoided the plethora of *Star Trek* books as reference tools, since their veracity quickly became questionable as I began to accumulate a substantial body of independent research and eyewitness testimony.

Anecdotes in which the people listed below participated were related directly to me; unless otherwise indicated, the use of quoted dialogue came from the participant as he or she recalled it:

Leonard Nimoy, John D. F. Black, Mary Stilwell Black, Robert Justman, Herb Solow, Rick Berman, Christopher Knopf, Sam Rolfe, Dorothy Fontana, Norman Felton, E. Jack Neuman, Grant Tinker, Del Reisman, Forrest Ackerman, Kevin Ryan, Tracy Tormé, Jerry Sohl, Joan Winston, John Trimble, Ray Ferry, Richard Arnold, David Gerrold, Jon Povill, Harlan Ellison, Harold Livingston, Howard Stevens, Phyllis Schlemmer, Sir John Whitmore, Susan Sackett, Herbert Schlosser, Ken Kolb, Michael Eisner, Jeffrey Katzenberg, Adam Malin, Sam Peeples, Johnny Dawkins, Sandy Fries, Herb Wright, Robert Lewin, Walter Jefferies, Lou Scheimer, Stanley Robertson, Douglas Cramer, Jesco von Puttkamer, Harve Bennett, Buzz Kulik, William Sackheim, Ralph Winter, Marc Scott Zicree, Alden Schwimmer, Jim Stacy, Fred Freiberger, Ted White, Ruth Carpenter, Howard Barton, Ralph Kamon, Albert Germann, Don Ingalls, Jack Kenney, Danny Galindo, Robert Wise, Lauren Weinstein, Eric Stillwell, Greg Strangis, Ray Gaston, Leon Rockwell, Ernest Wellenbrock, Campbell Larsson, Eugene Sharp, Jack Ferguson, Virgil Faulkner, Elmer Schoggen, Stanley Pietuck, Clifford Havenstein, James Kyle, Joc Jacobs, Lorri Goldman, Jill Bryant, Nita Myer, Liz Wahlstedt, Miriam Nordahl Post, Paulette Spyrell, Russell Moody, Eula Lee Geisert, Clifford Wynne, Dean Skur, Urban Moor.

E N D N O T E S

CHAPTER TWO: THE LIEUTENANT
1. *Los Angeles Times*, September 13, 1942.

CHAPTER THREE: ON THE OUTSKIRTS OF THE FINAL FRONTIER
1. Letter dated February 12, 1945.
2. Memo dated June 19, 1964.
3. Letter dated June 22, 1964.
4. Ibid.
5. Letter dated August 25,1964.
6. A speech to the LAPD titled "A View of the Immediate Police Future";
   March 21, 1984.
7. David Alexander interview with G. R., *The Humanist*, March/April
   1991.
8. LAPD speech of March 21, 1984.
9. Interview with G. R., *The Humanist*.
10. Ibid.
11. Ibid.
12. Ibid.
13. Ibid.
14. From an undated early draft, circa 1964, of the *Star Trek* series format.
15. Letter to Jack Whitener, RAND Corporation, dated June 30, 1964.

CHAPTER FOUR: LOST IN SPACE
1. Memo dated May 20, 1966.
2. From the Columbia Records album *Inside Star Trek*, 1976.
3. Comment in a speech given at the Museum of Broadcasting's Fifth Annual Televisionfest, Los Angeles, March 30, 1988.
4. *Los Angeles Times*, December 20, 1988, section 6, page 6.

5. MOB Televisionfest, March 30, 1988.
6. Letter to Prickett at Sandia Base in Albuquerque, New Mexico, dated May 28, 1964.
7. Draft dated March 15, 1966.
8. Letter to Alden Schwimmer, dated February 2, 1965.
9. Letter to Samuel Peeples, dated April 12, 1965.
10. Ibid.
11. Outline draft of "The Omega Glory," dated April 25, 1965.
12. *Inside Star Trek* album.
13. Writer-Director Information, March 15, 1966.
14. Museum of Broadcasting seminar, August 7, 1986.
15. Letter to Jeffrey Hunter, dated April 5, 1965.
16. Remark made to Dorothy Fontana.
17. Letter dated May 4, 1965.
18. Draft dated March 15, 1966.
19. Remark made by Gene Roddenberry to Robert Justman.
20. *Los Angeles Times*, April 15, 1984, section 4, page 1.
21. Speech given to the Los Angeles Police Department, March 21, 1984.
22. Letter to NBC sales vice president Don Durgin, dated July 19, 1965.
23. An undated series description, circa late 1964.
24. *Inside Star Trek* album
25. MOB Televisionfest, March 30, 1988.
26. Ibid.

CHAPTER FIVE: IMPRACTICAL JOKES

1. David Alexander interview with G. R., *The Humanist*, March/April 1991.
2. Remark made to Kevin Ryan, senior editor of Pocket Books, in May 1991.
3. Memo to Gene Coon, dated June 16, 1967.
4. Memo to Gene Coon, dated December 6, 1966.
5. Interview with G. R., *The Humanist*.
6. Tom Snyder's radio show, 1988 (exact date unknown).
7. One version dated March 15, 1966, plus several earlier versions.
8. Museum of Broadcasting's Fifth Annual Televisionfest, Los Angeles, March 30, 1988.
9. September 28, 1991, broadcast on the ad hoc television network of *Star Trek: The Next Generation* stations.
10. MOB Televisionfest, March 30, 1988.
11. Interview with Charles Champlin, *Los Angeles Times*, December 20, 1988.
12. Remark made to Robert Justman.

13. Memo dated December 13, 1966.
14. Internal Desilu memo dated May 23, 1966.
15. Letter to Don Mankiewicz, dated May 6, 1966.
16. Memo dated December 6, 1966.
17. Memo to Gene Coon, dated May 9, 1967.
18. Memo to Ted Sturgeon, dated July 5, 1966.

CHAPTER SIX: WHO IS JAMES T. KIRK?

1. Letter to Isaac Asimov, dated June 19, 1967.
2. Ibid.
3. Ibid.
4. Letter dated August 17, 1966.
5. All information in this section has been culled from documents filed by the Civil Aeronautics Board, the Federal Aviation Administration, Pan American Airways, and the U. S. Department of State.
6. Story told to Herb Solow.
7. Letter from Isaac Asimov, dated July 10, 1967.
8. Ibid.
9. Memo from Roddenberry to Edwin Perlstein, Desilu legal affairs, dated November 25, 1966; album on Dot Records.
10. Internal Desilu memo from Edwin Perlstein to Shirley Stahnke, dated December 30, 1964.
11. Letter to Alexander Courage, dated October 3, 1967.
12. Memo from Roddenberry to Edwin Perlstein, dated December 19, 1966.
13. David Alexander interview with G. R., *The Humanist*, March/April 1991, page 23.
14. Source, nationwide poll of more than 50,000 *Star Trek* viewers conducted by Paramount Pictures, July 1991.
15. Memo to Stan Robertson, dated February 20, 1968.
16. Memo to John Reynolds, dated February 20, 1968.
17. Letter to Andrew Porter, secretary of NYCON3, dated November 4, 1966.
18. November 17 and 24, 1966.
19. Letter from Ted White to Roddenberry, dated May 5, 1967.
20. Letter from Roddenberry to Isaac Asimov, dated June 19, 1967.
21. Letter to Alden Schwimmer, dated April 25, 1966.
22. Letter to Leonard Maizlish, dated April 22, 1968.
23. Article by John Stanley in *Miami Herald*, March 19, 1968.
24. Letter to John Stanley, dated February 19, 1968.
25. Memo to Emmet Lavery, Jr., dated March 12, 1968.
26. Ibid.
27. Letter to Herb Schlosser, dated February 1, 1968.

28. Memo to Gene Coon, dated July 13, 1967.
29. Undated cover memo to Herb Schlosser, attached to *Assignment: Earth* series outline, dated October 21, 1967.
30. Letter to Mort Werner, dated December 1, 1967.
31. *Inside Star Trek*, Columbia Records, 1976.
32. Speech excerpted in *The Man Who Created Star Trek: Gene Roddenberry*, by James Van Hise (Pioneer books; Las Vegas, Nevada, 1992).
33. Ibid.

CHAPTER SEVEN: A VIEW TO THE PANTHEON

1. *People* magazine, March 16, 1987.
2. David Alexander interview with G. R., *The Humanist*, March/April 1991.
3. *Los Angeles Times*, April 15, 1984, section 4, page 1.
4. Ibid.
5. Remarks made on the Tom Snyder radio show, 1988.
6. Ibid.
7. Ibid.
8. *Los Angeles Times*, April 15, 1984.
9. Speech titled "A View of the Immediate Police Future," given to LAPD, March 21, 1984.
10. *Los Angeles Times*, April 15, 1984.
11. *Beat*, September 1952.
12. Ibid.
13. *Los Angeles Times*, April 15, 1984.
14. Ibid.
15. *Parker on Police* (Charles C. Thomas, Los Angeles, 1957), page 148.
16. Ibid, page 14.
17. *TV Guide* quoted (undated) from *The Man Who Created Star Trek: Gene Roddenberry*, by James Van Hise (Pioneer Books, Las Vegas, Nevada, 1992, page 71).
18. *Los Angeles Times*, June 27, 1972, page 1.
19. *Los Angeles Times*, March 5, 1974.
20. Kevin Thomas in the *Los Angeles Times*, April 23, 1974.
21. *Questor* TV series format, revised August 3, 1973.
22. Ibid.
23. Ibid.
24. *Inside Star Trek*, Columbia Records, 1976.
25. Ibid.

CHAPTER NINE: SOON TO BE A MAJOR MOTION PICTURE

1. Interview with Jesco Von Puttkamer, the NASA scientist who was technical adviser on *Star Trek: The Motion Picture*, for a German-language magazine, 1979.
2. Comments made to Tom Rogers for *The Making of the Trek Films* (New York: Image Publishing, 1991).
3. Letter to von Puttkamer, dated April 2, 1979.
4. Excerpt from an unpublished coffee-table book written in 1990 by G. R. and Susan Sackett.
5. *Starlog*, November 1985.
6. Remarks made on Tom Snyder's radio show, 1988.
7. Museum of Broadcasting's Fifth Annual Televisionfest, Los Angeles, March 30, 1988.
8. David Alexander interview with G. R., *The Humanist*, March/April 1991.
9. MOB Televisionfest.
10. Roddenberry and Sackett coffee-table book.
11. Memo to Harve Bennett and William Shatner, dated August 31, 1987.
12. Roddenberry and Sackett coffee table book.
13. Von Puttkamer interview.
14. Roddenberry and Sackett coffee table book.
15. Ibid.

CHAPTER TEN: THE CLOTHES HAVE NO EMPEROR

1. Remark made on Tom Snyder's radio show, 1988.
2. Museum of Broadcasting Fifth Annual Televisionfest, Los Angeles, March, 30, 1986.
3. Ibid.
4. *Star Trek* convention, Los Angeles, June 4, 1989.
5. Ibid.
6. *New York Times*, November 2, 1986.
7. MOB Televisionfest.
8. *Millimeter* magazine, January 1988.
9. Memo dated November 10, 1986.
10. *New York Times*, March 27, 1988.
11. *Star Trek* convention, Los Angeles, June 4, 1989.
12. From a report filed with the Los Angeles Superior Court by Dr. Joseph Frawley, Schick Shadel's chief of staff.
13. Dr. Frawley's report was filed with the Los Angeles Superior Court in October of 1993 as an affidavit in Dawn Roddenberry's contesting of her father's will. She claimed that he could not have been mentally competent at the time he signed the will in August of 1990.

14. The departed staff were: Johnny Dawkins, David Gerrold, Dorothy Fontana, Greg Strangis, Sandy Fries, Robert Justman, Herb Wright, Bob Lewin, Hannah Shearer, Leonard Mlodinow, Scott Rubenstein, Burton Armus, Michael Gray, John Mason, Tracy Tormé, Robert McCullough, Maurice Hurley, Michael Wagner, Richard Manning, Edward Milkis.
15. Roddenberry's first draft bible, dated November 5, 1986.
16. Memo dated May 11, 1987.
17. Memo dated April 27, 1987.
18. Told to David Gerrold.
19. Memo dated May 11, 1987.
20. MOB Televisionfest.
21. *TV Guide*, February 6, 1988.
22. *Los Angles Times Magazine*, May 5, 1991.
23. *Millimeter* magazine, January 1988.
24. *New York Times*, October 5, 1987.
25. "Multiple cerebral infarcts" from Dr. Frawley's medical report filed with the Los Angeles Superior Court.

EPILOGUE

1. *TV Guide*, July 24, 1993.
2. *Los Angeles Times Magazine*, May 5, 1991.

INDEX